Augsburg Commentary on the New Testament

GALATIANS
•
Edgar Krentz

PHILIPPIANS, PHILEMON
•
John Koenig

I THESSALONIANS
•
Donald H. Juel

Augsburg Publishing House
Minneapolis, Minnesota

AUGSBURG COMMENTARY ON THE NEW TESTAMENT
Galatians, Philippians, Philemon, 1 Thessalonians

Library of Congress Cataloging-in-Publication Data

Krentz, Edgar.
  GALATIANS.

  (Augsburg commentary on the New Testament)
  Includes bibliographies.
  1. Bible.   N.T. Galatians—Commentaries.   2. Bible.
N.T. Philippians—Commentaries.   3. Bible. N.T.
Philemon—Commentaries.   4. Bible. N.T. Thessalonians,
1st—Commentaries.   I. Koenig, John, 1938–   —
Philippians, Philemon. c1985.   II. Juel, Donald.
Thessalonians. c1985.   III. Title.   IV. Series.
BS2650.3.K74   1985   227   85-11116
ISBN 0-8066-2166-4

Manufactured in the U.S.A.   APH 10-9028

1   2   3   4   5   6   7   8   9   0   1   2   3   4   5   6   7   8   9

CONTENTS

ABBREVIATIONS

HTR	*Harvard Theological Review*
IDB	*Interpreter's Dictionary of the Bible*, ed. G. Buttrick; 4 vols. (Nashville: Abingdon, 1962); *Supplementary Volume*, ed. K. Crim (1976)
JBL	*Journal of Biblical Literature*
LXX	The Septuagint (Greek OT)
NAB	New American Bible, 1970
NEB	New English Bible, 1961
NIV	New International Version, 1978
NT	New Testament
NTS	*New Testament Studies*
OT	Old Testament
RSV	Revised Standard Version, 1946, 1952, 1971
SBL	Society of Biblical Literature
TDNT	*Theological Dictionary of the New Testament*, ed. G. Kittel and G. Friedrich; trans. G. Bromiley; 10 vols. (Grand Rapids: Eerdmans, 1964-1976)
TEV	Today's English Version, 1966, 1971, 1976
WA	*Weimarer Ausgabe* (the Weimar edition of Luther's Works)
ZNW	*Zeitschrift für die neutestamentliche Wissenschaft*

FOREWORD

The AUGSBURG COMMENTARY ON THE NEW TESTA-
MENT is written for laypeople, students, and pastors. Laypeople
will use it as a resource for Bible study at home and at church.
Students and instructors will read it to probe the basic message
of the books of the New Testament. And pastors will find it to
be a valuable aid for sermon and lesson preparation.

The plan of each commentary is designed to enhance its usefulness. The Introduction presents a topical overview of the biblical book to be discussed and provides information on the
historical circumstances in which that book was written. It may
also contain a summary of the biblical writer's thought. In the
body of the commentary, the interpreter sets forth in brief compass the meaning of the biblical text. The procedure is to explain
the text section by section. Care has also been taken to avoid the
heavy use of technical terms. Because the readers of the commentary will have their Bibles at hand, the biblical text itself has
not been printed out. In general, the editors recommend the use
of the Revised Standard Version of the Bible.

The authors of this commentary series are professors at seminaries and universities and are themselves ordained. They have
been selected both because of their expertise and because they
worship in the same congregations as the people for whom they
are writing. In elucidating the text of Scripture, therefore, they

attest to their belief that central to the faith and life of the church of God is the Word of God.

The Editorial Committee

Roy A. Harrisville
Luther Northwestern Theological Seminary
St. Paul, Minnesota

Jack Dean Kingsbury
Union Theological Seminary
Richmond, Virginia

Gerhard A. Krodel
Lutheran Theological Seminary
Gettysburg, Pennsylvania

GALATIANS
Edgar Krentz

To Ernst Käsemann—
scholar, teacher,
Pauline interpreter
κατ᾽ ἐξοχήν

INTRODUCTION

Galatians was written in the heat of controversy; every line in it reflects that fact. Paul believed his gospel to be under a deadly attack that would destroy the churches he had founded and ultimately the gospel itself. Therefore he used all the arguments at his command to counteract that attack: personal experience, biblical interpretation of the OT, sarcasm and pathos, personal appeal, and apostolic tradition.

Paul's language and thought are shaped by the situation. An attack on his gospel is an attack on the validity of his ministry. His life and his gospel are closely tied together. The result is a letter that is personal, emotional, self-revealing. Of all of Paul's letters, only 2 Corinthians can equal Galatians in this respect. As a result, both are fundamental for understanding Paul's character and reconstructing his life story. Galatians provides the chronological framework for Paul's life prior to A.D. 49. Without it we could reconstruct little, if anything, of his early life.

Galatians was written in the heat of controversy. Because the controversy touched the core of the Christian gospel, Galatians is basic to any discussion of what is essential in Christianity. Paul was aroused because the attack was deadly. It would destroy the congregations founded by his missionary preaching and change the character of Christian faith and life. The attack was deadly because it was so pious. It was based on the OT and so accused Paul of preaching an incomplete gospel, one that set aside the law, part of God's own revelation to Israel (Gal. 3:1—5:12), and left life dangerously unregulated and without guidance (5:13-26). The law is essential, the opposition contended, for all Christians, Jew and Gentile alike. Therefore the demand was made that Gentiles be circumcised (2:3-5; 5:2-4, 12; 6:12-13) as a sign that they will observe the law (4:21). This opposition involved a group (6:12, 13) led by one person (5:10, "he who is troubling you"). Apparently the interpretation this group gave the law also led to the call to observe a ritual calendar (4:10). This demand for observance of the law on the basis of the OT strongly suggests that the opponents are Jewish Christians. That view has long been the prevailing one.

Some features in Galatians suggest that the converts were ethnically Gentile. Paul contrasts their present state as "knowing God" (4:9) with the former time when they did not know him, but were enslaved to "the weak and beggarly elemental spirits," a clear reference to Gentile gods (4:9; cf. 4:2). On the basis of this and the view that Paul in 5:3 tells the Galatians something new, that circumcision obligates one to keep the law, Walter Schmithals[1] has argued that the Galatians were Gnostic, essentially non-Jewish in their beliefs. Much earlier W. Lütgert had argued that there were two groups in the Galatian church, one Hellenistic and one Jewish.[2]

But all such views either must presuppose that Paul was badly informed about the Galatian situation or used arguments that were not completely relevant. Paul's argument from 2:15 through 4:31 is based on the OT. It addresses the question "Who is a son of Abraham?" The traditional view that the opponents are Jewish Christians who come into the congregations of Galatia from outside still accounts best for the data of the letter.[3]

This attack occasioned Paul's magnificent letter, written in haste to counteract the opposition. The attack raised fundamental questions about the gospel and the church. Is the gospel by itself sufficient to define Christians and determine their life? To whom is the gospel addressed, Jews only, or Jews and Gentiles? On what terms do those evangelized become Christians? What is the nature of Christian freedom? And what is its practical sense?

Paul's answer to these questions is given in fundamental, radical terms. There can be no compromise. The road to salvation is the same for all, through faith in Christ proclaimed in the gospel. Faith rests only and completely on what God has done. Paul formulates this in terms of a drastic either-or: either faith in Christ or works of the law, either God's action or human product. The law and its fulfillment is, as far as justification is concerned, on the same level as pagan religiosity; it is the counterpart to slavery to the elemental spirits. Christ has put an end to the function of the law (cf. Rom. 10:3,4).

Luther[4] resonated strongly to Galatians because of his own religious experience. He called this letter "my little letter to which I have entrusted myself. It is my Käte von Bora." Luther's reference to "entrusting himself" is a pun based on the similarity in German of the words meaning "to marry" and "to entrust something to someone." Luther's evaluation shows why the letter remains one of the foundation documents of the Christian faith that must be reappropriated in every generation.

■ Critical Questions about Origins

In one respect Galatians requires less of an introduction than any other Pauline letter. No doubts about Paul's authorship are expressed by any responsible analysis; it is securely established. Nor are there questions about the integrity of the text. While there are some debatable textual variants, there are no serious suggestions of interpolation or that the letter is made up of more than one prior document. The argumentation of the letter is so coherent that there is no doubt that we have the letter approximately as Paul wrote it.

There are, however, two questions concerning origins that require brief discussion. The first is that of the location of the churches in Galatia and of the accounts in Acts with which they are to be connected (if any). Galatians itself has only minimal information about Paul's earlier contacts with these churches. He calls them "churches of Galatia" (1:2) and addresses them as "Galatians," the proper name for ethnic Celtic tribes (3:1). In 4:13 he uses an ambiguous phrase, "at first," which means—if pressed—"on the first of two" occasions. But there are no other place-names that will identify the recipients.

Galatia is applied to two differing entities in Asia Minor. One is the region in the central highlands inhabited by Celts since 279 B.C. The chief cities were Ancyra (modern Ankara), Pessinus, Tavium, and Gordion. The Celts (Gauls, hence Galatia) were a fierce people who caused the more settled areas of Pergamum great problems until Attalos I defeated them about 240 B.C. (The victory was commemorated in a magnificent sculpture which showed a dying Gaul and, in a second piece, a Gallic chieftan who has killed his wife and is at the point of suicide to avoid capture and slavery. Now in the Vatican museum, they are among the treasures of Hellenistic art.) The Romans defeated the Gauls in 189 B.C., but later supported them in an independent client kingdom until the death of Amyntas in 25 B.C.

Acts refers to the territory of Galatia in the phrase the "region of Phrygia and Galatia" (16:6; 18:23). According to 16:6 Paul went through the region after the Holy Spirit had forbidden him to "speak the word in Asia," i.e., in southwestern Asia Minor, the region around Ephesus. While there is no word of missionary activity in 16:6 (Luke is interested in getting Paul to Macedonia), 18:23 mentions that Paul strengthened the disciples in Phrygia and Galatia. Paul must have made some converts, possibly the ones who later made up these Galatian churches. That is the so-called northern, regional, or territorial theory of the recipients.[5] It is the theory that was traditional until the 19th century and the rise of modern criticism. It is held today by most European and many American scholars, and is the position favored in this commentary.

In 25 B.C. Augustus created the province of Galatia, adding to the territory of the Galatians the territory of the Isaurians, Lycians, Pamphylians, Cilicians, etc., in order to create a larger administrative unit. Antioch in Pisidia, Iconium, Lystra, and Derbe, the cities of the so-called first missionary journey of Acts 13 and 14, all lie in this Roman province.[6] Scholars who were troubled by the differences between Gal. 2:1-10 and Acts 15 found a solution in identifying the recipients with these churches in the southern part of the province. Hence the name "southern" or "provincial" for this theory. It was thus possible to date Galatians 2 earlier than Acts 15, and to regard them as reporting two separate incidents. It implied that Galatians was written early, possibly as early as A.D. 48.[7]

Supporters of the provincial theory point to other data in support of the position. They think it unlikely that Paul would not have written a letter to these churches. Barnabas is named in Gal. 2:1, 9, 13. He was in the southern churches, but not in the territorial region, according to Acts. According to 4:13, Paul's ministry began in a period of illness. That might account for the silence of Acts 13 about work in Perga in Cilicia.

The arguments on neither side are absolutely persuasive. However, the references in Acts 16 and 18 accord well with the two visits suggested in Gal. 4:13. In addition, the content of Galatians is much closer to that of 2 Corinthians and Romans than to any other of the Pauline epistles. Moreover, it would be difficult to account for the character of 1 Thessalonians if it were written after Galatians; but as the first of the known Pauline letters it is quite comprehensible. The territorial theory also allows a setting for the chronological data of Galatians 1 in the period between his conversion and the writing of the letter—something almost impossible with the theory of early composition.

There is a second historical question that faces the reader of the letter, namely, that of the exact date and place of writing. The southern theory makes an early date about A.D. 48 likely, but not necessary. The territorial (northern) theory makes a date after Acts 18:23 mandatory. The epistle's similarity of content and argument to that of Romans usually leads scholars to date it close to that letter, but slightly before it. Scholars hold almost univocally that Paul wrote Romans in Corinth during his last visit there, just before his trip to Jerusalem at the end of the third missionary journey (i.e., A.D. 55/56). Paul had come to Corinth from Ephesus by way of Macedonia. Ephesus is geographically closer to Galatia than is Corinth; if Galatians were written in Ephesus (where information might easily reach Paul from Galatia), then Galatians dates from about A.D. 55. That date would be assured if we could know that Paul wrote from Macedonia after leaving Ephesus, but before arriving in Corinth and writing Romans.[8]

About 20 years ago Werner Foerster[9] presented a novel view that deserves more attention than it has received. He points to the unusual phrase "and all the brothers who are with me" in 1:2. None are named, because they would not be known by name to the Galatians. Paul cannot come to Galatia personally, much as he would like to (4:20), and he calls attention to his large handwriting (6:11). Foerster suggests that these brothers are the companions that are coming with Paul on the journey to take the collection to Jerusalem from Corinth and Macedonia at the end of the third journey. Paul learns of the problem in Galatia and writes the letter on board ship (hence there is no scribe to serve him, like Tertius in Rom. 16:22) in his own hand. He reaches back into the argument of Romans, there carefully worked out, to counteract the unexpected threat. He dispatches the letter from one of the ports touched by the ship in southern Asia Minor. And Paul himself goes on to Jerusalem, bearing the "marks of Jesus" (6:17) on his own body.

The virtue of Foerster's theory is that it accounts for a number of puzzling statements in the letter, accounts for the absence of greetings, and suggests that the ordered argument of Romans is the resource for Paul's more impassioned utterances in the letter of controversy.

OUTLINE OF GALATIANS[1]

Paul defends his proclamation that faith in the gospel is all that is needed to be Christian.

I. Salutation and Theme (1:1-12)
   A. Salutation: Greetings from the Apostle (1:1-5)
   B. Curse on Perverters of the Gospel (1:6-10)
   C. Theme: Paul's Gospel Is Not Determined by Human Standards; Transition to II (1:11-12)
II. Body of the Letter: Paul's Apology for His Gospel and Appeal to the Galatians to Live by It (1:13—6:10)
   A. Paul's Proclamation Ratified by His Life (1:13—2:21)
      1. Paul's Life Drastically Changed by the Revelation of God's Son (1:13-16a)
      2. Paul's Proclamation Vindicated by His Earlier Ministry (1:16b—2:14)
         a. In Arabia (1:16b-17)
         b. His Ministry Required No Corporate Approval by the Jerusalem Church (1:18-24)
         c. When Challenged, Paul's Gospel Is Recognized by the Jerusalem Leaders (2:1-10)
         Excursus: Historical Questions in Galatians 1–2
         d. Paul's Gospel Vindicated in Confrontation with Cephas at Antioch (2:11-14)
      3. Conclusion and Transition: Justification by Faith Works Drastic Change (2:15-21)

B. Stand Firm in the Liberty that Is Grounded Both in Experience and Scripture (3:1—5:12)
   1. Rebuke Based on Reception of the Spirit on Hearing the Gospel (3:1-5)
   2. Appeal to Support Paul's Message: The First Argument from Scripture (3:6—4:11)
      a. Abraham Was Justified by Faith—and So Are We (3:6-9)
      b. The Law Demands Perfect Performance, Not Faith (3:10-12)
      c. Christ's Death under the Curse of the Law (3:13-14)
      d. Promise Is Prior to and Superior to the Law (3:15-18)
      e. The Law Has a Restricted, Subsidiary Role (3:19-22)
      f. By Baptism Faith Frees Us from the Law and Makes Us Children of God (3:23-29)
      g. From Slavery to Adoption as Children of God (4:1-7)
      h. Do Not Relapse into Slavery (4:8-11)
      i. Transition: Appeal to Identify with Paul's Proclamation (4:12-20)
   3. Appeal to Maintain Freedom: The Second Argument from Scripture (4:21—5:12)
      a. Stand Fast in the Freedom Shown in the Allegory of Abraham's Two Sons (4:21—5:1)
      b. Circumcision Obligates; Faith Is Active in Loving (5:2-6)
      c. Conclusion and Transition: Troublemakers Impede Your Christian Life (5:7-12)
C. Exhortation to Loving Service (5:13—6:10)
   1. Loving Service as Fulfillment of the Law (5:13-15)
   2. Loving Service Is Life in the Spirit, Not the Flesh (5:16-26)

COMMENTARY

■ Salutation and Theme (1:1-12)

Salutation: Greetings from the Apostle (1:1-5)

Paul fashions his words to fit the Galatian problem from the very beginning. Ancient Greek letters normally opened with a very simple salutation: "A to B, Greetings" (cf. Acts 23:26; 1 Thess. 1:1). Paul expands this formula with two major additions, both of which place Christ into central prominence. Paul is **an apostle,** a term he uses especially in Romans and Corinthians; that is, he is commissioned by an authority. For Paul, apostleship means missionary work (2 Cor. 11:5, Rom. 11:3). He is "set apart for the gospel" (Rom. 1:1). No human commissioner made Paul an apostle (**not from men nor through men**); though he does not say it here, he is as much an apostle as those commissioned directly by Jesus himself. He is apostle **through Jesus Christ and God the Father.** As 1:15-16 will make clear, God is the ultimate commissioner of apostles because he is the one **who raised him** [Jesus] **from the dead.** This happens, however, through the resurrected Christ, whom Paul saw (1 Cor. 9:1; 15:7).[1] Therefore Jesus is mentioned first (cf. 1 Cor. 1:1). The phrase **who raised him from the dead** has confessional overtones and probably reflects an early Christian creed. God showed himself as God by the resurrection (cf. Rom. 4:24; 8:11; 10:9; 1 Cor. 6:14; etc.). In this addition Paul claims that he possesses all necessary qualifications for apostleship, and therefore is an authoritative proclaimer of the gospel. This stress on apostleship in the salutation is elsewhere found only in Romans, where Paul introduces himself to a congregation unknown to him. Here he defends himself against those who attack his gospel as coming from one who lacks the credentials of an apostle.

Paul is an apostle, but he is not alone, isolated from other Christians. **All the brethren who are with me** (v. 2) is a somewhat vague phrase, indicating no numbers. (**Brethren** is an unwarranted archaism. "Christians" would be better.) Nor are these Christians named later in the letter. Werner Foerster[2] suggested that this phrase should be taken very literally to denote all the traveling companions who are with Paul on his trip to Jerusalem at the end of the third missionary journey. The **brethren with me** would be those who had gathered the collection for Jerusalem and were designated to carry it there. The addressees are simply named **the churches of Galatia.** No mark of personal friendship, no praise, no qualifier is added to the simple naming of the addressees. The plural suggests that the letter is in some sense a circular letter.

Grace to you and peace from God the Father and our Lord Jesus Christ (v. 3) is the standard Pauline greeting in opening his letters (Rom. 1:7; 1 Cor. 1:3; 2 Cor. 1:2; Phil. 1:2; Philemon 3; Eph. 1:2). More than a mere pious wish, it, together with Gal. 6:16, forms a kind of framework that encloses the letter. **Grace and peace** combine the Greek (*chairein* = "greetings," *charis* = "grace," etymologically related) and Semitic (*shalom* = "peace"; cf. Dan. 3:31; 2 Macc. 1:1) forms of letter greeting. **Grace** is best explicated by a reading of Romans. 2 Corinthians 5 makes clear that peace is the result of the reconciliation accomplished in Christ. It is the state in which Christians live (Rom. 5:1).

The addition to the greeting in vv. 4 and 5 reflects pre-Pauline Christian worship. Verse 4 is creedal, describing Jesus as the mediator of salvation. It has ideas and language not used later in the letter (the expressions **will of . . . God, present evil age,**

deliver, and **sins** in the plural are non-Pauline and occur in citations). **Who gave himself** is a Semitic expression for voluntary death (Ps. 49:7,8; Exod. 12:1). It reflects Isa. 53:6 and 11, and suggests that Jesus' death was an offering, a sacrifice for the removal of sins (cf. Rom. 3:25 and 4:25, both creedal formulas of the early church). **The present evil age** is a Jewish apocalyptic idea. Apocalyptic thought divided history into the present evil age and the coming age (4 Ezra 7:50). Paul refers to this evil age elsewhere (Rom. 12:2; 1 Cor. 1:20), but rarely refers as such to the age to come (but see Eph. 1:21, a deutero-Pauline letter). This age is evil, under the power of Satan (cf. 2 Cor. 4:4). The death of Jesus, which delivers us from the threat and power of the old age, frees us for living in the Spirit as we await salvation. Thus Paul both uses and breaks the Jewish apocalyptic schema.

This deliverance is not by chance or accident. It is the will of God who therefore is also **our Father.** It is the work of Christ that shows what God is. The only proper response (v. 5) is a doxology. This is a traditional Jewish ascription of glory, but is not a normal part of an introduction to a letter. God properly receives doxologies (Rom. 11:33-36; 1:25; 9:5), but Jesus almost never in Paul.

Curse on Perverters of the Gospel (1:6-10)

After the doxology the emotional impact of vv. 6-10 is as blunt as a blow to the face. Formally it is not out of place. Ancient letters normally have a thanksgiving for the health of the reader at this point. Paul usually has a thanksgiving for his readers that leads into the theme of the letter (cf. Rom. 1:8-17; 1 Cor. 1:4-11; Phil. 1:3-11). The curse that Paul utters in this paragraph is the reverse of the blessing and serves the same function.[3] It ironically, even bitterly, describes the present situation in Galatia as the backdrop for the theme Paul will state in vv. 11, 12. The very ad hoc nature of the letter is clear; Paul presupposes a knowledge of affairs in the churches and plunges right into the middle. We have to reconstruct the situation.

There is no word of transition. Paul is **astonished** that they could **so quickly desert** (the Greek term behind this denotes a "shameful change of mind") the God **who called . . . in the grace of Christ.** This corresponds to the thanksgiving for faith in Rom. 1:8. God calls through Paul's preaching of the gospel, as he had called Paul (1:15; 5:8). God is present in the gospel; to change the gospel for another is to leave God. The Galatian move shocks because it is so rapid, so drastic (**so quickly**). No measuring point is given. The call comes in **grace** (the expression **of Christ** is not found in many ancient manuscripts), that is, both by means of proclaimed grace and into a relationship with God that is determined by grace (cf. Rom. 5:15; 1 Cor. 7:15; 2 Cor. 1:12; 1 Thess. 4:7). Their desertion was shown by their accepting "another" (**different**) **gospel,** which is no gospel. "Gospel" in the New Testament is the oral proclamation of Jesus Christ. (In secular Greek it occurs in the ruler cult and in the healing cults.) But that other "gospel" is nothing else than, concretely speaking, that there are some people "who disturb [**trouble**] you" (5:10 suggests a specific individual) and **want to pervert the gospel of Christ.** Change is in this case destruction. There are not varieties of Christian gospel, but only one. It is the **gospel of Christ**, that is, the gospel which has Christ as its content (cf. 1:1,4) and as its moving force (cf. Rom. 15:19; 1 Cor. 9:12; 2 Cor. 2:12; 9:13; 10:14; Phil. 1:27; 1 Thess. 3:2; elsewhere Paul speaks of the gospel of God, e.g., Rom. 1:1; 15:16).

There is no middle ground: either one proclaims the gospel of God's grace in Christ or one is **accursed.** Paul says it twice, hypothetically in v. 8 and concretely in v. 9. The gospel does not get its value from the speaker, but from the one proclaimed. The phrase **an angel from heaven** may be an implicit reference to fascination with the law, the "word given through angels" (Heb. 2:2; cf. Gal. 3:19; Acts 7:38), which the disturbers might be urging on the Galatians. The Galatians had received Paul as an "angel of God" (4:14); now they were listening to others who bring a different gospel. **Let him be accursed** (cf. 1 Cor. 16:22). The translation has a rather archaic ring. To be *anathema* is to be cursed to hell, put out of the community, committed to destruction (cf. the *herem* of the OT, Josh. 6:17; Lev. 27:28). This passage has played a key role in the Lutheran Confessions, where it is used to justify disobedience to church authorities (*Apol.* 28.20; 7-8.48). Verse 9 shows that this anathema is not an incidental idea on Paul's part. He had made this a part of his earlier teaching; now he calls the Galatians to recognize the serious nature of a turn to another gospel. In form, vv. 8 and 9 are both sentences of holy law.[4] The use of this form gives an impressive solemnity to the thought, and the repetition underscores Paul's seriousness.

Paul had apparently been accused of reducing the full message of God in his gospel because he wished **to please men** by not making any demands on them for rigorous ethical action. That accusation Paul rejects in the bitterly ironic questions of v. 10. The curse in the form of a legal prescription can scarcely be **seeking the favor of men.** Nor is Paul seeking **to please men;** the sense is made clear from 1 Thess. 2:4-6. **To please men** is to seek glory from them. But Paul is **a servant of Christ** (cf. Rom. 1:1; Phil. 1:1), proclaimer of the gospel, as the "servants of God" in the OT were the prophets (Amos 3:7; Jer. 7:25), and so responsible to God. That is why Paul can pronounce such a curse. He is unconcerned with human reputation.

Theme: Paul's Gospel Is Not Determined by Human Standards; Transition to II (1:11-12)

Paul could not only bless and thank, but also curse. This curse is the reverse side of the gospel that can bring life. It is also the transition to the theme of the letter. Verses 11 and 12 give the basis of Paul's curse (in vv. 8-9), announce the motif of the letter, and form the transition to the major subject that concerns Paul. **For** indicates that the material is the basis for the preceding and also marks a new stage in thought. **I would have you know** is a disclosure formula that Paul uses to mark off a fundamental statement of basic importance (cf. 1 Cor. 15:1; 12:3; 2 Cor. 8:1). Paul is not ironic or sarcastic in this verse, but speaking as the "servant of Christ" to **brethren** (fellow Christians). The sexist tone of both phrases in English is not present in Greek. **Brethren** connotes members of the same association or group; it does not recur again until 4:12. Indeed, Galatians is singularly lacking in terms of affection throughout the first part of the letter, a mark of Paul's emotional involvement.

Paul begins with a negative statement. His gospel is not normed by human beings. **According to man** (RSV footnote) is the literal translation of the Greek. **According to** is the preposition used in Greek to refer to an ethical standard (cf. Rom. 3:5). Paul knows his gospel is not his personal possession or his creation, but has divine origin and character (1 Thess. 2:13). He preaches what all the apostles preached (1 Cor. 15:11).[5] Verse 12 makes clear what Paul regarded as the issue, as Paul narrows the sense of **according to man.** While the gospel is Paul's, its source was not human, whether Paul himself or some other human. Like that of all other apostles, Paul's apostolic mission and message goes back to an appearance of the resurrected Christ (**through a revelation of Jesus Christ**). 1 Cor. 15:1-10 is the fuller statement of this position (see also 1 Cor. 9:1). That rules out two other possible modes of transmission. He did not **receive it from man** (a technical term for the reception of oral tradition; cf. 1 Cor. 11:23; 11:2; 1 Thess. 4:1; 2 Thess. 3:6). Jewish tradition referred to the transmitting of oral traditions from Moses through all the generations into the early Christian period.[6] Paul's gospel did not come by such a chain of tradition. Nor was it given to him by some form of education (**nor was I taught it**). It is no esoteric, hidden teaching that belongs only to some initiated group. His gospel is public, open, known, proclaimed. Paul knows of teaching in the church (Rom. 6:17; 12:7), but his gospel was not even mediated by the people of God. It came directly by **a revelation of Jesus Christ** that made clear God's plan of salvation. (Paul also uses the term *revelation* to refer to a particular revelation, e.g., Gal. 2:2.) Paul's gospel came neither by a charismatic experience nor through a gradual process.[7]

■ Body of the Letter: Paul's Apology for His Gospel and Appeal to the Galatians to Live by It (1:13—6:10)

Paul articulated his theme in vv. 11-12; what follows unfolds that theme. Paul demonstrates in the first major section of the letter, 1:13—2:21, that his gospel is not from humans. His gospel is also not proclaimed in accordance with any human standard. Paul shows that in two major arguments: (1) His gospel brings liberty that destroys human legalism, 3:1—5:12. (2) His gospel impels Christians to true loving service, 5:13—6:10. Thus Paul takes up two points made in vv. 11-12 in reverse (chiastic) order.

Paul's Proclamation Ratified by His Life (1:13—2:21)

In this section Paul shows the truth of 1:12 by surveying his own career in proclaiming the gospel. He shows that the shift in his own life was drastic. Then follows a chronologically oriented survey of his career in relation to Jerusalem and other apostles; cf. **when** (v. 15), **then after three years** (v. 18), **then** (v. 21), **then after fourteen years** (2:1), and **but when** (2:11). Then, in 2:15-21, Paul states the significance of this biographical survey in theological terms that serve as the transition to 3:1—5:10.

1. Paul's Life Drastically Changed by the Revelation of God's Son (1:13-16a).

Paul's gospel came to him as an unanticipated interruption in his life as a Jew. Paul claims here, as elsewhere (cf. Phil. 3:5-6; 2 Cor. 11:22), that he was an exemplary Jew, as the Galatians knew (**for you have heard of my former life in Judaism**). Paul's drastic change was not caused by a failure as a Jew. His Jewish way of life was expressed in two ways, both of which showed his fidelity to Judaism. First, he **persecuted the church of God violently and tried to destroy it** (v. 13). The term translated **vio-**

lently might well be paraphrased "to the nth degree" (this Greek term is used only by Paul in the NT: Rom. 7:13; 1 Cor. 12:31; etc.). The Greek verbs indicate repeated, customary action. Given Paul's hostile attitude to the church, he could not have learned of the gospel from any one of the earlier apostles. In referring to the church Paul uses an OT phrase, "assembly of God" (Deut. 23:2), with which we may compare "Israel of God" in 6:16. During the time Paul was persecuting the church, he thought it to be the enemy of Israel, God's people and congregation (for Paul as persecutor cf. 1 Cor. 15:9 and Phil. 3:6).

In v. 14 Paul gives the basis for his persecution and the second mark of his outstanding Jewishness, his precocious advancement in the faith because he was **extremely zealous . . . for the traditions of** [his] **fathers.** Paul's Judaism was neither half-hearted nor unsuccessful. As a Pharisee (Phil. 3:5) he was by his own witness "as to righteousness under the law, blameless" (Phil. 3:6). Paul does not apologize for his Jewish life; indeed he speaks of it with pride, even after his conversion (see 2 Cor. 11:22; Phil. 3:5-6).[8] **The traditions of my fathers** comprehends the entire tradition of the law (Torah) and the halakic exposition of it, a tradition that claimed to stem from Moses and be passed on in unbroken continuity through a succession of teachers.[9] The written law of Moses and the oral tradition about it constituted an unbreakable whole that demanded diligent observance.

Paul's life as a Jew was drastically interrupted, in a completely unexpected way. **But when he** shows that Paul did not gradually come to the gospel. God had marked Paul out for preaching the gospel from before birth, even as the Servant of the Lord (Isa. 49:1 "from my mother's belly," the literal translation that stands behind the RSV's **before I was born**) and Jeremiah (Jer. 1:5) had been marked out from conception to bear God's word to Gentiles. God **called** Paul **through his grace** (1:15), and that amazed Paul ever after. "By the grace of God I am what I am" (1 Cor. 15:10). Paul speaks of his work as "grace and apostleship" (Rom. 1:5) or as the "grace given to me" (1 Cor. 3:10). When God was **pleased to reveal his Son to me** (Paul) is Paul's way of underscoring that it was God's decision and action that changed the direction of his life. The Greek term used here for "reveal" has the sense of uncovering something hidden; it underscores the unexpected experience Paul had. God revealed **his Son;** the title here probably stresses the exalted character of the risen Christ (cf. Rom. 1:3). Paul met the Lord in this revelation ("Have I not seen the Lord?" 1 Cor. 9:1; the risen Lord appeared also to Paul, 1 Cor. 15:8).

The experience of the risen Christ made Paul the proclaimer of the gospel **among the Gentiles.** It was not, strictly speaking, a conversion, but a call (v. 15) or commissioning to apostleship (cf. Rom. 1:1). Paul did not worship a different God than before, though he now knew him as the "Father of our Lord Jesus Christ" (Rom. 15:6; 2 Cor. 11:31; etc.). That knowledge marked a complete caesura in Paul's life. What had been gain was now loss because of the surpassing excellence of the knowledge of Christ Jesus (Phil. 3:8). Paul gives no details of this experience. Acts mentions Ananias of Damascus (9:17) as the one who transmitted the Holy Spirit and Paul's call to him. There is a tension between Acts and Galatians at this point.[10]

2. *Paul's Proclamation Vindicated by His Earlier Ministry (1:16b—2:14)*

After asserting that the gospel came to him directly by God's action, Paul now shows that he proclaimed this gospel with positive results before he came to Galatia. The argument proceeds both chronologically and conceptually.

a. In Arabia (1:16b-17). The effect of the call is instantaneous. "Immediately" (the term is omitted in the RSV) Paul **went away into Arabia** (**Arabia** at this time means the region east and south of Syria). Paul sets up an antithesis between conferring with any human being (**flesh and blood,** cf. Matt. 16:17) or going **to Jerusalem to those who were apostles before me,** on the one hand, and his trip to Arabia, on the other. He went to carry out his task as apostle, a title he implicitly claims in v. 17. His call led to immediate proclamation of the gospel that required no human approbation. When finished there, he returned to Damascus, not Jerusalem.

b. His Ministry Required No Corporate Approval by the Jerusalem Church (1:18-24). But Paul did not stay away from Jerusalem in perpetuity. **After three years** he spent two weeks in **Jerusalem,** where he visited **Cephas** (Aramaic for "Peter") and also saw **James.** Paul makes it clear without stressing it that this trip was his decision. His purpose was **to visit Cephas** (RSV). The Greek term *historēsai,* from which our noun *history* derives, means "to inquire into" something, "to do research." It suggests that Paul first became acquainted with Peter on this visit. The subject matter of the conversations is not given, although Paul implies that it was not apostolic (i.e., Petrine) approval of his message.

It was not a visit to the Jerusalem church as the mother church of Christianity. (Paul remained personally unknown to the large majority of members in Jerusalem, 1:22.) No community approval was sought for his mission. Almost incidentally Paul mentions that he saw **none of the other apostles** in Jerusalem, **except James the Lord's brother.** Paul's visit was a private visit. Was James an apostle? The language is unclear. In 2:9 he is in a position of leadership in Jerusalem (cf. Acts 15:13-21). Paul singles him out in 1 Cor. 15:7 as the recipient of a special resurrection appearance, while the "brothers of the Lord" are mentioned in the context of the apostles in 1 Cor. 9:5. The texts are not decisive. 1 Corinthians 9 seems to exclude James from the group of apostles, while 1 Corinthians 15 (and Gal. 1:19) seem to include him. At all events, James was an important leader in Jerusalem, one of Jesus' own family.

This minimal contact with the Jerusalem church is significant for Paul. He underscores his truthfulness with a sacred-oath formula, **before God** (v. 20). He uses similar oaths in 1 Thess. 2:5 ("as God is witness"); and 2 Cor. 1:23; 11:31. In each case a point of extreme importance to Paul occasions the oath; here it is his continued independence from the Jerusalem church.

Paul next went to **the regions of Syria and Cilicia** (v. 21). Syria is the region around and south of Antioch on the Orontes, while Cilicia is the area around Tarsus on the southeastern coast of Asia Minor.[11] Barnabas brought Saul from Tarsus (Acts 9:30) to Antioch, according to Acts 11:25-26. But Galatians makes no mention of the so-called first missionary trip reported in Acts 13–14. The correlation of Acts and Galatians is very difficult at this point.

Paul is not concerned to spell out all his movements. The purpose of his account in Galatians is to demonstrate his independence of human authorities, especially Jerusalem authorities, and thereby to show that his gospel is not from humans or through humans. His statements in vv. 22-24 make that clear. Even after his visit to Jerusalem, he remains **not known by sight to the churches of Christ in Judea.** This unequivocal statement is clearly contradicted by Acts 7:58; 22:3; and 26:4-5 (Lietzmann, p. 9). Even more striking is the statement in Acts that Barnabas brought Paul to Jerusalem from Damascus and introduced him to the apostles. There in Jerusalem Paul preached so boldly that he had to be sent out of the city for his safety (9:26-30). Paul claims that they knew of him by hearsay, but would not recognize him face to face. **They glorified God because of** him; the reason is the drastic change from persecutor to proclaimer of the gospel (v. 23). Only God could have caused such a reversal of actions.

It is a reasonable suggestion that Paul's opponent(s) in Galatia came with credentials or, at the least, a claim to credentials from Jerusalem. They may have invoked the names of Cephas and/or James to support their attack on Paul's message as incomplete or less than adequate. Paul has now shown that his message was divinely given, led to proclamation in Arabia, and that its effects were a reason for doxologies in Judea.

c. When Challenged, Paul's Gospel Is Recognized by the Jerusalem Leaders (2:1-10). Paul's next (**then, again,** v. 1) visit to Jerusalem took place **after fourteen years.** His activity in the intervening years is not mentioned, since Paul is not writing an autobiography, but an apology. His companions are Barnabas and

Titus. Barnabas had introduced Paul to Antioch, according to Acts 11:22, and had been with Paul in Cyprus and Pisidia on the first journey (Acts 13; 14). Outside of Galatians Barnabas is mentioned by Paul only in 1 Cor. 9:6 and Col. 4:10. Titus is never referred to in Acts, but is mentioned eight times in 2 Corinthians. He is entrusted there with delicate negotiations on Paul's behalf. Paul implies that this is only his second visit to Jerusalem since his call, a chronology that is difficult to correlate with his visits in Acts. The matter will be discussed below after the comments on v. 10.

The events that led to the decision of vv. 9-10 are less than clear, and the details that are given are complicated by the differences between the account here and that in Acts 15:1-29. It will be argued below that Acts 15 and Galatians 2 recount the same event. It is for the moment assumed as a theory to be tested. Paul says he **went up by revelation;** his decision to go was of the same order as his call (1:16). He does not make the mode of revelation clear (prophet's word, Acts 13:1-2;[12] dream, Acts 16:9; ecstasy, Acts 22:17; 2 Cor. 12:2f.), for what is important is that the decision to go came not from Jerusalem, but by revelation at Antioch. Nor was it a personal decision; it was related to his apostolic work. In Jerusalem Paul **laid before them . . . the gospel;** that is, his gospel he preached to the Gentiles was the point of the trip. A negative decision would mean that Paul's many years of missionary work would have been lost. Paul uses the figure of **running** to describe the missionary work he does in Phil. 2:16 and (possibly) Rom. 9:16. Paul's language about the meeting is less than clear. **I laid before them** seems to refer to the Jerusalem Christians mentioned in 1:22—2:1. This would accord well with the account in Acts 15. But then Paul inserts the qualification **but privately before those who were of repute** that suggests a small, private meeting with the Jerusalem leadership. Acts makes no mention of this private conference. The leaders are referred to again in vv. 6 and 9 and are there named: **Cephas, James,** and **John.**

Two important decisions took place at Jerusalem. The first concerned Titus, a Gentile-Christian companion of Paul whose case in principle involved the situation of all Gentile Christians. He **was not compelled to be circumcised** (v. 3). Some interpreters[13] hold that Titus was voluntarily circumcised; others more correctly hold that Paul would not yield in this matter of conscience (cf. v. 5; this issue will return with force and biting sarcasm in 5:12). Paul's intense emotional involvement in the question of circumcision is indicated both by the language and the broken sentence structure of vv. 4-5. He begins the sentence in v. 4 with **but because of false brethren,** interrupts that with a relative clause, and then never completes the sentence (as indicated by the dash at the end of v. 4). The RSV mistranslates a second relative clause that begins v. 5 in order to bring order into Paul's language and provide the main clause that is not there. Paul's emotions have disturbed his grammar.

The sense is nevertheless clear in general. Christians (**false brethren**) whom Paul regards as traitors to the gospel (cf. 2 Cor. 11:26; false apostles in 2 Cor. 11:13), people who had no right to be there (**secretly brought in**), apparently raised a demand. They are distinct from the Jerusalem leaders. They infiltrated Gentile churches (Antioch?) and demanded that circumcision also apply to the·Gentiles—with all that this implied (cf. Acts 15:1-2). Apparently they were now active in Galatia (5:10; 6:12-13). Paul regards this demand of circumcision as enslavement (**bring us into bondage**), the annulment of the **freedom which we have in Christ.** Paul thus introduces an opposition that will be very important later in the letter. Christ liberates; to add the law to Paul's gospel puts humans in slavery (cf. 4:1-6). That is what the demand of circumcision meant. Small wonder that Paul's excitement leads him to suspend rules of grammar (more evident in the Greek than the RSV). The abiding validity of **the truth of the gospel** (the truth is the gospel: 2:2; 1:6-9) requires absolute rejection of the demand (v. 5). Paul was stubborn because anything less would have meant that the gospel was destroyed.[14] The demand to circumcise Titus showed the radical, destructive impact of legalizing the gospel. Paul could not accede to the demand.

The second important decision at Jerusalem is given in one long, involved sentence (vv. 6-10) that is also grammatically broken. The leaders of the church, James, Cephas, and John, are variously identified in that sentence: **those who were reputed to be something** (v. 6), **those . . . who were of repute** (v. 6b), **who were reputed to be pillars** (v. 9). Though Paul disclaims being impressed with their reputations, for God has no regard for social position (v. 6, cf. Rom. 2:11; Col. 3:25), he clearly regards their recognition of his law-free gospel of prime importance. They are the **pillars** (v. 9). This term ascribes to these three the leading role in the Jerusalem community.[15] They **added nothing to** Paul (v. 6), that is, placed no additional burden on him. Paul's gospel is accepted as he proclaimed it, because they recognized that he **had been entrusted with the gospel to the uncircumcised** (the term is particularly appropriate after vv. 3-5, more pointed than "Gentiles" would be), just **as Peter had been entrusted with the gospel to the circumcised** (v. 7, restated in v. 8). Paul claims that the "pillars" recognized his message to the non-Jews as on a par with the proclamation to the Jews. Gentiles are not second-class Christians and Paul not a second-class apostle. They **perceived the grace given to** him, a very Pauline formulation for apostleship (v. 9). And they took a symbolic action (**gave the right hand of fellowship**) that publicly ratified this agreement and openly proclaimed that the two missions did not lead to two Christian communities, but one. It was not an agreement to disagree, but rather a recognition of divided responsibility.

The sentence ends with a kind of codicil that does lay an obligation on Paul and the Gentile churches: **only . . . remember the poor.** Paul adds that he **was eager to do it.** The only problem here is the identification of the poor. It is clear that the poor are in Jerusalem. Paul works at collecting for them, as 1 Cor. 16:1-4; 2 Corinthians 8–9; and Rom. 15:25-27 demonstrate. The collection by the Gentiles for the poor in Jerusalem is a mark of the unity of faith and commitment. Two views about the identity of

the poor are held. One is that they are the economically deprived in the Jerusalem church. The other is that "the poor" is a translation of the Hebrew *ebyonim,* a title of honor the early Jewish Christians in Jerusalem had borrowed from earlier Judaism (cf. Ps. Sol. 10:6; 15:1; 18:2). Keith Nickle[16] has argued that the collection had an even greater theological significance: the collection from the Gentiles would fulfill the eschatological expectation that the wealth of the nations would flow to Jerusalem at the end-time (cf. Isa. 18:7; Hag. 2:7; Sib. Or. 3.772). The collection thus ratifies Paul's gospel, which brings such eschatological hopes to fulfillment.

Excursus: Historical Questions in Galatians 1–2. Paul's narrative in 1:13—2:10 reads like a straightforward account. Yet it raises a series of historical and chronological questions. Paul records two visits to Jerusalem (1:18f.; 2:1-10), the second being the one at which his gospel is recognized. Acts records three visits before the second missionary journey (9:26-30; 11:30—12:25; 15:1-29) and two later visits (18:22; 21:17ff.). Paul solemnly swears (1:20) that he has truthfully reported the entire account of his relationships with Jerusalem. But the third visit in Acts (chap. 15) seems to correlate with the second visit in Galatians (2:1-10).

This commentary argues that Galatians 2 and Acts 15 are variant accounts of the same meeting. In both cases Paul, Barnabas, Peter, and James play key roles. (Titus is never mentioned in Acts. His mission in Acts 15 shows that his case was not recognized as significant by others.) The problem is the same—circumcision as sign of the abiding validity of the law for all Christians. The outcome is the same—recognition of Paul's gospel as legitimate. There are differences. Paul does not mention the unrest at Antioch reported in Acts 15:1-2. Paul speaks of a revelation leading to the trip, Acts of a decision by the Antioch community. The most significant variation lies in the formulation of the outcome. Acts 15:20, 29 records four prohibitions laid on the Gentiles: abstinence from pollution by idols, from blood, from strangled animals, and from fornication. These were regarded by later Jews as universally binding on the entire human race since the days of Noah.[17] Acts does not mention the division of labor, while Paul does not mention the fourfold prescription in Galatians and does not refer to it in 1 Corinthians 8-10 when discussing the eating of meat offered to idols. With all the similarity, the differences are striking.

There is a second complicating problem of chronology.[18] The following data have to be taken into account. Paul's arrival in Corinth is dated approximately A.D. 50, based on the proconsular year of Gallio (Acts 18:12). The meeting in Acts 15 thus is dated about A.D. 49 (Caird) or 48 (Ogg). The 3-year interval between the conversion and Paul's visit to Jerusalem and the 14-year interval mentioned in 2:1 suggest that Paul's conversion took place somewhere between A.D. 32 and 34 (the variation is caused by the inclusive reckoning that counts a partial year as a full one). The famine visit (the second in Acts) in either A.D. 45-46 or 46-47 (Ogg, *Odyssey*, p. 53) is too early to fit the chronological schema of Galatians.

Various solutions have been proposed—and none of them satisfies entirely. One solution identifies Gal. 2:1-10 with the second visit of Acts. It solves the chronological difficulty by including the 3 years of Gal. 1:18 in the 14 years of Gal. 2:1, a solution that contradicts the chronological structure of Galatians. Proponents argue that Galatians 2 is essentially a private consultation between religious leaders, while Acts 15 is an open, public meeting of the Jerusalem church. The second meeting is necessary because the agreement reached in the first did not hold, as Gal. 2:11-14 shows. That view founders on the statement of Acts 11:29 that Barnabas and Saul visited the "elders" in Jerusalem, a term that will simply not fit Peter (if it may fit James). And Acts 15 in no way suggests that there had been an earlier discussion or solution.

A second solution (more possible) rests on a theory of different source documents. One form suggests that the second and third visits in Acts are actually the same visit, but known to Luke through two different accounts used by him to mark off stages of development in his narrative. There is no textual evidence for this suggestion. It appears to be a case of explaining the difficult by the obscure. There is a greater textual basis for the suggestion that the reports of Paul and Acts are based on variant memoranda of the same event, neither of them absolutely complete. Acts 15 records the event from the Jerusalem perspective. The fourfold prohibition (15:20, 29) would be highly important to the Jewish-Christian community there, but not to the Gentile churches served by Paul. Paul is dependent on an Antioch source that can be recognized in Gal. 2:6-8, where the Greek name *Peter* is used of the apostle. Paul elsewhere uses the Semitic *Cephas* (Gal. 1:18; 2:9, 11; 1 Cor. 9:5; 15:5). The Gentile church in Antioch remembered that the Pauline gospel was approved without the addition of Jewish legal obligations. Paul himself recalled the case of Titus (which became a point of honor for him) and the remembrance of the poor. Jerusalem might well stress the separation of Jewish and Gentile missions and the universally binding legal prescriptions. The variations are such as local pride and interests might well cause; they are of the type that historians know well in other contexts. Thus Gal. 2:1-10 and Acts 15 record the same incident from different perspectives. (It is a minor point in favor of this solution that it was universally held until the 19th century.) This solution fits well the territorial theory of the recipients. It leaves some problems unresolved, but fewer than any other historical reconstruction.

d. Paul's Gospel Vindicated in Confrontation with Cephas at Antioch (2:11-14). Paul's apologetic recounting of history has one more scene to unroll. At a later, though unspecified, date in Antioch, Paul publicly maintained his position against an attack from Jerusalem that swayed Cephas. Paul stood up to him in public because he was wrong (v. 11). While the text nowhere explicitly says so, it implies that Paul was successful in his opposition to Peter's compromising cowardice. The bold summation of v. 11 is explicated in vv. 12-14. Cephas has come to Antioch, Paul's own center of operations. No reason for the visit is given. (Was it in some sense an official visit?) Paul mentions only such details as serve his purpose. The situation is one of table fellowship with Gentile Christians. Cephas upon arrival eats with the Gentiles, an act that has more than social significance. Meals began with benedictions of God and were thus regarded as worship by pious Jews. To eat together is to share an altar.[19] This meal is therefore an implicit affirmation of the Gentile form of Christianity. The arrival of **certain men . . . from James** changed Cephas' attitude. Paul is vague as to their identity and authority, a problem much discussed. The phrase suggests that James sent them; they are not the radical Jewish Christians of 2:4, but those who have in principle agreed to a different, law-free life-style for the Gentile Christians. Paul does not say that they demanded that Cephas change. Rather Cephas **drew back** and broke off the table fellowship, an action which in context is equivalent to rejection of the Gentiles. The basis for his action is not principle, but fear of the circumcision party. This phrase, describing Jewish Christians, looks back to 2:3 and forward to 5:3, 10; 6:12, 13. Circumcision is the symbol of fidelity to Jewish law.

Cephas' action leads the other Jewish Christians, who had eaten with Gentiles, to **act insincerely** (v. 13). The term is under-translated. It means to "play the hypocrite," to act in a false manner. The infection extends even to Barnabas, a leader of the Antioch community (2:1; cf. Acts 11:22-26; 12:25; 13:1-3). Paul does not say so, but the position represented by those from James and Cephas must have appeared compelling to the Jewish Christians of Antioch. It is reasonable to suggest that they now held that the Jerusalem accord of 2:8-10 implied that Gentiles and Jews could be Christian on different terms, but not in one community. The Antioch church is being split down the middle on theological grounds.

Paul intervenes (v. 14). The Jerusalem accord had recognized his gospel with the right hand of fellowship. The Jewish-Christian actions in Antioch call that gospel into question. **They were not straightforward about the truth of the gospel** (v. 14). The RSV obscures a point in Paul's language. **The gospel** is in some manner a standard or criterion of action that takes priority over other standards.[20] The verb "to be straightforward" means to "walk upright" and connotes correctness of action. ("Walk" is an ethical term in Hebrew.) The action of the Jewish Christians, above all of Cephas, calls the gospel into question. (This is the last of the seven occurrences of the term *gospel* in the letter. After this Paul speaks of "promise" or "freedom" or "grace" to denote the same position.)

Because others had followed Cephas' actions—even Barnabas—Cephas must be confronted publicly, **before them all.** Paul begins (v. 14) by quoting his own words, as the RSV punctuation indicates. Cephas' actions themselves have shown that Jewish Christians do not have to separate from Gentiles (**live like Jews**). Yet his actions now compel the Gentiles to recognize the Gentile/Jew distinction. They could preserve unity in the community only by adopting Jewish life and law, by Judaizing. In effect Cephas is demanding more of the Gentiles than Paul's preaching had, an action that goes beyond faith.

3. *Conclusion and Transition: Justification by Faith Works Drastic Change (2:15-21)*

Paul concludes his historical apology with the confrontation at

Antioch. The gospel has shown its power to expose false conduct that divides the church. Verses 15-21 point out the theological significance of the confrontation at Antioch and provide a transition to the next section (3:1—5:12).[21] Paul begins by making affirmations that every Jewish Christian would accept (vv. 15, 16). **Jews by birth** have an advantage over the Gentiles. Jews are righteous (cf. Ps. Sol. 13), do what the law demands (Rom. 2:17-20, Josephus *Ag. Ap.* 2.178), and so have righteousness (Rom. 3:1,2; 9:4,5). By contrast the Gentile is a *sinner* (Ps. Sol. 1:1; 2:1) who does not possess the law (Rom. 2:14) and does not do righteousness (Rom. 9:30, 31, 1 Cor. 6:1; 9:21). The language is compressed to the point of loss of intelligibility. The Gentile is outside the covenant (cf. Paul's contrary argument in 3:15-18 and Rom. 4:9ff., based on the priority of promise) and so outside the system of forgiveness. Verse 16 also states a position held by Jewish Christians (**yet who know**): justification comes by **faith in Christ** and **not by works of the law.** That conviction is grounded in the OT, as indicated by Paul's free citation of Ps. 143:2 with the addition of the words **by works of the law.**[22] As formulated in v. 16a the view is not specifically Christian, except for the reference to Jesus. Jews at Qumran held that God justified by forgiving sin: "I lean on Thy grace and on the multitude of Thy mercies, for Thou wilt pardon iniquity, and through Thy righteousness [Thou wilt purify man] of his sin" (1QH 4.36-37, Vermes; cf. 1QS 11.2-3, 10-15).[23] Jewish Christians are distinguished by their faith in Jesus.

They showed this distinction, argues Paul (v. 16b), in that they **have believed in Jesus Christ** (better, "came to believe") **in order to be justified by faith in Christ, and not by works of law.** Paul follows this by restating the principle that they **know,** i.e., confess. This verse is seminal for what follows in the next three chapters. New and important terminology is introduced that will dominate the subsequent chapters. *Justification* is first mentioned in Galatians in v. 16 (to recur in 3:8, 11, 24, and 5:4). **Faith** first appears here in the letter, and as the antonym to **works.** **Faith** is directed to Christ, that is, has a specific content: the

unique work of Jesus Christ. **Works** are those **of the law.** Thus
the law is set in opposition to Christ as works are to faith. These
oppositions will run throughout the next chapters. They make
clear that for Paul justification is not earned by actions, that works
do not complete justification, and that faith is not itself the su-
preme work of humans. Verses 15-16 lay the base for what follows.

Paul clarifies his interpretation of this common starting point
by ruling out false ideas in vv. 17-18. To **endeavor to be justified
in Christ** is a difficult phrase that has been taken in quite opposite
senses. It might describe Christians who think their own efforts
partly enable God's acceptance of them. They will simply discover
they are **sinners.** One cannot accuse Christ of being a servant of
sin because of their attitude. But, attractive as it is, this interpretation does not account for Paul's sharp rejection (**certainly
not!** is far too weak a translation). The "God forbid" of the KJV,
though archaic, is closer to Paul's horror. It must be that **endeavor
to be justified in Christ** is a good description of Paul's own view.
But a false conclusion has been drawn: since God justifies the
ungodly (Rom. 4:5), then a positive value is placed on sin and
Christ leads men to sin. That is simply too wrong for Paul to
accept it as a possibility.

Verse 18 makes clear why. What was torn down is **the law,**
that to which works relates. To bring human achievement back
into justification is to reestablish the law. But it reveals that a
human is **a transgressor** (cf. Rom. 7:7). Indeed the law increases
trespass (Rom. 5:20).

Paul's own position is stated powerfully in vv. 19-20. The personal "I-language" dominates. But Paul's thought is more than
autobiographical here, for his experience is exemplary for all
Christians. (Similar language is found in Rom. 7:7-25; 1 Cor. 4:1-
7; Gal. 6:14; and elsewhere.) Four lapidary statements are made;
they are expanded later in the letter. **I through the law died to
the law, that I might live to God.** The break with the law (Torah)
is so complete that only the language of death and (new) life is
adequate to describe it. Later, in 3:19-25, Paul will make clear
that the law's function and power belong to a person's pre-Chris-

tian existence. That comes to an end by death in Baptism (Rom. 6:2,3). Death brings the force of law to an end (cf. Rom. 7:1-6). A new life is the result of this death, a life lived by the power of God to the honor of God (cf. Rom. 6:10-22). Paul is no Christ monist. Ultimately, for him God is the one before whom man lives and to whom he owes love and life (cf. Rom. 6:11,13,22, for the language of slavery to God). What that life means is described in 5:13—6:10. But the new life has a historical basis; it is not just Paul's feeling. **I have been crucified with Christ** is Paul's second affirmation. He explains the significance of this death of Christ in 3:10-13. Paul uses the motif of dying and rising with Christ a number of times (cf. Rom. 6:1-14; 2 Cor. 5:15; Gal. 6:14; Rom. 7:4ff.).[24] It stresses the sharp break that comes with faith in Christ, a break of abiding significance as the perfect tense underscores.

Verse 20 makes one of the most drastic assertions about this change in all of Paul's letters. **It is no longer I who live, but Christ who lives in me.** The language is mystical in tone. It can best be paralleled in John (cf. John 17:23) and in the "mystery religions" of the Roman empire. This is not subjectivity on Paul's part; rather Paul underscores the sharp break every Christian feels; Baptism means a new power is at work that cannot be accounted for from within the human individual. A new "life power" is at work, **Christ in me.** In 4:6 Paul speaks of the "Spirit of his Son" coming into human hearts. The Spirit individualizes what the Christ has done. (Cf. the role of the Spirit in 3:1-5.)

And the life I now live in the flesh I live by faith in the Son of God, who loved me and gave himself for me. Paul's mystic language differs from that of contemporaries. He does not feel that divine indwelling removes the person's own mind and will.[25] Paul retains self-awareness in the world (**flesh**) of normal human life, yet lives out of faith directed to the Son of God. Faith here is the grasping of Christ's work so that it becomes effective in life. Paul cites familiar creedal phrases to describe the work of Christ (cf. Eph. 5:2; Gal. 1:4; etc.). This alert life of faith in the real world shows that Paul does not **nullify,** set out of the way, the grace of God (v. 21). **Nullify** is a legal term for setting aside a will (Gal. 3:15), the law (Heb. 10:28), or a commandment (Mark 7:9).

The phrasing is ironic. **If justification were through the law,** that would nullify God's grace. The clash between **nullify** and **grace** sharpens Paul's point. The death of Christ and the law are mutually exclusive. If the law is in effect, the death of Christ is futile. If the death of Christ is significant and powerful, then the law can no longer have force. Paul here draws the great either-or of the Christian faith that flies in the face of much so-called common sense. [26] The themes for the next two sections of his great apology are thereby laid before the Galatians.

Stand Firm in the Liberty that Is Grounded Both in Experience and Scripture (3:1—5:12)

The second section of Paul's apology turns to consideration of the effects of Paul's preaching among the Galatians. The section contains two major arguments from the OT, both based on God's promise to Abraham (3:6-18; 4:21-31). There is exquisite theological thinking here, as well as in the passage dealing with the law (3:19-29). But these are all in the service of the appeal to the Galatians to **stand fast** (5:1). Ironic description of the Galatians' attitudes (3:1-5), descriptions of God's action for them (4:1-6), and expressions of fear for them (4:8-11) all serve this appeal, which is made twice in different terms (4:12-19; 5:1-12). The tone of irony, sarcasm (5:12), and appeal shows the extreme danger Paul sees in the Galatians' position. His entire work for them is at stake (4:11) and he is at his wits' end (4:20). Paul's language shows that this letter is a letter of last resort in the Galatian situation.

1. *Rebuke Based on Reception of the Spirit on Hearing the Gospel (3:1-5)*

Paul's emotions are running high, as his initial **O foolish Galatians!** shows (v. 1). [27] He repeats the charge in v. 3. In his initial question he asks with rhetorical exaggeration whether someone

has bewitched them. Paul cannot imagine that a Christian would knowingly desert the gospel. Paul appeals in these verses to the Christian experience of the Galatians, both their past experience of the Spirit (v. 2) and their present experience of the gift of God: **who supplies the Spirit to you and works miracles among you** (v. 5). This appeal (v. 4) assumes that the Spirit produces effects in Christians that can be phenomenologically verified. In Galatians the Spirit is first mentioned in this paragraph; it will recur 14 times. Paul introduces the Spirit as a well-known entity—the powerful presence of the resurrected Christ in the Christian (cf. 4:6, "Spirit of his Son"). The Spirit is the power of the new age in the present, the demonstration of the reality of God's work in Jesus.[28] Galatians 5 will show that the Spirit is both the power and the standard for the Christian life.

The Spirit came to people **before whose eyes Jesus Christ was publicly portrayed as crucified** (v. 1; cf. 3:13, 14). Jesus' death is the decisive redemptive event in Galatians (1:4; 6:12, 14). It is the vivid, public pronouncement of that Jesus (cf. 1 Cor. 1:18, 23; 2:2; Gal. 5:11, 24), heard by the Galatians (**hearing with faith,** v. 2) that brought the Spirit. It required no actions (**works of the law,** v. 2) on their part. The Spirit is not induced, but given with faith that responds to the proclamation of Christ as crucified redeemer. Experience of the Spirit's activity shows that one has moved from the realm of *flesh* (v. 3) to a new existence. Note that flesh and law are put into the same category: both belong to the past left behind with the gift of the Spirit. To reintroduce works of the law is to have the experience of the Spirit and his miracles (better, "acts of power," v. 5) without benefit (**in vain,** v. 4). It is not a matter of the proclamation having the complementary addition of works of the law; rather, the one negates the other.

2. Appeal to Support Paul's Message: The First Argument from Scripture (3:6—4:11)

The appeal to experience (3:1-5) opposed "works of law" and

"flesh" to Christ crucified, Spirit, and faith. Paul now goes on to show that this opposition is based on the OT story of Abraham (3:6-18). The Abrahamic promise leads to an understanding of the proper role of the law (Torah) in relation to Christian existence (3:19—4:11) that issues in a broad appeal to remain with Paul's proclamation (4:12-20). Thus the OT argument is used as a springboard for an appeal. The apologetic character remains preeminent; Paul writes Galatians as a concerned pastor, not an abstract theologian.

a. Abraham Was Justified by Faith—and So Are We (3:6-9). Paul introduces Abraham as the great OT exemplar of what he has just argued in 3:1-5 (**thus,** v. 6). Abraham is the "rock from which you [Israel] were hewn" (Isa. 51:1-2); Israel is the "seed of Abraham" (Jer. 33:26; Isa. 41:8). Abraham, according to later Judaism, was "faithful when tested, and it was reckoned to him as righteousness" (1 Macc. 2:52, citing Gen. 15:6). Sir. 44:20 claims that he "kept the law of the Most High, . . . tested he was found faithful. Therefore the Lord assured him by an oath that the nations would be blessed through his posterity." The promise is based on prior fidelity and keeping of the law. Abraham is the "forefather [of Israel] according to the flesh" (Rom. 4:1). Paul's selection is carefully made.[29]

Abraham is an example of "hearing with faith" (3:5), as Gen. 15:6 says: **Abraham "believed God and it was reckoned to him as righteousness"** (3:6). Paul understands Abraham's faith as a response to God's prior promise. Thus it is antithetical to acts of conformity to law as a means of being recognized as righteous. The best commentary on Paul's view is Romans 4. Abraham did not have to present anything to God; he had only to believe. God's response was therefore an accounting that was an act of grace, not payment. (This is another place where Paul and James part company; cf. Jas. 2:21-23.)

Abraham is both model and father of all believers. The RSV
so you see is very weak in 3:7; it is rather something like "Therefore understand this." The descendants of Abraham foreseen in
Genesis are those who are **men of faith,** that is, who share Abraham's posture. No other qualification is necessary. In 3:8 Paul
speaks of **the scripture** in the sense of a particular passage and
cites Gen. 12:3. **"In you shall all the nations be blessed"** is there
in Genesis because the passage "foresaw" that God **would justify
the Gentiles by faith.** Paul personifies Scripture. It testifies that
all persons are justified in the same way as Abraham, Jew and
Gentile alike. Paul seems to interpret the **in you** of Gen. 12:3 in
the sense of corporate personality in 3:9. **With Abraham men of
faith** are blessed. The description of Abraham, **who had faith,**
underscores the essential point for Paul: people of faith get the
same blessing as Abraham, justification (cf. Rom. 4:16).

*b. The Law Demands Perfect Performance, Not Faith (3:10-
12).*   Paul often supports a point by assuming the opposing position and showing that it will not bring about the desired conclusion.[30] So here vv. 10-12 discuss justification on the basis of
the law to show that it contradicts the action of God with Abraham
(vv. 6-9). **All who rely on works of the law** stresses the universality
of the insight. However, they are not justified, but **under a curse**
(v. 10). Paul carefully avoids saying that the law itself is a curse
or evil. Paul holds that the law is good (Rom. 7:12). The law
demands absolute, total fulfillment, as Deut. 27:26 states. Paul
inserts the word **all** into the citation and replaces **words** of the
OT text with **things written in the book of the law.** Both changes
reflect Paul's experience with the law. He inferred the **all** from
the complementary statement on Deut. 28:1, while he knew the
law in the form of written document (cf. 2 Cor. 3:4-6; Rom. 7:6)
from the past. The law assumes one can keep its demands (cf.
Deut. 28:1); not keeping the law brings the curse (cf. Jas. 2:10;
Rom. 2:25ff.). The curse is very simply not receiving the blessing
mentioned in 3:9, i.e., not being "blessed with Abraham."

Paul reinforces this conclusion by interpreting two citations of the OT. Hab. 2:4 is cited (3:11) in a slightly edited form: **"He who through faith is righteous shall live"** (cf. Rom. 1:17). The Hebrew had said "the righteous shall live by HIS faith,"[31] while the Greek OT read "the righteous shall live by my [God's] faith." The omission of the possessive pronoun allows the interpretation the RSV puts on the passage. Faith means holding fast to God's word and deed. But since the law works on the principle of doing, of action, **it is evident that no man** [one] **is justified before God by the law.** Verse 12 states the conclusion that **the law does not rest on faith** (better, "is not on the side of faith") because it operates on the principle of fulfillment, of action, of doing, as Lev. 18:5 states: **He who does them shall live by them** (cf. Rom. 10:5). Thus Paul makes certain that the exclusivity of works and faith is clear, that faith cannot be related to the law, and that justification must be by faith apart from works of law. The proof from the effect of the opposite is complete.[32]

c. Christ's Death under the Curse of the Law (3:13-14).

Abruptly, without any transition (quite contrary to good Greek style), Christ's soteriological act of death is introduced into the discussion. It is viewed under two aspects. On the one hand it is the act of redemption (**redeemed us**); on the other hand it shows that Christ was under the curse of the law (**having become a curse**). This paradoxical death is the ending of the power of the law and the opening of the promise to the Gentiles. How can that be? The **curse of the law** is that it keeps people from receiving the promise. Christ's death freed us from that curse. Redemption is properly the buying free of a slave or a captive. (The term is used again in 4:5 of freedom from the law; for the sense cf. 1 Cor. 6:20; 7:30.)[33] Christ has **redeemed us.** The first-person object rings of creedal language (cf. the "we" in 4:5); it may be a reflection of the creed underlying 4:5. In context the **us** refers specifically to those **who rely on works of the law** (v. 10), that is, Jewish Christians, among whom Paul numbers himself (cf. 2:15). (Galatian Gentiles were in slavery to the "elemental

spirits," not the law; cf. 4:9.) This makes the passage very pointed.
The one innocent, righteous Jew (cf. 2 Cor. 5:21) is made a **curse
for us,** i.e., the Jewish Christians, so that Gentiles might obtain
the promise.

That Christ became a curse is demonstrated by the manner of
his death ("crucified," v. 1). Deut. 21:23 originally referred to
the custom of hanging a dead criminal's corpse on a tree to publish
the punishment as warning to others. It was evidence the person
had been "accursed by God." Paul drops the words "by God."
An innocent man cannot be so treated by God. But his innocent
death **on a tree** meant that his death was a curse **for us.** The
death of an innocent Jew, according to Jewish belief, had atoning
effect.[34] Jesus' death is interpreted as **for us,** i.e., as a death that
buys us free from the enslaving force of the law. The basis is a
text from the Torah itself, cited with the formula **it is written** (cf.
3:10; 4:22, 27).

This death on the cross had two effects, as v. 14 makes clear.
Once the death of Jesus removed the curse of the law, the way
was clear to achieve God's purpose, the inclusion of the Gentiles
in **the blessing of Abraham** (Gen. 18:18; 12:3). The logic is clear.
Justification is either by works of law or by faith. The death of
Jesus shows that the law brings a curse, not a blessing. Therefore
the blessing must come by faith, and that opens the blessing to
all, to the Jew because of the redemptive death of Christ and to
the Gentile because it is hearing and faith (3:2) that bring the
blessing. The purpose of God is effected, as the experience of
the Galatians makes clear. The Spirit is present (3:1-5) **through
faith** (v. 14). Paul here combines two terms that he usually keeps
separate: **promise** and **Spirit. Promise** is usually reserved for all
that Christ was to accomplish, while **the Spirit** is the anticipatory
power of the end-time in the present (cf. 2 Cor. 1:22; 5:5).

Verse 14 heaps up the great terms of the discussion on the side
of faith: **blessing, Abraham, promise, Spirit.** The reference to
Spirit recalls 3:1-5, but does not serve to close the argument, as
the reference to the Spirit in 4:6 shows. While the passage is
justifiably regarded as a high point in soteriological thinking, it

must be interpreted as part of the larger apologetic argument of which it is a part. One therefore should not engage in speculation about such unasked questions as to whom the redemption money was paid. The language is mythological in the ancient sense; it expresses a truth of such high order that it can be done only metaphorically.

d. Promise Is Prior to and Superior to the Law (3:15-18). A Jewish Christian has an objection to Paul's position. Both the promise and the law are words from God. The later law of Moses, precisely because it is later, is either a specifying of the covenant with Abraham or a modification of it that is legally binding. Later Jewish tradition spoke of Abraham as one who kept the law long before it was given. [35] Does not the law supersede the earlier covenant? In that case the position Paul had arrived at in v. 14 would be negated completely.

Paul needs to show that this objection is impossible. He does it by invoking a legal principle that is universally recognized in the secular realm. **To give a human example** might better be translated "to give a commonly accepted human principle" (cf. Rom. 3:5). The use of the term **brethren** is the first indication of positive relationship to the Galatians since 1:11; the term will recur in 4:12, 28, 31; 5:11, 13; 6:1, 18. Paul is seeking the assent of the hearers to his analogical reasoning. He introduces a legal principle. Once a will has been properly put in force (**ratified**) no one can **annul** it or **add** (a codicil) **to it.** These are all technical legal terms, as are a second Greek term for **annul** (v. 17), and **will.** Paul is dealing with the law of inheritance.

Gen. 17:1-11 calls the promise made to Abraham a **covenant** made with him and his seed (**offspring,** v. 16). (The Greek term translated **will** in v. 15 is the term used in the Greek OT for "covenant," the legally binding agreement between an overlord and his subject or servant.) [36] This covenant is to be eternal (Gen. 17:7), and therefore not subject to change or annulment, if Abraham and his seed keep its terms. Paul stresses the fact that the word **offspring** ("seed" in Greek) is singular. It refers **to one,**

"And to your offspring," which is Christ. The argument from the singular is less than persuasive philologically, but compelling theologically. "Seed" could easily be a collective noun referring to the nation Israel (it is used collectively in 3:29!). The theological clue lies in the relationship of the **offspring** to the **promise.** The offspring must be the bearer of the promise that includes the nations of which Abraham is father (cf. Gen. 17:5,6). That came to pass with Christ (3:22,23,24,27). Abraham received the promise, the seed realizes it, and through him others come to share in the promise and be included in the seed (3:29).

Verse 17 applies the human analogy to the problem directly (**this is what I mean**). The later law (Torah, the Sinai legislation) cannot annul the **covenant previously ratified by God, so as to make the promise void.** The language is striking for what it does not say. The covenant with Abraham was ratified **by God.** But there is no mention of either God or Moses in connection with the later law. (The phrase "law of God" occurs only in Rom. 7:22,25; 8:7 in Paul.) Moses is alluded to in 3:19,20 ("intermediary"), but not named; the great hero of faith dwelt on at length in Acts 7:20-44 and Heb. 11:23-29 is named only in Romans (5:14; 9:15; 10:15,19), 1 Corinthians (9:9; 10:2), and 2 Corinthians (3:7,13,15) in Paul.[37] 2 Corinthians shows that Moses is a figure of glory who can be a threat to Christ, while Rom. 5:14 identifies Moses with the law through which sin is reckoned. Only in 1 Cor. 10:2 is he viewed positively as a type of Christ. In our passage Paul avoids saying that the law is not from God, but neither does he affirm that it is. The lateness of the law[38] is stressed to affirm that it cannot nullify the heart of the covenant with Abraham, the promise. God does not change his mind about the promise.[39]

Verse 18 introduces a new term, **inheritance,** into the discussion as Paul draws the conclusion. It is suggested by the use of the term **offspring** in v. 16; it prepares the way for the use of the term "heir" in v. 29 and in 4:1-7. Once again Paul sets up an alternative: **by law** or **by promise** (cf. Rom. 4:14). Compromise is impossible. If by law, it must be produced by actions, works. But **God gave it to Abraham by a promise.** Jewish Christians and Paul alike supported the idea of promise. Paul's point now is that the mode of giving ruled out any idea of works of law to merit the promise. Its origin as gift means that the realization of the promise must also be as a gift, by faith.

e. The Law Has a Restricted, Subsidiary Role (3:19-22). The caesura between promise and law is so sharp in Paul's argument that the question of v. 19 is inevitably raised by any pious Jewish Christian, **Why then the law?** The law in Paul's argument appears useless. Does God speak useless words and do useless things? Jews (and Jewish Christians) stressed the eternity of the law. It existed before the world was made. "Seven things were created before the world was created, namely, the Torah, penance, paradise, hell, the throne of glory, the [heavenly] temple, and the name of the Messiah."[40] The law is the source of wisdom (Sir. 51:19, 23-27) and life (Sir. 17:11). It is permanent and unchanging (Matt. 5:18). It will be observed in the messianic age, or replaced by a new Torah.[41] The Torah (law) is the cornerstone and foundation of Judaism (and Jewish Christianity). "R. Jose said: He that honours the Law is himself honoured by mankind; and he that dishonours the Law shall himself be dishonoured by mankind" (M. Aboth 4:6, Danby's trans.). The question is a cry from the heart of Jewish Christians.

Every word of Paul's response in vv. 19-20 is, as Oepke says, like the blow of a fist. Four points are made about the Torah that fly in the face of Jewish-Christian piety:

(1) The law **was added because of transgressions.** The law is later than the promise and deals only with the breaking of explicit demands (**transgressions**). Paul's words elsewhere clarify these. The law makes transgressions known and so stimulates them (Rom. 7:7f.). Where there is no law, there are no transgressions (Rom. 4:15), but where the law is present, it multiplies transgressions (Rom. 5:20). Jews held that the law restrained sin, served as a boundary and curb (cf. Josephus, *Ag. Ap.* 2.174). There is in Paul no word of this. For him the law is the "law of

sin and death" (Rom. 8:2), the "power of sin" (1 Cor. 15:56) from which we need deliverance.

(2) The law is not eternal, but has only a restricted period of validity in human history. It was added after the promise (cf. Rom. 5:20) and lasts only **till the offspring should come to whom the promise had been made** (cf. v. 16). While Jews held that "the law . . . endures for ever" (Bar. 4:1), Paul argues that the law is a temporary expedient.

(3) The law **was ordained by angels.** Exod. 19:16 does not mention angels, but speaks of thunder, lightning, clouds, and a trumpet blast (all marks of a theophany). Later Jews seem to interpret these phenomena as being (or including) angelic beings; cf. Deut. 33:2 in the Greek OT; T. Dan 6:2 speaks of the angel who is a mediator between God and man. Acts 7:53 and Heb. 2:2 speak of the angels participating in the giving of the law. In Judaism the introduction of the angels served two purposes, to exalt God and to glorify the law.[42] Paul has a different stress, as v. 20 will make clear. The angelic origin means that the law has an origin inferior to that of the promise. God gave the promise directly to Abraham; the law is not directly from God, but from God via angels.[43]

(4) The law did not come to Israel directly from the angels, but **through an intermediary** (a mediator, arbitrator, middleman). The mediator is clearly Moses, though he is not named (Exod. 31:18; 32:19; Lev. 26:46). Moses as mediator of the covenant (and so the law) was a glorious figure; cf. 2 Cor. 3:7ff.; As. Mos. 1:14; Philo, *Vit. Moys.* 3.19. Verse 20 indicates that Paul regards Moses' mediation as proof of the secondary character of the law: **Now a mediator implies more than one; but God is one.** "God is one" is the acclamation that summarizes the creed of Judaism (Deut. 6:4; Mal. 2:10; Rom. 3:30; 1 Cor. 8:6; etc.). The existence of a mediator for the law implies that God is not the law's originator (or at least not directly). A mediator is not of one, therefore the mediator did not mediate between God and Israel, but between the angels and Israel. A mediator negotiates between parties and the result is a compromise document. The law is at best from

God only at third hand; the promise comes directly without intermediaries.

Every one of these four statements about the law is a direct affront to Jewish-Christian sensibilities when Paul says that the law is "a temporally limited addition to the primary promise which has the function of bringing sins to consciousness and so to spread them out, a testament from the mediating angels and Moses," not of God.[44]

One can almost hear the sarcasm in the Jewish-Christian response. **Is the law then against the promises of God?** That appears to be the position to which Paul must come. But Paul recoils in horror: **Certainly not** (v. 21) and adds a description of the function of the law. The law does not have the power to **make alive;** life is on the side of those righteous by faith, not works (3:11, 12). The Spirit which gives life (1 Cor. 15:45) does not come by works of law but by faithful hearing (3:2). Righteousness does not come by the law. The promise is "in fuller agreement with God's own character than was the Law."[45] Luther's suggestion that the law is a word of the *deus absconditus* (the hidden God), but the gospel a word of the *deus revelatus* (the revealed God) accords with Paul's interpretation of the law.[46]

The law brings a curse (3:13). It is "for the sake of transgressions" (3:19, my translation). It does not make alive (3:21), but "proved to be death" (Rom. 7:10). As far as justification is concerned it is no alternative to the promise; its function must be drastically different. **The scripture consigned all things to sin** (v. 22 RSV). The NEB is better: "But Scripture has declared the whole world to be prisoners in subjection to sin." The Scripture here is the law, as the context demands. It has a power; it imprisons man with sin as the jailor (note that the same function is ascribed to the law in 3:23). **All things** is a standard phrase to denote the totality of the creation (cf. Rom. 8:19-22). This imprisoning power of the law makes clear that the promise can only come to believers. **What was promised to faith in Jesus Christ** (3:22) is a paraphrase that misses the point of Paul. Literally it reads "the promise from faith of Jesus Christ," stressing the tie of promise to faith. It is not clear whether this refers to faith in Jesus Christ or (more likely) the faithfulness that Jesus Christ shows to the promise (cf. 3:23 and its use of *faith*).

f. By Baptism, Faith Frees Us from the Law and Makes Us Children of God (3:23-29).   Verse 22 cannot be Paul's last word on the law, because it is essentially negative. In 3:23—4:7 Paul uses three interrelated pictures to show that the law has a temporary but useful role to play in relation to the significance of Christ. The pictures show that Paul is thinking in terms of chronologically distinct periods (cf. 1:4). While Paul does not make it explicit, the reader will be reminded of Paul's autobiographical description in 1:13-16, though the terminology varies. Paul's experience is not unique; it is in small compass what God is doing in all human history.

The first picture (v. 23) describes the law as holding humans "in protective custody" (**confined,** RSV). Humans were **under the law** (as they were "under sin" in v. 22), **kept** (the same term as "consigned" in v. 22), locked up in jail with the law as jailer. That lasts, however, only **until faith should be revealed, before faith came.** The phraseology is striking. Had there not been faith already in Abraham's case? How can faith "come"? Paul makes the sense clear in v. 24 where the parallel phrase, **until Christ came,** draws an equal sign between faith and Christ. Paul plays verbally on different senses of the Greek term *pistis.* It denotes the act of believing or trust in many places in Paul. But the term can also refer to fidelity or faithfulness, reliability. In judicial language it means "proof" or "pledge."[47] That "proof" on God's part calls for the response of faith by humankind. Christ, according to Paul, is the ultimate demonstration that righteousness comes by belief, not by law (3:21,22). Christ reveals the end of the rule of the law as custodian. This means that a new era has come in history that calls for the corresponding human reaction: faith, not works.

The second picture, the *paidagōgos* in vv. 24-25, clarifies the first and draws a conclusion from it. The law is a **custodian,** like the slave who is assigned supervision and responsibility for a minor son in a Greek family. He makes the boy behave modestly, sees to it that he goes to school without loitering on the way, carries his slate, protects him against pederasty in the gymnasium, and teaches him manners. He could exercise disciplinary force on the boy. The regimen lasted for the boy from about 6 to 16 years of age.[48] This picture clarifies the role of the law. The law is not a teacher that prepares for faith. It is transitory in its authority, lasting only **until Christ came.** One might have many *paidagōgoi*, but only one father (1 Cor. 4:15). Paul is thinking of the role of the law for Jews and Jewish Christians (**we** in v. 23; **our** in v. 24; **we** in vv. 24, 25). They are the people who "boasted in the law" (Rom. 2:18), "whose are the . . . covenants and the giving of the law . . ." (Rom. 9:4). Since the law lasted only until Christ, it had no justifying force; it belongs to the premessianic age in order **that we might be justified by faith.** Thus the radical opposition of works of law and faith is given a historical basis. When faith comes (v. 25), the law loses its authority. This is no incidental, ad hoc position on Paul's part. He opposes being "under law" and "under grace" in Rom. 6:14 and stresses that "Christ is the end of the law, that every one who has faith may be justified" (Rom. 10:4). Jewish Christians can no longer plead the authority of the law; its power is over and past.[49]

Paul is drawing close to the end of the apologetic that began with a personal word in 3:1-5. Now, after the Galatians had disappeared from Paul's language, they suddenly reappear in v. 26, directly addressed as **you** (this direct address continues to 4:21). Paul had been discussing the significance of Christ for Jewish Christians who had been under the law. Now his language broadens to prepare the appeal to the Gentile Galatians not to move into slavery to that law.

Paul draws a conclusion about the Galatians from the picture used in vv. 24-25 (**for . . . you**). They are free from the law. How did that freedom come to them? They are **all sons of God, through faith.** (The son of God motif is explicated in 4:3-7.) As sons of God they are no longer under the law. **In Christ Jesus** they also achieved new status. The RSV correctly pulls the phrase to the head of the sentence: the point at issue here is not that faith is directed to Jesus, but that Jesus' coming means the opening of the era of faith also for the Gentiles (2:16, 20-21 lies in the background).[50]

That new era is entered by Baptism. All the Galatian Christians (**as many of you as were**) were baptized. Their Baptism was an act of drastic consequences. Theologically, it meant a change of lords. Once under the power of law (or elemental spirits, 4:3), Baptism meant that they were now the "possession of Christ" (Oepke). That change of lordship is expressed in the phrase **into Christ** (cf. Rom. 6:3; "into Moses," 1 Cor. 10:2; cf. 1 Cor. 1:13, 15; 6:11). Rom. 6:3-11 is a fuller discussion of the significance of Baptism as an act that radically changes one's status. Baptism moves one into a new relationship that alters the baptized. That is expressed in the phrase **have put on Christ.**[51] This "most daring" passage (Guthrie) suggests that they have been enveloped by Christ and live in him as in an environment in which all is new (cf. 2 Cor. 5:17: "If anyone is in Christ, he is a new creation," which expresses it well).[52] The language is drawn from early Christian baptismal liturgy.[53]

Baptism into Christ gives Christians value and significance. Differences among them no longer matter, as v. 28 shows. Paul says that three different, fundamental polarities are overcome in Christ. The repetition of **there is neither . . . nor** with each polarity gives a dignity and elevation to the language that ancient rhetoric prized. The linguistic form highlights the conceptual importance. The ethnic division of **Jew** and **Greek** no longer exists.[54] The division is formulated in a Jewish fashion, as Paul's opponents in Galatia might well state it. Paul's apologetic concern surfaces. There is **neither slave nor free;** social distinctions do not apply. Philemon shows that this is not the announcement of a radical, new social program, and also not mere intellectual exercise. (The refusal to allow a rich/poor division in the Corinthian church is a social parallel; cf. 1 Cor. 11:17-22.) There is **neither male nor**

female. Paul surprisingly uses the neuter case in Greek, equivalent to something like "the masculine" and "the feminine." Jews (and other ancient people) were often strongly male oriented. One synagogue prayer includes thanks that the worshiper is not a woman.[55] All these distinctions disappear because **you are all one** [human] **in Christ.**[56]

Baptism is mentioned in Galatians only in 3:27. Verse 28 shows that it is nonetheless of fundamental significance in Paul's thought. To be baptized is to be incorporated into Christ, to become part of a larger whole that determines attitudes and actions. That whole provides a unity of interrelated service that leaves no room for the recognition of divisive differences, not even those that ancient people felt were religiously (Jew/Gentile), economically (slave/free), or naturally (male/female) based. There is in Christ a new creation (2 Cor. 5:17) that brings Christians into a unity, despite earlier polarities. The same approach is applied to a different problem in 1 Corinthians 12 (key verses are 13 and 27). Faith is a great equalizer; it does not respect persons. Paul does not from this insight develop a social reform movement in the Roman world. However, the leaven of his insight would ultimately have its effects. Christians led the way to the abolition of slavery in the 19th century; in our time this insight has stimulated Christians to attack the sins of racism and sexism in the church.[57]

Paul closes this section on unity by showing how it relates to the idea of the offspring in vv. 16-17. Baptism means that one belongs to Christ. Therefore, one is incorporated into Christ, and so into **Abraham's offspring.** The singular **offspring** contains many people. The promise to Abraham is open to many through the "one human" of v. 28. In him we also are heirs of the promise. With the word **heirs** Paul also provides a link to his third illustration (4:1-2) and its application to the Galatians (4:3-11).

g. From Slavery to Adoption as Children of God (4:1-7). Paul continues the direct speech to the Galatians begun in 3:27. He gives a third illustration suggested by the use of the word **heir**

(4:1-2). By his introduction Paul indicates that he is extending the use of that language (**I mean that . . .**). The illustration turns on the difference in status of the heir to a wealthy father, contrasting a minor (**as long as he is a child**) with an adult in control of the property. The minor is under the protection and authority of **guardians and trustees; he is no better than a slave,** since neither is in charge of himself. Only when the "fixed time" is past, **the date set by the father,** does he come into the full use of the inheritance. The two periods of history of 3:23ff. are still in play.

The Galatians were like enslaved children (**so with us**) before their Baptism and conversion. They **were slaves to the elemental spirits of the universe** (v. 3), who exercised over them the power Jews experienced in the law. The Greek term *stoicheia* (RSV "elemental spirits") has the root meaning "what is put in a row," "what is put in order." It came to have a long series of applications, e.g., the letters of the alphabet, numbers, and elemental materials out of which the universe is made (for the Greeks: earth, air, fire, and water; cf. 2 Pet. 3:10,12). Two additional senses of the term deserve attention because they are regarded as possible meanings in this passage. *Stoicheia* is used of the basic principles, the elementary teaching in a discipline (cf. Heb. 5:12, where it is opposed to advanced teaching, adults' food). Some interpreters prefer this sense to the RSV translation because the *stoicheia* are set parallel to the law, which is a type of teaching.[58] On this interpretation the Galatians are returning to a childish status when they accept the law, and so are in bondage once again. But this interpretation does not take adequate account of the accusation that being under the law is equivalent to returning to a status in which they do "not know God" (4:8,9); that is not a matter of elementary teaching.

Another view is based on the statement that the Galatians had been slaves to "beings that by nature are no gods" (4:8). The term is used of "elemental spirits," that is, spirits who serve as the "guardians and trustees" (4:2) of the universe.[59] Col. 2:8 implies that these **elemental spirits** are the "fulness of the Godhead."

The term is applied to the 12 signs of the zodiac as the heavenly bodies that control human destiny[60] (cf. the ritual calendar in Gal. 4:10). They are probably to be identified with the "world rulers" of Eph. 6:12, and possibly with the angels whom the Corinthians are to judge (1 Cor. 6:3).[61] Humankind is in slavery to these lords and needs deliverance.

Deliverance has come by a change in status. The rule of law and the elemental spirits has been allowed its full period of authority. **But** the moment of destiny has arrived. God has ended their rule by the sending of his Son. Verses 4-7 restate what Paul had already said in 3:13-14 in a form fitted to explicate the illustration used in 4:1-2. Here are two earlier creedal formulations, united in their use of son/father terminology. The first is the formula **God sent forth his Son . . . that we might receive adoption as sons.**[62] It is reflected also in Rom. 8:3; 8:32; and John 3:16. The formula, before Paul used it, stressed that the Son was sent into the world to achieve a kind of *quid pro quo* exchange for humanity: the Son becomes a human that humans may become children of God. Therefore, **born of woman** is probably part of the original formula. The Son becomes human by divine commission. (There is no agreement as to whether the sending formula implies [heavenly] preexistence for the Son.) The term *son* in Paul is always used of Jesus in relation to God (cf. 1 Cor. 1:9; 2 Cor. 1:8; Rom. 1:2; etc.).

Paul inserts **born under the law** to interpret **born of a woman.** To be human is to be a slave under the law. He also adds **to redeem those who were under the law,** to recall 3:13. Without that insertion the formula has no reference to the cross, the place where the law lost its lordship. The end purpose is **that we might receive adoption as sons** (4:5). The first-person verb is significant: it is often a mark of creedal affirmation. The formula shifted the image from growing into maturity (4:2) to that of adoption. Adoption of an adult was one option in ancient law to insure survival of the family. It also is grist for Paul's mill. Adoption is completely by gift, not by merit. An adopted son has no prior claim on the father.

Paul introduces the second formula in 4:6, "**Abba! Father!**" The verb **crying** is highly significant; it means shouting, even screaming. It is the correct verb to use with an acclamation, the shout of a formula that identifies a community (cf. the acclamation of the Artemis cult in Acts 19:28, "cried out, 'Great is Artemis of the Ephesians' "). Such shouts are used in religious assemblies to indicate unity of mind and belief. The Jewish acclamation was "God is one" (Rom. 3:30), while Christians used "Jesus Christ is Lord" (1 Cor. 12:3; Phil. 2:11) and possibly "One Lord, one faith, one baptism" (Eph. 4:5). **Abba** is colloquial Aramaic for "father" or "our father."[63] The Christian community addresses God as "Daddy," and that implies sonship. The same acclamation is found in Rom. 8:15, while Jesus himself addresses God this way in prayer (Mark 14:36).

Paul uses this acclamation of the Galatian community (which contains a Semitic word) also in the service of his apologetic. Verse 6 is drawn up in a form parallel to vv. 4-5. **Because you are sons** is resumptive, underscoring the reality of the adoption in v. 5. **God has sent the Spirit of his Son** is formed in absolute parallel to v. 4. The parallel is underscored by naming the Spirit **the Spirit of his Son,** an almost unique phrase (cf. "Spirit of Christ" in Rom. 8:9, set parallel to "Christ . . . in you" in Rom. 8:8). **The Spirit** is not independent, but closely tied to Christ. He actualizes in the individual the cosmic work of Christ by bringing one to shout the acclamation (for the idea cf. 1 Cor. 12:3). The mention of the Spirit closes the circle begun in 3:1-5.

Paul can now draw the conclusion in v. 7. **So** by adoption and therefore **through God** who is Father (note that Spirit is the mode of God's action in the individual) the decisive movement from slavery to sonship has taken place. The verse is cast in the second person. Paul addresses the Galatians directly, as he had in 3:1-5. **If a son then an heir** recalls the language of 3:18. To be an heir means to inherit the promises to Abraham. And that is the basis for the severe warning (4:8-11) and strong appeal (4:12-20) which follow. The theological argument is complete.

h. Do Not Relapse into Slavery (4:8-11). Paul now moves to a direct attack on the Galatian position.[64] It is dominated by the contrast between the past (**formerly,** v. 8) and the present (**but now,** a strong transition in Greek that denotes the actual state of affairs, v. 9). The past condition is illuminated by the present. They have become sons and heirs through God (4:7). That makes clear that their past pagan life was one without knowledge of God (cf. Rom. 1:18-23; 1 Cor. 1:21) and of slavery to **beings that by nature are no gods** (v. 8). **By nature** is the opposition in Greek to "by convention" or "by agreement." At best these gods are demons (cf. 1 Cor. 8:5,6).

But now by the Spirit they **have come to know God** (v. 9). This is no mere intellectual discovery on their part, but the recognition that God has acknowledged them (**known by God**). God is no passive object, but one known by his doing. But now, given that, **how can you turn back again to the weak and beggarly elemental spirits?** The question is both ironic and sarcastic. **Turn back again** is the language of conversion (cf. 1:6). But this conversion would be regression to the pagan state, a willing slavery to gods who are weak and lowly. Paul transfers to the elemental spirits the characteristic features of their worshipers.

That this return is an act of will on their part is shown by v. 9: **whose slaves you want to be.** They have begun to observe a ritual calendar of set times and festivals. No specific festivals are named, but chronological points (**days, months, seasons, years**). While it is likely that it is a Jewish festival calendar that Paul has in mind,[65] the language is not specifically Jewish and also describes many ritual calendars in Asia Minor. In this way Paul makes Judaism's calendar approximate that of the religiosity of their Gentile past. Paul distinguishes sharply between religion and faith. In religion, means such as festivals become ends, obligations regulated by law. Such are a betrayal of the gospel.

And they can be a sign that the gospel has not created faith— or that Christians are regressing into paganism. That is what underlies the profoundly ironic expression of fear in v. 11. **I have labored** does not have the picture of birth pains (though see 4:19).

It is rather a technical term for missionary work (cf. 1 Thess. 5:12; Rom. 16:6,12; Phil. 2:16, and the analogous "run" in Gal. 2:2). Paul fears that all his proclamation would go for nothing. The ritual calendar is that bad! In it the law becomes once more a living force in the life of the Galatians. That means the absence of the Spirit and of the confession "Abba! Father!"

i. Transition: Appeal to Identify with Paul's Proclamation (4:12-20). In many ways 4:12-20 is the most difficult paragraph in Galatians. It appears disjointed, without clear structure. After the argument from 3:1—4:11 it appears curiously personal, almost maudlin. Indeed, some commentators feel that Paul's emotions, held in check since 1:10, now break the dam and rush to expression. There is much validity in that.[66] But this personal appeal, based on friendship, is a familiar motif in ancient rhetoric.[67] The difficulties are often caused by our lack of knowledge about Paul's earlier relations with the Galatians (would that Acts reported that first missionary contact!). But the main lines are clear.

Brethren, I beseech you ("brothers" occurs earlier in 1:11 and 3:15) shows Paul's pastoral heart coming to the fore. He has been arguing; now he makes an appeal (the term is not the normal one for exhortation, *parakalō*, but the more rare *deomai*, which means "to ask" or even "to beg" [cf. 1 Thess. 3:10; Rom. 1:10; 2 Cor. 5:20; 8:4; 10:2]). Paul wants them to be like himself, i.e., to have experienced the move from slavery to sonship, to prize freedom from the law (cf. 1:13-17). Verse 12 in itself is gnomic, capable of many senses, but in context it must mean the freedom Paul will soon so strongly stress.

Paul recalls their past relationship in vv. 12b-14. It had been positive: **you did me no wrong** (v. 12b), not even when Paul's physical condition might have been a possible reason for putting him down (vv. 13-14). When he **first preached** to them, he was sick (**bodily infirmity** is as vague in Greek as in English), though the illness is not defined. Paul's sickness was a "temptation" (RSV's **trial** is a bit underplayed, v. 14) because sickness in the ancient world was often regarded as a sign of divine anger or displeasure. But they did not **scorn** him. The term **despise** translates a term that literally means "spit out." Paul may suggest that they did not use an apotropaic action to ward off the demonic from themselves (spitting when one passes a graveyard is such an action to this day), but affirmed that he really was **God's messenger** (*angelos* can denote either messenger or angel) and **received him . . . as Christ Jesus.** (This is scarcely to be identified with Acts 14:12!)

Given that reception, their present actions and attitudes to Paul are mystifying. Their former **satisfaction** (with Paul) is gone. The RSV translation implies some such sense. But the Greek *makarismos* can also mean "blessing," either on Paul or on God. Their praise has disappeared. That question of puzzlement is grounded in their prior attitude of support for him. Paul uses an oath formula (**I bear you witness,** v. 15) to introduce in ironic fashion a commonplace to remind them that true friends are willing to sacrifice for each other, even to plucking out their **eyes** (symbol of the precious, v. 15). The change in attitude suggests the question, **Have I then become your enemy by telling you the truth?** Among friends one should be able to speak frankly. The exact situation in v. 16 is unclear. **Telling . . . the truth** may refer to some blunt exchange, now lost, that occurred earlier, or to the frank language of Galatians itself, or to the gospel itself.

At stake is Paul's relationship with the Galatians; that dominates the last four verses of the paragraph. Suddenly in v. 17 the "opponents," **they,** appear for the first time in the letter. (They appear again in 5:10 and 6:12f.) **They make much of you,** are eager for you, court you (cf. 2 Cor. 11:2), but their motivation is evil (**for no good purpose**). They want to **shut** them off (better than **out**), to monopolize them. In context this must mean to wall them off from Paul so that the Galatians will **make much of them.** There is a right way to be eager for others (v. 18), **for a good purpose** (contrast to v. 17). Paul had shown that when in Galatia—and his present activity carries it on (**not only when I am present with you**).

Paul shifts the picture to that of pregnancy and birth in v. 19, the only place where he calls his converts **my little children.** The whole paragraph from 4:12 on has dealt with close relationships. By the maternal image Paul claims the closest of human relationships to the Galatians. He is laboring in birth with them again—**until Christ be formed in you** (cf. 2:20, the best commentary on the phrase). This is not some mystical experience; rather Paul wishes them to be as he is (4:12), moved and normed by Christ in him, that is, by the Christ he preached to them. Verse 20 expresses in a kind of desperate tone Paul's concern for them. He would like to be with them and use only the language of intimate friendship (**and to change my tone** [of speech]). At a distance Paul feels himself handicapped, without resources or plans to deal with the situation. **I am perplexed** translates a verb that is better rendered "I am at a loss because of you."

3. Appeal to Maintain Freedom: The Second Argument from Scripture (4:21—5:12)

Verses 19-20 form a sort of transition. "Christ in you" (v. 19) reminds the reader that faith is also expressed in action. Paul is moving toward a discussion of Christian life as freedom under the guidance of the Spirit. This third argument first presents a scriptural basis for using freedom as a category for Christians (4:21—5:1) and on that foundation describes life as active faith (5:2-6) that issues in a condemnation of the Judaizing teachers (5:7-12). The apologetic character of the letter demands that the scriptural argument be followed by an appeal. It is possible, alternatively, to find a radical break in the argument at 4:20 and argue that the second scriptural interpretation is in itself already the beginning of the paraenesis.[68] But 5:13 marks a new beginning as it brings in the law in a new and different manner.

a. Stand Fast in the Freedom Shown in the Allegory of Abraham's Two Sons (4:21—5:1).

Paul's interpretation of the OT in 3:6ff. is congenial to modern interpreters. He argues on the basis of a grammatical (cf. 3:16) reading of the text in its own order (3:17).

In this paragraph he interprets the Abraham narrative in a quite different manner by using a method that is allegorical midrash (to coin a term). The literal sense is not stressed or used; instead, individuals in the narrative assume a deeper significance. Paul calls his method **allegory** (4:24). He takes for granted that his readers know and respect the method which is widespread in the ancient world.[69]

Paul begins (4:21) with an almost reflective question (not sarcastic!), **Tell me, you who desire to be under the law** (cf. the "under" phrases tied to the law in 3:10, 22, 23; 4:4, 5), **do you not hear the law?** The question appears abrupt at first, so much so that commentators have trouble accounting for it. C. K. Barrett[70] found in 4:21 the implication that the passages Paul treats here allegorically (4:24) are the very passages the new teachers were using to argue the necessity of following the law. In that case, the argument is climactic and comes properly at the end of the discussion. It is the ultimate argument that finally cuts the ground out from under the Galatians' feet.

Paul introduces the biblical material by a formula (**it is written**) that usually introduces a direct citation (cf. 4:27), but here introduces a summary of the tradition (vv. 22-23). The summary is based on Gen. 16:15 and 21:2, 9). (Paul makes no reference to Abraham's six other sons, by Keturah, Genesis 25). The mothers have different status, one **slave** and the other **free.** They also differ in manner of conception (4:23). The slave's son was **born according to the flesh,** that is, by natural generation (there is no connotation of evil in this usage). The free woman's son was born **through promise.** The change in preposition is significant. **Promise** is more than a word about the future; it is an active force in the generation of the free woman's son. Therefore the son can also be described as **born according to the Spirit** (4:29). The two women are not yet named; indeed Sarah never is. Her name is not important for Paul's argument.

Verse 24 highlights the concepts *slave* and *promise*, both significant earlier in chaps. 3 and 4. Now Paul gives an extended interpretation (4:24-27) that he calls **an allegory** (4:24). *Allegoria* in Greek means that which says something else, i.e, that has a meaning beyond the immediate sense. Paul presupposes the historical reality in vv. 22-23; but now he turns to a more profound sense. The two **women are two covenants.** Their sons then represent groups for whom the covenants are valid. They represent all humanity, though Paul does not say this expressly. The two women differ in the geographical ties. Hagar is **from Mount Sinai** (v. 24). Since she is a slave, her children are slaves—and the covenant tied to Mount Sinai is a covenant of slavery. **She is Hagar.** Her name is significant because (4:25) **Hagar is Mount Sinai in Arabia.** The latter identification is difficult, since v. 24 had affirmed that she was *from* **Mount Sinai,** not identical to it. There is probably some kind of punning allusion to a Semitic name that escapes us, or some form of numerical acrostic, also lost. The precise sense is unclear,[71] but the goal Paul has is clear. Hagar represents geographically the locus for the giving of the law, and theologically slavery. That is why she also **corresponds to the present Jerusalem,** the Jerusalem of Judaism— and possibly also of Judaizing Christianity (2:1). She represents the slavery of the law.[72]

There is a contrasting Jerusalem (**but,** 4:26), **the Jerusalem above.** Paul uses an idea from the OT (Isaiah 54 and 60) and later Jewish apocalypses (4 Ezra 7:26; 10:40ff.) that is reflected elsewhere in the NT (Heb. 12:22; Rev. 3:12; 21:10-14). But Paul deapocalypticizes the motif. **The Jerusalem above is free** and **our mother.** Paul claims this side of Abraham's offspring for himself and those who believe his gospel (cf. 3:29). In v. 27 he cites Isa. 54:1, a passage some Jews understood to refer to the changed future of the nation of Israel. Paul claims this status for his Galatian Gentile converts (cf. "Israel of God" in 6:16). There is scriptural debate going on.

Paul makes direct application of his allegory by a typological interpretation of Isaac and Ishmael in vv. 28-30. Since **we** have the free woman for our mother, we **like Isaac are children of promise.** Verse 29 offers a curious proof for that: the persecution of Isaac by Ishmael back there (**at that time**) is repeated **now.**

The OT says nothing of this persecution, though Jewish exegesis did find it in a sort of wordplay in Gen. 21:3. This use of extra-biblical tradition supports the suggestion that Paul is citing his opponents' biblical argument in order to turn it against them.

Only the free son (and his "descendants," the "seed" of 3:29) is the legitimate heir of the promise. Paul cites Gen. 21:10 in v. 30 to support that claim. He does not suggest that the opposition should be excommunicated. Rather, the direction of his argument is made clear in the summation of v. 31 and the strong appeal in 5:1. **We are . . . children . . . of the free woman.** Paul wants the Galatian Christians to recognize their true identity. They are meant to be free, as the story of Hagar and Sarah makes clear.

Paul underscores his concern with the brilliant, lapidary terseness of his summary and appeal in 5:1: **For freedom Christ has set us free.** The formulation is abrupt (as it is in 3:13); some have seen in this the indication that a new section begins here, and support it with the fact that 5:1b continues with an appeal, a trumpet call to **stand fast.** However, not every abrupt transition means the opening of a new section; moreover, 5:1-12 serves as the concluding appeal to the argument of 4:21-31 in the same way that 4:8-20 made a concluding appeal to take the theological argument in 3:1—4:7 to heart. Paul will conclude by making the problem facing the Galatians absolutely clear in 5:2-12. The strictly paraenetical third section begins at 5:13.[73]

Paul uses the term *freedom* to sum up his entire argument (cf. 2:4; 4:22-31; 5:13). But his view of freedom is quite different from the idea in the Greek world. It is not the realization of one's true self (as in Stoicism), not freewheeling independence. It is rather the result of the redemptive work of Christ. **Christ has set us free.** It comes via the preaching of Christ crucified, ratified by the gift of the Spirit (3:1-3). Thus freedom is the radical alternative to life without Christ. It is the work of the Spirit (2 Cor. 3:17). But that freedom can be lost. **Therefore,** says Paul, **stand fast** (cf. 1 Cor. 16:13, and 1 Cor. 15:1; the latter passage makes clear that such standing means preservation of the liberty).[74] The alternative is submission to the **yoke of slavery.** In antiquity captives in war were sometimes marched beneath an ox yoke as a symbol of entry into slavery.[75] Slavery is the situation of the Galatians prior to faith (4:9). Paul sees the situation he confronts as jeopardizing the entire Christian existence of the Galatians. He calls them to preserve their new Christian status; that means they must make a decision for faith and freedom. The precise nature of the danger is given shape in the paragraph which follows.

b. Circumcision Obligates; Faith Is Active in Loving (5:2-6). The scriptural argument is complete. The true descendants of Abraham are those who, like him, have faith in the promise of God. There is no other mode of sonship. Paul now concludes the argument that began at 3:1. He opened with an appeal to their experience of the Spirit. He closes with a direct personal appeal to the Galatians.

The problem is now somewhat clarified. Someone ("he who is troubling you," 5:10) has suggested to the Galatians that Paul's gospel of faith needs to have circumcision added to it to make it complete. Details are unclear. Paul opens his evaluation of the significance of circumcision for them by setting his entire apostolic authority in the balance. His opening word is an attention getter, stronger than the underplayed **now** of the RSV (cf. NEB, "Mark my words"). **I, Paul, say to you** is emphatic in Greek (compare the opening words of 2 Cor. 10:1, an equally emotion-charged passage). He reinforces the opening by using an oath formula to open v. 3: **I testify. . . .**

Three implications of accepting circumcision are pointed out. The first is expressed in v. 2. **If you receive circumcision** suggests that Galatians are considering the option, but have not yet made the decision. Paul is seeking to prevent it. Here circumcision enters the discussion thematically for the first time in the book. (It had been mentioned in 2:3 in connection with Titus and as an identifying mark of the Jerusalem church. There was no suggestion there that the Jewish Christians ought to give it up as a wrong practice.) It is not the minor physical operation per se to which Paul objects, as 1 Cor. 7:18f. makes clear. Rather it stands here for a whole way of being that is antithetical to Paul's gospel. **Christ will be of no advantage to you.** If circumcision is necessary, Christ's work is inadequate. Any addition to Paul's proclaimed gospel destroys the gospel. Gal. 1:6-9 is here made more specific; the addition is circumcision and all it stands for.

The second implication is the reverse of the first and so explicates it, as the **again** suggests. Circumcision obligates the one who has it performed **to keep the whole law.** Circumcision is of value only if you keep the law (Rom. 2:25). Given the argument in 4:21-31 the Galatians must have heard that circumcision was the way to become a son of Abraham. Paul has placed that sonship on the side of faith and Christ. Circumcision means the loss of Christ and the gaining of the obligation to law. And that means accepting the premise that justification is by the law, since circumcision is only the starting point for keeping the law. Christ and the law are mutually exclusive.

The third radical consequence of giving in to the agitators' demand would be to be **severed from Christ** and to fall **from grace.** Paul uses the same verb in Rom. 7:2 and 6 to describe the break with the law made by death. The verse (5:4) sums up the entire letter's antithesis between justification **by the law** and by **grace** (cf. Gal. 2:16, 21; 3:11, 24). The Christian life is a standing in grace (Rom. 5:2), in the gospel (1 Cor. 15:1). The law excludes grace (3:12). Functionally, therefore, the Galatians are in danger of apostasy, of leaving Christ and returning to a condition like their pagan slavery to the elemental spirits (4:9).

Gal. 5:5-6 is an epigrammatic summation of Paul's gospel. **For through the Spirit, by faith, we wait for the hope of righteousness.** Each word sums up some earlier, longer statement or argument. **The Spirit,** received by the Galatians when they heard the gospel (3:2-5), enables the acclamation "Abba! Father!" (4:6) and shows that Christians are children of God. Spirit becomes the leitmotif of 5:13-25. **Faith's** hearing brings the Spirit (3:2); faith has figured throughout 2:16-21; 3:10-14, 23-29. It will recur in 5:6, 22; 6:10. Faith is the basis of hope and the gift of the Spirit.

Therefore it is not listed in the fruit of the Spirit in 5:22-23. By shifting to the first person plural, Paul includes himself in those who **wait for the hope of righteousness.** The phraseology is at first surprising. It seems to push righteousness off into the future and so make it uncertain; but that is a misreading of the words. Paul's formulation does not regard righteousness as at all uncertain. The verb would be better translated "eagerly expect with anticipation" (cf. Rom. 8:19,23,25). **Hope** is the "strong assurance" (Guthrie, p. 130) about the future (cf. Rom. 5:2,5; 8:24). The formulation of v. 5 places Christian existence in the tension between the accomplishments of Christ's death (5:1) and the full realization of his benefits. That delivers the Christian from boasting (cf. Rom. 3:27) into a life of responsible action.

This is underscored in 5:6. **In** the sphere determined by **Christ Jesus** the old distinctions no longer have validity (cf. 3:27,28). Circumcision, in itself, is indifferent (1 Cor. 7:18,19), no longer has force, is not decisive in relations to God, **is of no avail** (cf. 6:15). There is neither threat nor value in being uncircumcised; it gives no second-rate status before God. All that has power is **faith working through love.** The formulation is pointed, compressed, evocative. In contrast to circumcision and uncircumcision only faith has power. The law does not empower life; **faith** (here a summary term for all that Christ and the Spirit mean) empowers **love, love** is **faith** determining life. **Faith** is therefore not an intellectual or theoretical abstraction. "Faith active in love" is a phrase that describes the life-style of the Christian (cf. 2:20). It is the realization of the righteousness of God, the expression of that righteousness between the resurrection of Christ and the arrival of the hope of righteousness. Luther said it well: "O what a live, creative, active, powerful thing faith is."[76] Love is mentioned here for the first time in Galatians (it recurs in 5:13,22 as the major fruit of the Spirit). Paul thus opposes to the agitators' demand of circumcision and law the adequacy of faith not only to appropriate the freedom of the gospel, but also to empower life. The law cannot do that. A starting point is set for the discussion in 5:13ff.

c. Conclusion and Transition: Troublemakers Impede Your Christian Life (5:7-12). After the closely reasoned theological summation in 5:2-6, Paul concludes the second section with a loosely structured personal appeal and expression of feelings (5:7-12). The style is much more oral. There are no connecting conjunctions or particles to indicate how the sentences interrelate. Yet the entire effect is powerful.

Paul begins with a glance back at their past, using the picture of a race. **You were running well** (cp. 2:2; 1 Cor. 9:24, 26; Phil. 2:16); **who hindered you from obeying the truth?** The question is rhetorical, like that of 3:1. The **truth** is the gospel (2:5, 14). Paul formulates sharply, using the verb *obey* with *truth* (for the formulation, cf. Rom. 2:8). As Rom. 1:5 formulates it, the obedience which correlates with the truth of the gospel is faith. The answer to the rhetorical question, **who hindered you?** is suggested by 1 Thess. 2:18: Satan. In v. 8 the term **persuasion** is based on the same stem as "obey" in Greek. The verbal play makes the formulation rhetorically sharp. This persuasion to nonobedience could not be from God; according to 1:6 he is the one who called them by Paul's gospel (see also 1 Cor. 1:9). That means that God called "by grace"; a call to disobey grace can only be from Satan, God's great enemy. Verse 9 (like v. 8) is attached without any indication of how it is related to the preceding. **A little leaven leavens the whole lump.** Paul's use of the statement in 1 Cor. 5:6 suggests that it is a proverb. Proverbs take their specific sense from their context. Here the sense is something like "You cannot make a minor concession in respect to grace (faith, freedom, promise); any concession (or addition) loses the whole. (One is reminded of the popular saw, "You can't be a little bit pregnant.") The reference is not to the small number of the opponents infecting a large number of Galatians.[77]

The next sentence (v. 10), also added without a conjunction, seems to change tone rapidly. Paul concludes with a statement of confidence: **I have confidence in the Lord that you will take no other view than mine.** At first reading it sounds like bravado or whistling in the dark. The emotional tone of the whole letter up to this point suggests that there is every likelihood that some at least will think differently, else Paul's long argument is unnecessary. A second reading, however, shows that Paul's confidence does not rest on his knowledge either of their ability or of their backbone. It rests **in the Lord** (cf. Phil. 2:24 and Rom. 14:14 for similar statements of trust). It is God who empowers Paul's gospel (cf. Gal. 4:14; Rom. 1:16,17; 1 Thess. 2:13). It is God's own fidelity to the promise that is at stake, and he has shown himself faithful to that promise in the revelation of his son (Gal. 3:23-25; 1:15,16). Therefore Paul is sure that they will support unity in the gospel, an idea he often expresses in the phrase "think the same thing" (Rom. 12:16; 15:5; 2 Cor. 13:11; Phil. 2:2; 4:2). In spite of all his antagonists have done, in spite of his realism about the Galatians, Paul has hope for a good outcome.

Paul's mood shifts again. **And he who is troubling you will bear his judgment, whoever he is.** It is outsiders who are responsible for the threat in Galatia. Paul elsewhere (1:7; cf. 4:17; 5:12; 6:12f.) refers to troublers in the plural. It is therefore futile to try to identify a single named opponent, as some have done.[78] Paul himself is not concerned about the identity (**whoever he is** is a kind of generic expression). What is significant for Paul is that any opponent of the gospel will **bear his judgment** (only here does Paul use this particular phrase). The same idea is expressed in 1 Cor. 3:13. The falsification of the gospel will be made clear on the Day. The consideration of this falsification leads to a final outburst on Paul's part: **But if I, brethren, still preach circumcision, why am I still persecuted?** (5:11). The use of **brethren** shows that Paul's kindly feeling for the Galatians perdures (cf. 1:11; 3:15; 4:12,28,31; 5:13; 6:1,18). But the reality behind the rest of the statement is obscure. Paul himself is somehow accused of being for circumcision. Paul's language (**preach circumcision**) is almost a parody of "preach Christ" (1 Cor. 1:23; Phil. 1:15). That phrase sums up Paul's entire understanding of his message of the gospel. The phrase he uses here is sarcastic in the extreme. What might it refer to? The case of Timothy (Acts 16:3) is never mentioned in Paul's letters. (In fact, Timothy is never mentioned outside of 1 and 2 Timothy, the deutero-Pauline, late letters.) To invoke this case, the circumcision of a half-Jew in Acts, would be to explain the obscure by the unknown. Does the textual difficulty in 2:2 about the (non)circumcision of Titus lie behind it? Is it a reminiscence of Paul's pre-Christian zeal as a persecutor of Christians on behalf of the law?[79] Is it a reflection of the fact that Paul does not demand that Jews who are also Christian must give up circumcision, i.e., that he is in that case essentially neutral? Oepke[80] suggests that all difficulties are resolved if we give the conditional sentence a *future* reference. But that seems to make no sense of the present conclusion. We remain in the semi-darkness with which we began. The reference to **persecution** with the twice-used **still** supports the idea that it is present persecution that Paul has in mind. And that probably refers to what the agitators are doing as persecution (a pointedly sarcastic statement). The harsh words of 2:4, 11-14 and 4:29 need to be recalled. Were Paul to preach circumcision, then **in that case the stumbling block of the cross has been removed.** That would be to please men (cf. 1:10; 6:12), whether others or oneself. The "offense of the cross" (cf. 1 Cor. 1:23) is that which makes the cross manageable. This is the first mention of the cross in Galatians (it recurs in 6:12, 14). It is mentioned each time in the context of persecution. A cross whose proclamation arouses no opposition would be one without curse (3:13, 14). To add circumcision to the cross would make the cross the enabler of piety, of works, or conformity to the law. Then grace would be gone. Christ would have died in vain (2:21; cf. 5:4; 1:6-7); it would not be a matter of a different gospel, but no gospel at all.[81]

Small wonder that Paul concludes this section with an outburst that cannot be matched elsewhere in his letters for its sheer animosity, bitterness, and venom. **I wish those who unsettle you** (this time in the plural) **would mutilate themselves.** The translation in the RSV removes Paul's somewhat salacious, bloody joke. The word translated **mutilate themselves** is a joke on the basic sense of the word for circumcise ("cut around"). One should translate it "Would that they would excise [i.e., castrate] themselves!"

The sarcasm is almost blasphemous. Paul suggests that it would be good if circumcision, the sign of sonship to Abraham and membership in Israel, would be transformed into castration. According to Deut. 23:1 that would be enough to disqualify them for membership in Israel. It would put them permanently in the class of pagans. A grim joke indeed![82] But it purifies and cauterizes Paul's emotions. When he begins the third and final section of the letter his mood is once again calm, disciplined, and contained (5:13—6:10). And he is able to keep that mood until he refers to the agitators for a final time in 6:12-13.

Exhortation to Loving Service (5:13—6:10)

Paul's sharp insistence on freedom from the law and its directives left a flank exposed. His opponents could accuse him (and apparently did) of trimming and shaping his message to make it more readily acceptable ("pleasing men," 1:10; "according to men," 1:11). He annuls part of God's revelation to be popular. Moreover, his sharply contoured position on the (temporally) restricted validity of the law (3:19-29) and the correlative freedom he stresses (5:1, 13) might seem to leave no controls over or guidance for life. The accusation might well arise in both Jewish and Gentile circles that Paul leaves the door open for an individualistic, "anything-goes" attitude that would destroy the Christian community.

Paul meets the objection by arguing that Christians have a comprehensive guide for life—the Spirit—and that they meet the basic demand of the law for love. He prepared for this earlier in the letter when he pointed out that life must conform to the gospel (the case of Peter in Gal. 2:14) and spoke of faith being "active through love" (5:6). Now Paul explicates these hints. The Spirit gives both guidance and power for Christian lives of service. No human standard determines conduct, even though the law is no longer valid; love defines and limits liberty (5:13-26) and maintains life in community.

1. Loving Service as Fulfillment of the Law (5:13-15)

After his outburst against the ones causing difficulties among the Galatians, Paul in 5:13 sounds the theme of the hortatory section: **For you were called to freedom, brethren** (cf. 5:1). The **for** calls attention to its character as summation of 3:1—5:12. **Brethren** (in our time better translated "sisters and brothers") calls attention to the communal character of the recipients (cf. 3:26-28). They are a community because God has **called** them (1:6, 15; 5:8) **to freedom.** Freedom is to be both their status and their task (the **to** is used in the same sense in 1 Thess. 4:7). Though that freedom is first and foremost freedom from the law (3:19—4:11), it is not a rejection of discipline. In 3:26-28 Paul defined the post-law existence of the Galatians as that of unity in Christ in which all Christians are "children of God." Now Paul expands that insight by defining the ethical task as "preservation of freedom"[83] over against one another. Freedom is communal.

Paul clarifies freedom first by giving a caveat: **only [do not use] your freedom as an opportunity for the flesh. Opportunity** in Greek could connote the "staging point" for a military operation (Thuc. 1.90; Polybius 1.44.6); more generally it came to mean "starting point" or even "pretext" (cf. Rom. 7:8; 2 Cor. 11:12). **Flesh** in Paul is the antonym of "Spirit" (3:3; 4:23; 5:17); the two cannot coexist in the same human being. **Flesh** is for Paul the unrestrained egoism, the individualistic self-assertion of a person who is under the dominating power of sin.[84] It is the source of self-serving lust and desire (5:16-17). Freedom is not the possibility of self-expression in Paul, but the opportunity for true obedience to God.

Paul introduces his positive statement about freedom with the strongest adversative conjunction in Greek: *alla*, **but. Through love be servants of one another.** This is Paul's fundamental response to the attack on his position. Freedom is now defined in terms of slavery (the term should be translated "be slaves to") to others, the activity Paul had in mind in 5:6. True freedom involves both love and slavery. Love without the service is an abstraction or narcissistic self-congratulation; service without love is bondage. Freedom is not something an individual possesses; it is an activity that benefits others. Paul's formulation is sharp, bringing two concepts together that appear to be mutually exclusive (freedom and slavery, a rhetorical oxymoron). The combination reveals how much Paul loads into this position.

Paul clarifies his position by two additional comments. In 5:14 he reinforces his claim by evidence from the law itself. He is not advocating a life-style that determines conduct by rules. He does not legislate new laws. Rather, he argues that **the whole law is fulfilled in** love which serves. That law is summed up (cf. Rom. 13:9) "in one statement" (the Greek *logos* is better translated "statement" or "point" than "word"): **You shall love your neighbor as yourself,** cited from Lev. 19:18 (also found in Rom. 13:8-10). Paul does not express his argument at length here. First he states that the law can be fulfilled in one statement; he then identifies Lev. 19:18 as the summation.[85] Active love fulfills the entire law (that may be what he means by the "law of Christ" in 6:2). Paul here pays no attention to varieties of legislation—moral, cultic, political. Nor does he cite specific commandments. In 3:10,12 and 5:3 he seems to assume that the Jew must keep ("do") every detail of the law while the Christian fulfills it by doing good to all people (6:10). Thus the law is not specifically done by the Christian; but neither is it disregarded or transcended. Rather it is taken up into the serving love that begins in Christ.

Paul's second comment (5:15) is an *argumentum e contrario*, the demonstration of his own position by showing the evil result of taking the opposite side (Paul does this earlier in 3:10-12; cf. also 1 Cor. 15:13-19). The present tense of the verbs may reflect the actual state of affairs in Galatia. The language Paul uses (**bite, devour, consume**) are metaphors from animal behavior, the law of the fang. Live according to them and you have a vivid portrait of self-interest that destroys. It is also a type of freedom, but it issues in every person's hand being raised against every other's. Paul sets up two divergent views of freedom to make his hearer affirm love through service as the only true possibility.

2. *Loving Service Is Life in the Spirit, Not the Flesh (5:16-26)*

Paul now turns to two questions that follow from the basic

position he has given: (1) How does day-to-day existence deal with the power of the flesh (5:16-26)? (2) What are the practical implications for community life (6:1-10)? His fundamental position is clear. Freedom is not simply the absence of restraining forces; positively, it is a life directed to Christ (2:20) and one's neighbor (5:13) in loving service.

a. Flesh and Spirit Are Antithetical Powers (5:16-18). Paul now concretizes the position laid out in 5:13-15. **But I say** would be better translated "Now, this is what I mean" (5:16; cf. 1:9; 3:17; 4:1). The stated position is put in a new way—by the sharp antithesis of **flesh** and **Spirit** that runs through vv. 16-26. The human being is a battleground in which two opposing powers contend. **Walk by the Spirit** is in the form of a command that functions as a conditional clause ("if you walk by the Spirit . . ."). **Walk** is an OT expression for "live," "conduct yourself." Paul uses the term some 18 times (in the authentic letters) in this sense. To **walk by the Spirit** is to live by the power that enables confession to God (4:6, 7), that comes with the hearing of the gospel (3:2-3). To walk by this Spirit is thus to be open to Christ's Lordship—and then one certainly will not "fulfill the desire of the flesh." The RSV translation here (**and do not gratify . . .**) is simply wrong. The second part of v. 16 is not a second command, but a very strong statement about a sure result in the future.[86] Where Spirit is in charge flesh has no power.

Paul is not a romantic about this. As 5:17 makes clear, he does not underestimate the flesh. **Flesh** and **Spirit** are actively hostile to one another; orientation to one's self and orientation to God's will (expressed in loving slavery to one another) are two irreconcilable powers; **these are opposed to each other.** The last phrase of 5:17 is extremely difficult: **to prevent you from doing what you would.** Is it the flesh alone that prevents the human from doing what he would, or is it Spirit and flesh? Or is it the contest, the struggle between the two? No solution seems fully satisfactory, but it is probable that the contest between the two is what does the preventing. That opposition is what leads to the result described.[87] Each "power" tries to prevent the other achieving its end. The only effective solution for the Christian is to be open to the Spirit's leading: **But if you are led by the Spirit,** that is, if the Spirit is the ruling power and produces his desire, then **you are not under the law** (5:18). To be **under law** is to be led by the flesh. It is to be back in the pre-Christian realm in which the law was slave master (3:23), to be under the elemental spirits of the universe (4:3-6), to be functionally back in pagan, fleshly existence. To be **led by the Spirit** is to be "sons of God" (Rom. 8:14; cf. Gal. 4:4f.). By contrast, to be under law or led by flesh is to be an enemy of God, a point that Paul underscores in the following list of vices and list of virtues.

b. Works of the Flesh Lead to Loss of God's Kingdom (5:19-21).   Paul drives the point of vv. 16-18 home by the use of a traditional catalog of vices (5:19-21) to illustrate the power of the flesh.[88] He balances it with a catalog of virtues (**fruit of the Spirit**) in 5:22-23 to show the complete incompatibility of flesh and Spirit, as demonstrated by their effects. The illustrative character of both lists is indicated by the transitional conjunction **now. The works of the flesh** (5:19) sounds harsh at first; we anticipate works conjoined to law or desires to flesh (v. 17). The term **works** could just as well be translated "effects" or "products." The list is exemplary and not complete. What characterizes it, says Paul, is **plain.** The effects of the flesh are open to public inspection. There is no need of an argument beyond the mere listing. Paul's claim is verifiable. Lists of virtues and vices are known from different groups in the New Testament environment, both Greek and Jewish.[89] Such lists are frequent in Paul: 1 Thess. 4:3-6; 1 Cor. 5:9-13; 6:9-11; 2 Cor. 12:20f.; Gal. 5:19-22; Rom. 13:13; 1:29-31; Col. 3:5-8; Eph. 4:17-19; 5:3-5.[90] Vice catalogs can also be found in the Gospels (Matt. 15:19; Mark 7:21-22) and the non-Pauline letters (1 Tim. 1:9,10; 2 Tim. 3:2-5; Titus 3:3; 1 Peter 2:1; 4:3,15; Rev. 21:8; 22:15). In form they are similar: mere listings without

argumentation, on the basis of which a general conclusion is sometimes drawn. They are not systematic in structure, indeed often
go far beyond the argument of their context. Here, for example,
after 5:15, one would expect the vices listed in v. 20 (beginning
with enmity) to come first as directly describing the Galatians.

Paul's list falls into four groups, though he himself does not
call attention to the fact. The first three are sexual vices.[91] **Fornication** specifically means cohabiting with a prostitute, but
comes to have a broader sense (cf. 1 Cor. 5:1; 6:13,18; 7:2; 2 Cor.
12:21; 1 Thess. 4:3) of sexual irregularity. **Impurity** (Rom. 1:24;
6:19; 2 Cor. 12:21; 1 Thess. 2:3; 4:7) is any kind of sexual aber-
ration, the opposite of sanctification (Rom. 6:19). **Licentiousness**
(Rom. 13:13; 2 Cor. 12:21) is that attitude that loses all shame
and parades its incontinence.

Verse 20 adds two effects of flesh that relate directly to religion.
Idolatry (1 Cor. 5:10,11; 6:9; 10:14; Col. 3:5) enters the vice lists
through Judaism. For Greeks and Romans polytheism was the
norm. Idolatry is often tied to immorality (cf. Acts 15:29), which
may be why it is mentioned in fourth place. **Sorcery** is an interpretive translation of the Greek term *pharmakeia*, the use of
drugs. It probably does not denote the mixing of poisons but
rather the use of artificial means to induce religious ecstasy or
exercise power over the gods or people. Love philtres might be
a possibility.

The next eight vices all reflect attitudes that are contentious,
argumentative, or divisive. At times the distinction among them
is very slight. **Enmity** (plural in Greek; cf. Rom. 8:7, "hostile" to
God) is the attitude of the one who has trouble getting along with
others, while **strife** (Rom. 1:29; 13:13; 1 Cor. 3:3; 2 Cor. 12:20;
Phil. 1:15) is the characteristic of one who is regularly cantan-
kerous. **Jealousy** (Rom. 13:13; 1 Cor. 3:3; 2 Cor. 12:20), *zēlos* in
Greek, describes the attitude of one who is greedy, envious,
appetitive. **Anger** (2 Cor. 12:20) might more generally be translated "given to strong emotions," of which wrath is a major example. **Selfishness** (Rom. 2:8; 2 Cor. 12:20; Phil. 1:17; 2:3) in
English denotes an acquisitive character. The term might better

be translated as "pushy attitude," "self-assertiveness," or "aggressiveness." **Dissension** (Rom. 16:17) is a political term in origin; it stresses division within what should be a group. **Party spirit** (1 Cor. 11:19) translates a Greek term (*hairesis*) that originally meant "choice." It comes to mean selecting a group or party with which one allies oneself. At a later period in church history it comes to mean a false position, i.e., "heresy." **Envy** (Rom. 1:29; Phil. 1:15) is the sour reaction of one who begrudges another some success or position.

The final two vices describe excesses in alcohol (**drunkenness,** 5:21) or in celebrating (*kōmoi*) The latter term is often used of religious celebration. In the New Testament it occurs in close proximity to "drunkenness" (Rom. 13:13; cf. 1 Peter 4:3). Paul adds **and the like** to his list. He is not presenting a complete list, and suggests that many more vices could be given. Paul goes on to make clear the drastic consequences of these products of the flesh. **I warn you, as I warned you before** translates a term that literally means "say in advance." Paul is probably referring back to some of his initial teaching, most likely given in connection with instruction surrounding Baptism. (Similar warnings occur in Gal. 1:9; 2 Cor. 13:2; 1 Thess. 4:6.) The linking of instruction in behavior to Baptism is evident in Rom. 6:4ff.; 1 Cor. 6:11 in context, etc.[92] **Those who do such things shall not inherit the kingdom of God** (v. 21) is the content of the warning. Paul does not use the phrase **kingdom of God** frequently. 1 Cor. 6:9 introduces another sort of vice catalog with the rhetorical question "Do you not know that the unrighteous will not inherit the kingdom of God?" (cf. 1 Cor. 15:50). The term occurs also in Rom. 14:17; 1 Cor. 4:20; 15:24; 1 Thess. 2:12; and 2 Thess. 1:5. The concept played a central role in Jesus' teaching, but not in Paul's, where its occurrence is almost an anachronistic remnant. It refers to the rule of God, public and powerful, which is to be realized at the end of the present age (cf. 1:4). David Aune suggests that the verb translated as **warn** by the RSV ought here be translated "predict" and suggests that what follows is an oracular threat of an early Christian prophet, perhaps Paul himself.[93]

c. The Fruit of the Spirit Shows the Effect of Christ's Death (5:22-24). Paul counterbalances the 15 works of law with 9 qualities that are the fruit of the Spirit (5:22). The singular *karpos* contrasts with the plural *works* (v. 19). The term **fruit** is not used of the results of the Spirit's power in the life of the Christian elsewhere in Paul. Where he speaks of qualities that are not common to all Christians, but are produced by the Spirit, he uses the term *charismata,* "gifts" (1 Cor. 12:4). Apparently Paul is not thinking of the nine items as separable, distinct items, but as coming from one Spirit who produces one effect with a variety of manifestations. Paul uses the term **fruit** to describe a good result (cf. Phil. 1:11,22; 4:17; Rom. 1:13). Paul also does not repeat the term *plain* from the introduction to the catalog of vices (used in sense of public, manifest, and clear, 5:19). In a sense the qualities that follow can be expressed in many different acts; their presence is thus less evident.

There are other catalogs of virtues in Paul (1 Cor. 12:4-11; Rom. 12:6-13) but none is a simple listing like the one here.[94] The most recent edition of the Greek New Testament prints the nine virtues as three triads. The first triad is **love, joy, peace.** They are basic to the other six. **Love** has been mentioned earlier in 5:6 as the mode of action for faith, and as the fulfilling of the law in 5:13. Here, in its final mention in Galatians, it heads the list for **the fruit of the Spirit. Love** is the greatest of the triad in 1 Cor. 13:13. Rom. 13:8 suggests it is for Christians the major mode of relating to others.[95] Its universal application puts it properly at the head of the list (Col. 3:14 buries it in the middle of a list). **Joy** is for Paul a characteristic mark of Christians (Rom. 12:12; 14:17; 2 Cor. 6:10; Phil. 3:1; 1 Thess. 1:6; the last regards the Spirit as its source). Rom. 14:17 links joy to **peace,** as Paul does here also. Peace is not simply the absence of struggle or battle; it is rather the result of the justifying activity of God in Christ. Rom. 14:17 links righteousness, joy, and peace, while Rom. 5:1 makes clear the tie to Christ's work described in Rom. 3:21—4:25. Peace is thus the condition in which the Christian lives and the condition he or she seeks for others; Rom. 14:19 therefore urges Christians to pursue what makes for peace and edification.

The Spirit has empowered; therefore the virtues are **the fruit of the Spirit. Peace** is expressed in three modes in the second triad: **patience, kindness, goodness** (5:22). **Patience** is the quality of putting up with those who try to provoke you (of God, Rom. 2:4; 9:22; of humans, 2 Cor. 6:6; 1 Thess. 5:14). **Kindness** is friendliness based on God's friendliness to sinners (cf. Rom. 11:22 and, for the idea, Rom. 15:7); 2 Cor. 6:6 links it to patience. **Goodness** is a more unusual term, appearing in the NT only here and Rom. 15:14; Eph. 5:9; and 2 Thess. 1:11). It practically forms a hendiadys with **kindness,** together describing that attitude that refuses to react in kind to attacks or insults or just plain boorishness. Gal. 6:10 catches its sense very well.

The third triad, **faithfulness, gentleness, self-control** (5:22-23), is three virtues that appear in Hellenistic ethics. **Faithfulness** (the same Greek term is usually translated "faith") is here a social virtue: reliability, trustworthiness (cf. 1 Cor. 12:9; Rom. 12:3, 6). **Gentleness** is the mean between allowing anything to occur and the ready anger that reacts rapidly to every hurt.[96] Paul uses the term to describe the non-proud attitude that is concerned for another's well-being more than for personal position (cf. 1 Cor. 4:21; Gal. 6:1). It is not to be confused with humility (*tapeinosophrynē* in Greek) or servility. Paul closes the list with **self-control,** a term with a long tradition in Greek philosophy. In Plato it denotes mastery over desires and pleasure. The mention of **passions and desires** in 5:24 suggests that Paul knows the philosophic tradition; elsewhere he uses the term in a more general sense (1 Cor. 9:25) and of control of sexual desire (1 Cor. 7:9).

Paul concludes with a needling comment: **against such there is no law.** These virtues are not unlawful; but neither are they the result of law's demands, nor do they function as a new law. They belong in the realm of the Spirit. The Spirit is thus not impractical, mere ecstatic experience. He is the intensely life-oriented power for the good and the true.

Verse 24 makes clear that the fundamental reorientation from the law and the flesh took place at the time people are baptized. **Those who belong to Christ** are those who are "in Christ," who have been "crucified with Christ" (2:19-21). To be baptized into Christ (Gal. 3:27) means a whole new mode of existence. Baptism, as Rom. 6:3ff. makes clear, is death. It means a new way of life. The **flesh** dies in Baptism along **with its passions and desires.** This one verse sums up the entire argument of Gal. 3:19—4:11 under the figure of crucifixion and the flesh. It underscores the radical gulf between the works of flesh and the fruit of the Spirit. They cannot coexist.

d. Conclusion and Transition: Living by the Spirit (5:25-26). Paul sums up his entire position on ethics in one magnificent sentence in chiastic structure. **If we live by the Spirit** sums up all that has been said in 5:13-24. The Spirit was the one who enabled hopeful waiting (5:5), by whom Christians walk (5:16), and by whom they are led (5:18). No Galatian Christian would disagree with this statement of reality. But given this statement, then Christians are to actualize what has been stated. **Let us also walk by the Spirit** uses a different term for *walk* than that used in 5:16. **Walk** (Greek *stoichein*) is a military term. A *stoichos* is a straight line; the verb means to walk in such a straight rank. The dative gives the person from whom the file draws its position. The Spirit is the one by whom the Christian "dresses right," to use the modern military command. Life must conform to him; thus the Spirit is the standard of the Christian life.

Verse 26 applies this to self-evaluation. Paul exhorts the Galatians not to have a false self-estimate (**self-conceit**). Such self-delusion is expressed in attitudes and actions that challenge the person and value of one's fellow human, either by **provoking** him or her to false competition or by **envy** (cf. 5:21) that does not give another person proper and legitimate recognition. Walking by the Spirit expresses itself in very practical, down-to-earth actions and attitudes.

3. *Directions for Life in the Community (6:1-10)*

The discussion in 5:13-26 leaves one major topic untouched. If there is no law code by which a community monitors itself, then how does one deal with the community member who breaks the community standards? While the Spirit is indeed a power that impels the individual Christian to positive action, in the real world some Christians fall short. How does a community freed from law deal with such an issue? Paul turns to the question of the sinner in this last section of the argument—at least, that is where he begins. But in a series of what appear to be loosely strung together, lapidary sentences, Paul moves from how to deal with the **brethren** to a consideration of the motivation for action inside the community.

The paragraph at first glance contains almost no overtly Christian motifs. Only the phrase **law of Christ** in 6:2 gives an indication of Paul's Christian basis. Most of the other statements could be found in non-Christian Jewish or Hellenistic philosophic ethics. Christianity differs not in formal, outward actions, but in the inner compulsion to action.

a. Loving Forgiveness (6:1-5).   Paul turns to a series of specific problems in the Christian community, as is indicated by his use of an initial **brethren.** He opens with this winning form of address as he introduces a new topic (cf. 1:11; 3:15; 4:12; 5:13). The conclusion to the preceding section (5:25) spoke of "walking in the Spirit"; 6:1-10 shows how this Spirit-directed life works out in community. He introduces the case (in the legal sense) of an errant Christian: **if a man is overtaken in any trespass.** The conditional sentence is a standard literary form for presenting casuistic law in the OT (e.g., see Exod. 21:1—22:16). The term **trespass** is Paul's term for the breaking of a specific directive of God; this is the only occurrence of the term in Galatians (2 Cor. 5:19 is a close parallel).[97] **You who are spiritual should restore him.** Paul addresses not the sin of the one presented in the case, but the Christians who are to deal with him. The **spiritual** are those who have received the Spirit through hearing the gospel

(3:2), that is, any Christian. The Spirit produces fruit (5:22-23). In this case the fruit is the effort to **restore him;** here the term implies aiding the errant Christian himself to walk by the Spirit.

In this passage Paul is more concerned with the attitude of the non-errant Christians than with the sinner. He does not introduce a form of excommunication or the severing of fellowship.[98] He does not use the law. Instead he identifies the attitude that the spiritual are to demonstrate, the **spirit of gentleness.** The fear underlying Paul's comment comes out in the directive **look to yourself, lest you too be tempted.** The failure of one Christian may become an occasion for others in the community to have a false self-evaluation (6:3). Paul does not spell out the exact nature of the temptation, but urges that mildness, one of the fruits of the Spirit in 5:23, should characterize one's reactions to the errant Christian. (Paul used the same phrase of his own attitude to the Corinthians in 1 Cor. 4:21.) The Spirit is no one's certain possession. The boasting (cf. 6:4) that tempts one opens the way to the works of the flesh of 5:19ff.

Verse 2 is introduced without any connective to v. 1. That makes **bear one another's burdens** sound much like maxims in non-Christian ethical writing.[99] Paul's application of the maxim in v. 2b makes it specifically his own—and Christian: . . .**and so fulfil the law of Christ.** The formulation is striking, a pointed summary of Gal. 5:14. Paul uses similar formulations in other places: "under the law of Christ" (1 Cor. 9:21); "the law of the Spirit of life in Christ Jesus" (Rom. 8:2). After Gal. 3:23-26 the use of **law** in association with **Christ** indicates that something very significant is at stake for Paul.[100] The only law that applies in this case is the law that is expressed in the one word *love* (5:14). Thus one should not look for a specific saying of Jesus to serve as this law, nor should one seek a specific application.[101] The phrase may well have been suggested either by the use of the legal formulation of the case in 6:1 or by the opponents' use of the phrase to include the Torah in the full Christian message. In either case, Paul's formulation spells out clearly that the only law that he recognizes is that love which is unconcerned with personal status or superiority.

The next three verses (6:3-5) make the consequences of not "looking to one's self" clear. Verse 3 is a call to sober self-evaluation. One's opinion and reality must coincide; anything other than that is self-deception. **For if anyone thinks he is something, when he is nothing, he deceives himself.** The folk-wisdom character of the maxim is underscored by the shift to the third person. In its generic sense the sentence means "know your own limitations." Paul makes use of this idea in several contexts: 1 Cor. 3:18; 8:2; 10:12; and possibly 14:37. All of these are spoken to people in the Greek world, where the commonplace was at home.[102] In context it means that love which seeks the neighbor's good is the reverse side of humility. Failure to love is the expression of deceptive pride. What is demanded is rigorous self-examination. **But let each one test his own work** (6:4). This demand too was frequent in the philosophic schools, whether Pythagorean, Stoic, or other. It stresses personal responsibility. Paul uses a similar motif in 1 Cor. 3:13: "the fire will test what sort of work each one has done." The principle of responsibility applied there to missionary work here is applied to every Christian. The term **work** stresses the reality of what is tested. In Greek it is often the antithesis of *word.* Not what you say (or others say about you), but what you actually do is the basis for testing. The results of this testing have eschatological significance. **And then** refers to the judgment, as "the Day" does in 1 Cor. 3:13. Judgment will operate on the basis of one's own deeds. Therefore they alone are the basis for pride or boasting: **his reason to boast will be in himself alone and not in his neighbor.** Paul is not urging boasting. He is rather enunciating a principle of responsibility. Paul himself boasts only "in the cross of our Lord Jesus Christ" (6:14). He twice cites Jer. 9:23 (1 Cor. 1:31; 2 Cor. 10:17) to argue that people should boast only in God (Rom. 3:11). Verse 5 makes clear that personal responsibility in the judgment is at issue. Paul cites another maxim current in the ancient world. There it urges self-sufficiency: **For each man will have to bear his own load.** The burden is not that of weakness and sin; rather one's action will show whether one is or is not walking by the Spirit (5:25). Relations to other Christians are decisive (cf. 1 Cor. 8:11; Rom. 14:15; 15:7) in the judgment. The question is not how we compare to other Christians (2 Cor. 10:12); it is rather whether we walk by the Spirit (Gal. 5:25) and conclude as we began (Gal. 3:3).

b. Mutual Interdependence (6:6-9). Paul introduces a second example and sets it into an eschatological framework (much as he did with the first). From 6:5 one might infer that Paul prized that independent self-sufficiency (*autarkeia*) so highly valued by the Stoics. Indeed, Paul's own life-style seems to model it.[103] "I have learned, in whatever state I am, to be content" (Phil. 4:11). "Content" here translates the adjective *autarkēs*. His working to support himself as he preached is well known (1 Thess. 2:9; 1 Cor. 9:13-18), perhaps also to the Galatians. But self-sufficiency is not the same as the individual responsibility that Paul urges in 6:5. Self-sufficiency may develop into arrogant unconcern for others. Paul abruptly introduces the matter of supporting their teacher(s) to prevent that development. The brief treatment in v. 6 uses vocabulary that is almost technical. It suggests that the Galatians were already supporting their teacher(s). Paul gives no reason for introducing the topic; there is apparently no problem in this area in Galatia. From a good work already being done well, Paul generalizes to an attitude that should be found in all Christian actions.

He uses the Greek verb *katēcheō* (from which the English term *catechumen* is derived) both for the student (**let him who is taught**) and the teacher (**him who teaches**) in 6:6. The term is unusual, found elsewhere in Paul only in Rom. 2:18 and 1 Cor. 14:19, both times in the sense of "inform" or "educate." (It later becomes the technical term for the education of adults preparing for Baptism.) **Let him . . . share all good things** is an imperative; that is, it gives a command in Greek. The precise sense is not clear. The verb *koinōneō* has two possible connotations. The related noun *koinōnia* means "fellowship," the close personal relationship based on common faith commitments. The noun is used in that sense in 1 Cor. 1:9 and 2 Cor. 13:13. But all other occurrences of the verb in Paul imply the sharing of money or other tangible goods (e.g., Rom. 12:13; 15:27; Phil. 4:15). Thus the command here probably urges care for the physical needs of the teacher of **the word,**[104] that is, the word of God (cf. 1 Thess. 1:6; 2:13; Phil. 1:14).

The next three verses attach directly to v. 6.[105] Paul unites the picture of sowing and reaping with the flesh/spirit antithesis of 5:16-25 to give an eschatological warning about the need for action that is congruent with the fruit of the Spirit. The language is clear. Only a few comments are needed. **Do not be deceived** might better be translated "Don't deceive yourselves." The Greek expression regularly introduces a warning, often cast as a general principle (1 Cor. 6:9; 15:33). How the Galatians treat their teachers is an index of their attitude to the flesh (for similar warnings based on a specific item see 1 Cor. 11:31-33 and Phil. 2:1-10). **God is not mocked** should be punctuated as an independent sentence, a gnomic statement probably drawn from folk wisdom. That would account for the unusual verb, used only here in the New Testament. It is based on the term for an animal's nostril or snout. The term might picturesquely be translated "turn up one's nose," or even "be sneered at." God doesn't let himself be led around by the nose, as if he were some animal. You cannot outwit God, **for whatever a man sows, that he will also reap.** The first proverb is now interpreted by a second, well-known agricultural metaphor. It is a warning proverb, full of prudential wisdom. It is found in the OT (Hos. 8:7) and in Greek folk wisdom.[106] Paul himself uses the figure more than once (cf. 1 Cor. 9:11; 2 Cor. 9:6), as does Jesus in the Gospels (Luke 6:43; 19:21). The future tense suggests the principle that what one does in the present will call forth a corresponding judgment in the end times. Thus the principle of divine judgment in 6:4-5 is reinforced by a principle of recompense. Judgment is simply getting what you deserve. God's judgment is not vindictive, but a reaction to the human's action; in that sense love removes judgment.[107]

Paul interprets the two maxims of 6:7 in v. 8. He expounds both possibilities of judgment under the categories of flesh and Spirit used earlier in 5:13, 16f., 19. **For he who sows to his own flesh will from the flesh reap corruption; but he who sows to the Spirit will from the Spirit reap eternal life.** Paul adds to the picture the two types of soil into which seed is sown. **Flesh** is that in the human which is against God, the Spirit, the good, and makes man subject to sin and death (see the comments on 3:2-4 and 5:16-17). If human action is under the control or direction of the flesh, the payment it gets in the judgment **from the flesh** is **corruption.** The **flesh** is thus a power, something more than one's own personal inclination. **Corruption** is here the antonym to eternal life, that is, it does not mean moral decay, but eternal destruction. The term is used in that sense in Rom. 8:21. Conceptually Rom. 8:13 and 1 Cor. 15:50 are precise parallels in Paul. **Eternal life** is not as frequent in Paul as in John. In addition to this passage the phrase occurs in Rom. 2:7 (where it is the antithesis to *wrath* and *anger*), 5:21; and 6:22-23 (the best commentary on our passage). Elsewhere Paul uses the term *salvation* for what he calls **eternal life** here (cf. Rom. 13:11; 1 Thess. 5:8, and the use of the verb *save* in the future tense in Rom. 5:9, 10; 10:9; 1 Cor. 3:15; etc.). Finally, it should be pointed out that here Paul, formulating freely his own interpretation of the folk wisdom in v. 7, casts the verse in the form of casuistic law. There are good examples of the sentence form in Exod. 21:12-17. Paul thereby implies that there is a principle of legal retribution that also covers the community that lives by the Spirit. The Spirit is not a guarantee of eternal life; he does not make Christians divine, incapable of sin. While he is the down payment on eschatological salvation (so 2 Cor. 1:22; 5:5; cf. the "firstfruits" of Rom. 8:23), he does not work willy-nilly. Rather he sets people into a position of free responsibility before God.

Gal. 6:9 draws the consequence in terms of Christian action. **And** (better, "And so") **let us not grow weary in well-doing.** It would be more literal to translate "let us not relax in doing the good." That translation makes clear that Paul uses the very verb, *doing*, for Christian life that he had used earlier of the demand of the law (3:10, 12). Christians do have a moral obligation. "The good" is the morally right (1 Thess. 5:21 uses it as the antithesis of the *evil* in 5:22; Rom. 7:19, 21). Paul appeals to the Galatians to continue in what they are doing. Perseverance is necessary, **for in due season we shall reap, if we do not lose heart.** Paul reiterates the principle of reward. The Galatians should not "relax, become tired" (a better translation than **lose heart** for a term that occurs only here in Paul) because future judgment depends upon present action. So long as faith precedes, Paul (like Jesus in Matt. 5:11-12) has no fear of the idea of reward at the judgment (cf. 1 Cor. 3:14; 2 Cor. 9:9).

c. Final Admonition (6:10). The use of law-code forms (vv. 1 and 8) and the concept of "doing" suggest that there is a guide to conduct that functions in Christian life. The principle of reward stressed by Paul in 6:1-9 shows that this guide is effective. With that argument Paul has completed his defense against the attack that his gospel was "according to man" (1:11) or that he formulated it so as "to please men." Gal. 5:13—6:9 has established his message as an effective guide to life that holds human beings responsible before God at the judgment. That is what underlies the **so then** of 6:10, which begins the final appeal to responsible freedom. **As we have opportunity, let us do good to all men.** There are no limitations to the appeal. All people are the objects of Christian action. Once again, *doing* is the form in which *love* (5:14) is to be shown; it is the form in which "walking by the Spirit" (5:25) is demonstrated. Love and the Spirit are not warm feelings or ecstatic experience. Both are active practice, deeds. Paul adds not an exception, but an emphasis in his last phrase: **and especially to those who are of the household of faith.** While this sounds paradoxical (does it not set a priority over **all men?**), it would not have seemed so in antiquity. Both Epicureans and Pythagoreans recognized that communities are held together by a special bond. Paul shows that *the faith* creates community (**faith** here seems to equal *Christian*). As such, Christians meet people who are the objects of love within the community first, but not only there.

■ Concluding Autograph Appeal and Blessing (6:11-18)

The argument of the letter is ended. With v. 11 Paul turns to the conclusion of the letter. Normally the conclusion contained personal notes, greetings, requests for intercessions, short exhortations, and a concluding blessing. Almost none of these elements are present here. The letter is as distinctive in its conclusion as in its beginning. However, as we shall see, it is likely that each of the elements in this concluding paragraph is an apologetic modification of the standard letter form, much as 1:6-10 was a reverse form of the normal prayer of thanksgiving (curse; see comments on 1:6-10).

Summary Review in Paul's Own Handwriting (6:11-14)

It is not easy to determine the structure in 6:11-18, unless one compares it to the standard letter form. This first part of the conclusion (6:11-14) is a summation of personal matters; Paul describes both himself (6:14) and the opposition teachers (6:12-13). In the latter part of the paragraph he turns to a description of the community (6:15-16). The whole is framed by two personal comments, one about his handwriting (6:11) and one about his suffering (6:17), while the letter concludes with the normal blessing in v. 18. The tone of the entire section is emotional. It is compressed, gives the feeling that the writer is rushing along, under strong emotions raised by the problematic situation he has addressed. The paragraph is like the "last outbreak of a powerful thunderstorm."[108] The metaphor is apt. Precisely because of its strongly emotional character the paragraph is also a key to what Paul thinks the fundamental issues in the Galatian churches are.

1. Mention of the Autograph (6:11)

The RSV translates the first word literally (**see**), but misses the effect entirely. It is the imperative of the verb *to see,* a form used only here in Paul. Its effect is to demand the attention of the reader: "Mark this! Note well!" Either would be closer to the effect of the imperative. The verb is followed by an indirect question: **with what large letters I am writing to you with my own hand.** There are two possible interpretations of this statement. (1) It was normal practice to dictate a letter to a professional scribe, whose script was more legible and who knew the proper conventions in writing letters. The person sending the letter would then sometimes add a greeting or his own signature as an identifying mark.[109] Thus Paul here would be introducing what he writes himself (6:11-18) by calling attention to his script, so different from that of the professional scribe. Rom. 16:22, the greeting of the scribe Tertius, shows that Paul at times dictated. While he does not say so, the subscription may have been a mark of authenticity (cf. 1 Cor. 16:21; 2 Thess. 3:17; Col. 4:18). The unique note here is that he calls attention to the **large letters.** (2) The alternative is to argue that the large letters characterize the entire letter, which Paul has written from beginning to end without the aid of a scribe. If the theory proposed by Werner Foerster and supported in this commentary is convincing, Paul wrote on board ship.[110] He would not have had a scribe available. In either case the Galatians are to see in Paul's distinctive hand-writing a mark of his personal concern for them.

2. The Self-serving Character of the Opposition (6:12-13)

Paul opens his concluding remarks with another (final) attack on his opponents, calling attention to the selfish motivation underlying their message. The attack is a mixture of objective facts and subjective evaluations on Paul's part, as Betz points out (pp. 314-317). **It is those who want to make a good showing in the flesh that would compel you to be circumcised, and only in order that they may not be persecuted for the cross of Christ.** The same term is translated **want** in v. 12 and **desire** in v. 13. Paul does not name the opponents, but characterizes them by their intentions. (He applies the same verb to them also in 1:7 and 4:17.) The verb translated **make a good showing** is unusual. Only one occurrence earlier than this passage is known.[111] It might be paraphrased "play a good role" or "cut a good figure." **In the flesh** might mean "in your flesh," since the **circumcision** of the Galatians is the form it takes (cf. 2:3; 5:2-3). They put pressure on the Galatians as they seek to **compel** them **to be circumcised.** Paul elsewhere (1:7; 5:10) accuses them of disturbing or upsetting the Galatians. Paul assigns a motive to them: **in order that they may not be persecuted for the cross of Christ.** He introduces the motive by the word **only.** The word is always negatively argumentative in Galatians (cf. 1:23; 2:10; 3:2; 4:18; 5:13). Paul does not describe how he knows that this is their only motivation. E. P. Sanders argues on the basis of 1 Thess. 2:16; 2 Cor. 11:24; Gal. 5:11; and this passage that some non-Christian Jews persecuted some Christian Jews in some places.[112] Paul had been on both sides of the persecution. He was persecuted because he brought Gentiles into the people of God without demanding circumcision or obedience to the law. Apparently, Jewish Christians who required circumcision of Gentile converts were not persecuted. Paul infers that the avoidance of persecution was their sole reason for asking circumcision of Gentiles. His opinion may well be wrong at this point, but it is understandable, since he regarded the whole of the gospel as at stake (summarized in the phrase **the cross of Christ;** cf. 3:1-5).

Paul supports this negative interpretation in v. 13 by pointing to what he regards as a contradiction in his opponents. **For even those who receive circumcision do not themselves keep the law.** These must be the agitators that have come into the Galatian churches. The phraseology reminds the reader of Gal. 2:11-14. Stephen in Acts 7:53 accuses his hearers of receiving the law, but not observing it. It is possible that circumcision without the observance of the law might have been the position either of an extra-Palestinian Judaism or of a form of early Jewish Christianity. (That might explain the curious language of Gal. 5:3!) Paul then repeats his attack on their motives: **but they desire to have you circumcised** (better: "that you get yourselves circumcised") **that they may glory in your flesh. Glory** would be better translated "have a reason to boast." Again, one does not know how Paul has this information about his opponents' motivation. Rom. 2:17 might suggest that they claim to have a special knowledge of God and his will, but Paul's language in v. 13 does not make it explicit. Paul's attack accused the opposition of being heretics (**for the cross of Christ**), of being morally inferior and self-serving (to avoid persecution and to have a basis for bragging), and of being cowardly (to avoid persecution). His final blow is partly ad hominem, crediting moral lapses to the opposition on the basis of knowing their interior purposes. It is extremely effective; much interpretation of Galatians simply affirms it.

3. *The Cross of Christ Ends All Self-assertion (6:14)*

Paul contrasts himself to the opposition in 6:14. **But far be it from me to glory except in the cross of our Lord Jesus Christ.** The Greek is more emphatic: it begins, "For me however." He then presents a new short thesis. "May it not happen that I boast except in the cross." Paul had accused his opponents of wanting to boast in the flesh (6:13). That boasting is a form of self-assertion (attacked in 6:3-5). The Greek ideal was expressed in the person of Achilles: "always to be the best, and to stand head and shoulders above all others" (Homer, *Iliad* 11.784; cf. 6:208). Paul identified a boasting in the law (Rom. 2:23) and a boasting in the flesh (Phil. 3:4) as evidence of self-assertion, self-confidence. Such boasting betrays "the sin of self-reliance."[113] Paul says that he will boast **only in the cross of our Lord Jesus Christ.** The paradoxical character of that statement hits us only as we recall that the cross is the instrument of public execution for the worst criminals in the Roman empire.[114] It is the public demonstration of evil that puts an end to all self-recommendation before God. The cross is the saving act of God, whose radical salvation is the one basis for Christian boasting (1 Cor. 1:18; Rom. 5:2,3,11). It excludes all other boasting (Rom. 3:27; Phil. 3:3,4) because it shows that all the things in which people boast are as nothing (Phil. 3:3-11; 2 Cor. 11:16—12:10). All boasting must be in the Lord (1 Cor. 1:31; 2 Cor. 10:17) who is revealed on the cross. The cross means a radical upsetting of all prior categories: **By which the world has been crucified to me and I to the world.** The statement recapitulates Gal. 2:19-21. **The world**[115] is the antithesis to the rule of God. It is this present evil age, as Paul asserts in Gal. 1:4. The cross is the defeat of the "elemental spirits of the world" (4:3,9), the act of manumission that sets us free from slavery to the powers of the world. It is as radical a change as death and resurrection (2:20). There is a new life force, "Christ who lives in me." That keeps Paul—and by implication, all Christians—from boasting in anything except the Lord and his cross.

Conditional Blessing (6:15-17)

Paul immediately moves on to draw a general conclusion from what he has affirmed specifically about himself in v. 14. **For neither circumcision counts for anything, nor uncircumcision, but a new creation.** In this new situation *post crucem Christi* (after the cross of Christ) the old distinctions, which belong to the world, have lost all validity. Paul simply restates Gal. 5:6, the summary of the fundamental problem facing the Galatian churches. The antitheses of 3:28 might all have been cited. What does count is **a new creation.** With that phrase Paul introduces a new concept into the letter that he has not hinted at earlier. The **new creation** is used also in 2 Cor. 5:17; it is suggested by the language of dying with Christ to the world in 6:14, but goes beyond it. The creator God is at work in Christ (cf. the argument of Rom. 4:17-25). Something drastically new is present in the resurrected Christ, so new that the old cannot contain it. The **new creation** expresses this drastic newness. Christ has redeemed us from the powers of this world (4:3-7). He has enabled a new life ("Christ . . . lives in me," 2:20); in the Spirit there is a new power of life (5:18,25). New creation is a category to describe the sharp break with the past.

The translation of Gal. 6:16 in the RSV obscures some problems of interpretation. The literal translation would be "And as many as walk by this rule, peace upon them and mercy also upon the Israel of God." The order of the terms raises questions. It is clear that the **rule** referred to is the removal of the significance of circumcision and uncircumcision, as formulated in 6:15. The question is whether those who **walk by this rule** are the same group as **the Israel of God.** The question has also been raised whether there should be a comma after "them," so that **peace** is promised to the first group and "mercy" to **the Israel of God. Peace** is one of the blessings promised to Israel in Ps. 125:5 and Ps. 128:6, while Ezra 3:11 and Ps. Sol. 11:9 promise "mercy" to Israel. Both are part of the promise to Israel in the tradition.[116] Richardson calls attention to the 19th Benediction of the *Shemoneh Esreh,* the great prayer of the synagogue: "May God grant peace and mercy upon them, even upon all Israel his people."[117] Richardson regards Paul's formulation as a modification of this synagogue prayer and argues that Paul in the second half of v. 16 extends his blessing to Israel, that is, "those within Israel to whom God will show mercy" (p. 82). He thus inserts a comma between "them" and "and" in the translation given above. His reasoning is ingenious, but not convincing. Paul has just argued that the national distinctions and religious distinctions no longer apply (v. 15). He has claimed that all who believe the promise are Abraham's descendants (3:29). Thus **the Israel of God,** a unique phrase in Paul, must serve as the capstone to his argument and include all, Jews and Gentiles, who believe that the promise liberates them from law and its demands.[118]

That interpretation is supported by Paul's final outburst in 6:17: **Henceforth let no man trouble me.** The Greek verb is an imperative. Paul feels that his letter has solved the problem in the Galatian churches. There should be no more disturbance. The word for **trouble** can also mean "labor" or "work." Paul bases this command on his statement **for I bear on my body the marks of Jesus** (v. 17b). These marks are either the branded mark of ownership on a slave or the tattoo mark to identify one as member of a religious cult.[119] Paul is a slave of Jesus, purchased by him from his slave master, the law (3:13). He bears in his body the "dying of Jesus" (2 Cor. 4:10). His sufferings on behalf of the gospel have come from persecution (cf. 5:11) and the many specific acts of indignity and punishment he received (2 Cor. 11:23-27; cf. Phil. 3:10). His stigmata (real wounds or scars) are the evidence of his new creation and life.

Final Unconditional Blessing (6:18)

The letter concludes with a typical blessing. **The grace of our Lord Jesus Christ be with your spirit, brethren. Amen.** It is almost identical to those in Philemon 25 and Phil. 4:23; the addition of **brethren** breathes a note of community that the Galatians must have appreciated. The reference to **your spirit** is not unique, but unusual; it stresses their inner life. **Grace** is a traditional term, but Paul uses it to underscore the unconditional promise received by faith (cf. 1:3, 6, 15; 2:9, 21; 5:4). **Amen,** the concluding word, is the liturgical response by which a hearer makes what is heard his or her own. It is so used in 1 Cor. 14:16. And it is probably a liturgical direction to the congregation, giving it its response at the reading of the letter.

This concluding paragraph is unusual. In a normal letter Paul includes in his conclusion personal information about himself and his plans (see Rom. 15:14-29; 1 Cor. 16:5-9; Phil. 4:10-20), recommendations about other people (Phoebe in Rom. 16:1-2; Timothy and Apollos in 1 Cor. 16:10-12), greetings to and from various people (Rom. 16:3-16, 21-23; 1 Cor. 16:19-20; 2 Cor. 13:12; Phil. 4:21-22; 1 Thess. 5:26), requests and invitations for intercessory prayers (Rom. 15:30-32; 1 Cor. 16:18; 1 Thess. 5:25), short warnings or exhortations (Rom. 16:17-18, if authentic; 1 Cor. 16:13; 2 Cor. 13:11), and prayers and blessings (Rom. 15:33; 16:20; 1 Cor. 16:21-24; 2 Cor. 13:13; Phil. 4:23; 1 Thess. 5:23, 24, 28). In a few instances there is mention of Paul's signature in his own hand (1 Cor. 16:21; 2 Thess. 3:17).

Almost all of this is missing in Galatians. Better stated, there is often a kind of negative presence of these elements.

1. There is mention of his signature in v. 11.
2. There is neither commendation, nor greetings; instead there is an attack on the opposition (vv. 12-13).
3. Instead of personal details about Paul's plans there is a statement of Paul's basic theological position (v. 14).
4. This leads not to greetings, but to a description of the Christian community (vv. 15-16).
5. Instead of a request for intercessions or prayers on the readers' behalf, there is the demand in v. 17 not to make any more difficulties.
6. Only the blessing (and the signature) are typical.

All of this suggests that here, as in 1:6-10, Paul is inverting the ingredients of the typical letter. His letter is a parody of the normal letter, each element underscoring his concern with their attitude to the gospel and its corresponding life-style. In short, apologetic interests shape the form in a manner unique in Paul. That is part of what gives the letter its perennial freshness. The letter is no *pro forma* document, but the excited thoughts of a creative thinker and preacher.

NOTES

Introduction

1. Walter Schmithals, "The Heretics in Galatia," in *Paul and the Gnostics*, trans. John E. Steely (Nashville and New York: Abingdon 1972) 13-64.

2. On the heresy in Galatia see any recent introduction, e.g., Werner Georg Kümmel, *Introduction to the New Testament*, trans. Howard Clark Kee, rev. ed. (Nashville and New York: Abingdon, 1975) 298-301; Eduard Lohse, *The Formation of the New Testament*, trans. M. Eugene Boring (Nashville and New York: Abingdon, 1981) 59-61.

3. In addition to books referred to in n. 2, see Günther Bornkamm, *Paul*, trans. D. M. G. Stalker (New York and Evanston: Harper & Row, 1971) 82-83. Robert Jewett, "The Agitators and the Galatian Congregation," NTS 17 (1970/71): 198-212, argues that the Jewish Christians were pressured by Zealots to carry on the campaign for the law in the late 40s and early 50s to avert "suspicion that they were in communion with lawless Gentiles" (p. 205).

4. WA 1.146.

5. For a map showing the location of this territory see the *Oxford Bible Atlas*, ed. Herbert G. May, 3rd ed. (London and New York: Oxford University Press, 1984) 90-91 or the map of "Greece and Asia Minor, Mid-First Century A.D." bound at the rear of the *IDB, Supplementary Volume* (Nashville: Abingdon, 1976).

6. See the maps listed in n. 5 and M. J. Mellink, "Galatia," IDB (New York and Nashville: Abingdon, 1962), 2:336-338 or Hans Volkmann, "Galatia," *Der Kleine Pauly* (Stuttgart: Alfred Druckenmüller Verlag, 1967), 2:666-670.

7. For a convincing presentation of the provincial (southern) theory see A. H. McNeile, *An Introduction to the Study of the New Testament*, 2nd ed. rev. by C. S. C. Williams (Oxford: Clarendon Press, 1953) 143-146.

8. Kümmel supports the traditional dating, about A.D. 54 to 55 at the end of the so-called third missionary journey (pp. 301-304). H. D. Betz, *Galatians* (Philadelphia: Fortress, 1979) 11-12, gives a slightly broader range, A.D. 50-55.
9. "Abfassungszeit und Ziel des Galaterbriefes," *Apophoreta: Festschrift für Ernst Haenchen,* Beiheft 30 of ZNW (Berlin: Alfred Töpelmann, 1964) 135-141.

Outline

1. This outline seeks to make clear that Galatians is a defense of Paul's message and ministry against a massive undercutting of it in the Galatian churches. The defense is designed to support an appeal neither to desert Paul's gospel nor to add anything to it, as 1:6-12; 2:15-21; 4:12-20; 5:1, 13, 25; 6:10, 16 show.

For that reason the outline treats the body of the letter, 1:13—6:10, as one argument in three stages. Gal. 5:13—6:10 is not some kind of practical appendix. It is designed to show that the Pauline message results in a community that rigorously lives out the implications of the new creation. The first section, 1:12—2:21, is not a kind of reaction out of personal peevishness. Paul gives this autobiographical survey to show that the gospel he proclaimed in Galatia was powerfully able to sustain itself in the church. The interrelationship of the three sections is indicated in those passages that are labeled *Transition.* In each case they are not only a conclusion, but a first statement of the theme that will occupy Paul in what follows, thus serving to bind the argument together.

Many commentaries provide an outline that is little more than a listing of topics. Others distinguish what is biographical, doctrinal, and ethical (e.g., Guthrie, Hamann, Duncan, Cole) in a way that obscures the fact that the letter is one single, sustained apologetic argument with introduction and conclusion. The notable exceptions are the commentaries by Schlier, Oepke, and Betz. Betz analyzes the letter as a Hellenistic-Roman apology in an epistolary format. Betz provides the first major interpretive challenge to Galatians as a whole in a generation. In my opinion, his outline does not give adequate structural function to the appeals and warnings in the letter. Nonetheless, it richly repays careful study. I have been strongly influenced by the views of Nils A. Dahl put forward to the SBL Paul Seminar in 1974 in an unpublished paper titled "Paul's Letter to the Galatians: Epistolary Genre, Content, and Structure."

Notes

Commentary

1. Paul differs from Luke on this point. In Luke-Acts only the Twelve are apostles. Luke places Paul in the category of prophet (Acts 13:1) and evangelist, but not apostle.
2. "Abfassungszeit und Ziel des Galaterbriefes," *Apophoreta: Festschrift für Ernst Haenchen* (Berlin: A. Töpelmann, 1964) 135-141.
3. Nils Alstrup Dahl, "Paul's Letter to the Galatians: Epistolary Genre, Content, and Structure" (unpublished paper, SBL Paul Seminar, 1974) 33-35.
4. For the form cf. Ernst Käsemann, "Sentences of Holy Law in the New Testament," in *New Testament Questions of Today*, trans. W. J. Montague (Philadelphia: Fortress, 1969) 66-81. Klaus Berger, "Zu den sogenannten Sätzen heiligen Rechts," *NTS* 17 (1970/71): 10-40, questions the validity of Käsemann's formal analysis.
5. Contrary to Anton Friedrichsen, *The Apostle and His Message* (Uppsala: Uppsala Universitets Årsskrift 1947:3) 8-12.
6. "Moses received the Law from Sinai and committed it to Joshua, and Joshua to the elders, and the elders to the Prophets; and the Prophets committed it to the men of the Great Synagogue" (*Mishnah, Aboth* 1:1, trans. H. Danby [Oxford: University Press, 1933] 446). The terms "received from" (*qibbel min*) and "deliver to" (*masar le*) are technical terms for the transmittal of oral tradition.
7. Paul's stress on the nonhuman origin of his gospel does not mean that he avoids all use of earlier Christian material, as 1 Cor. 15:3-5 makes clear. Paul's letters are laced with citations of earlier Christian material. In Galatians Paul is concerned with the source of and authority for his gospel; an apostle needs no chain of witnesses to establish his authority. Tradition, however, can be used to show that Paul's message is not aberrant or odd, as 1 Cor. 15:11 makes clear.
8. Cf. Günther Bornkamm, "The Revelation of Christ to Paul on the Damascus Road and Paul's Doctrine of Justification and Reconciliation: A Study in Galatians I," in *Reconciliation and Hope*, ed. Robert Banks (Grand Rapids: William B. Eerdmans, 1974) 91-92.
9. Cf. M. *Aboth* 1:1 and Martin Hengel, *Judaism and Hellenism*, trans. John Bowden (Philadelphia: Fortress, 1974), 1:81, 136, 174.
10. Cf. Gerhard Krodel, *Acts* (Philadelphia: Fortress, 1981), 39 and 95. On the difference between call and conversion see Krister Stendahl, *Paul among Jews and Gentiles* (Philadelphia: Fortress, 1976) 7-23.
11. *An Atlas of the Acts* by John Sterling (London: G. Philip, 1966) 1, has an excellent map of the Roman provinces at Paul's time, as does *The Oxford Bible Atlas*, ed. Herbert G. May, 3rd ed. (London and New York: Oxford University Press, 1984) 91.

12. Ferdinand Hahn, *Mission in the New Testament*, trans. Frank Clarke (Naperville: Alec R. Allemson, 1965) 78.

13. E.g., George S. Duncan, *The Epistle of Paul to the Galatians* (New York and London: Harper and Brothers, n.d.) 45. Timothy was thus circumcised, Acts 16:3. See also Johannes Weiss, *Earliest Christianity* (New York: Harper and Brothers, 1959 = 1937), 1:270-271.

14. The authors of the Formula of Concord saw the significance of Paul's stand over against all demands that indifferent rites are mandatory, cf. FC, SD X, 11-14 (*The Book of Concord*, trans. ed. T. Tappert [Philadelphia: Fortress, 1959], 493).

15. They correspond to the three who with the council led the Qumran community; cf. Bo Reicke, "The Constitution of the Primitive Church in the Light of Jewish Documents," in *The Scrolls and the New Testament*, ed. Krister Stendahl (New York: Harper & Brothers, 1957) 150-153.

16. *The Collection: A Study in Paul's Strategy* (Naperville: Alec R. Allenson, 1966) 129-138. See also Leander E. Keck, "The Poor among the Saints in the New Testament," ZNW 56 (1965): 100-129.

17. Cf. F. F. Bruce, *The Acts of the Apostles* (London: Tyndale Press, 1951) 299; Ernst Haenchen, *The Acts of the Apostles* (Philadelphia: Westminster, 1971) 449.

18. New Testament chronology is a difficult topic, due especially to the infinitesimal amount of data in the original sources. The following is an introductory bibliography: George B. Caird, "Chronology of the New Testament," *IDB* 1:603-606; George Ogg, "Chronology of the New Testament," *Peake's Commentary on the Bible*, ed. Matthew Black and H. H. Rowley (London: Thomas Nelson, 1962), 730-732; George Ogg, *The Odyssey of Paul: A Chronology* (Old Tappan, N.J.: Fleming H. Revell, 1962); Beda Rigaux, *Letters of St. Paul: Modern Studies*, trans. S. Yonick (Chicago: Franciscan Herald Press, 1962) 68-99; John G. Gunther, *Paul, Messenger and Exile: A Study in the Chronology of His Life and Letters* (Valley Forge, Pa.: Judson, 1972). Robert Jewett, *A Chronology of Paul's Life* (Philadelphia: Fortress, 1979), presents a quite novel reinterpretation of the data, as did John Knox, *Chapters in a Life of Paul* (Nashville and New York: Abingdon, 1950). See also Gerd Lüdemann, *Paul: Apostle to the Gentiles*, vol. 1 (Philadelphia: Fortress, 1984).

19. Cf. Israel Abrahams, *Studies in Pharisaism and the Gospels*, Series I (New York: Ktav, 1967 = 1917) 55, 56.

20. The NEB is more accurate: "Their conduct did not square with the truth of the gospel."

21. Scholars have debated for centuries whether these verses are the words Paul used at Antioch or not. The problem is insoluble. The

"we" in v. 15 suggests that Peter is included and so is in favor of an Antiochene context. But the language of vv. 16-21 almost completely deserts the language of 2:11-14; there is no reference to table fellowship, and the term *gospel* is no longer used. A whole new series of words is introduced that are characteristic of the argument of 3:1ff.: "justify" (used 8 times), "law," (used 29 times), "faith" (used 20 times), "believe" (3 occurrences), "works" (8 occurrences). This change in terminology supports the idea that vv. 15-21 are not part of Paul's speech at Antioch, but an application of that incident to the problem that Paul faces in the Galatian churches.

Hans Dieter Betz, *Galatians* (Philadelphia: Fortress, 1979) 14-25, argues that Galatians is written in the form of an apologetic letter, based on the structure of apologetic speeches as described in Greek rhetoric and Quintilian. In his view these verses are the *propositio*, the statement of the theoretical points at issue in the apology and the basis for their solution (p. 114).

22. Paul works out his understanding of justification in greater detail in Romans. One reason for holding that Galatians is later than Romans is that statements in Galatians often can be understood only in the light of the fuller Romans material. For Paul's views see Roy A. Harrisville, *Romans* (Minneapolis: Augsburg, 1980) 29-33; Betz, pp. 116-119.

23. This view is not held by everyone. Some Jews stress that God justifies in view of what man has already done in conformity with the Torah's demands. See, for example, 4 Ezra 13:23; James 2:14.

24. Robert C. Tannehill, *Dying and Rising with Christ*, Beiheft ZNW 32 (Berlin: Alfred Töpelmann, 1967) is an illuminating study of the eschatological power of this Pauline language.

25. Contrast Philo, *De spec leg* 1.65; 4.49, and elsewhere. Cf. the important article by Johannes Leipoldt, "Die Frühgeschichte der Lehre von der göttlichen Eingebung," ZNW 44 (1952/53): 118-145.

26. Luther caught this insight; see "How Christians Should Regard Moses" and "Prefaces to the New Testament," in *Luther's Works* (St. Louis: Concordia, 1960) 35: 155-174 and 357-362.

27. The use of the term *Galatians* is appropriate for those ethnically Celtic in origin, but not as a description of non-Celtic inhabitants of the Roman province of Galatia. This is often used as support for the northern or territorial theory of the recipients of the letter.

28. See Edgar Krentz, "The Spirit in Pauline and Johannine Theology," in *The Holy Spirit in the Life of the Church*, ed. Paul D. Opsahl (Minneapolis: Augsburg, 1978), 47-57; Eduard Schweizer, *"pneuma*, etc.," TDNT 6:415-437: and E. Schweizer, *The Holy Spirit*, trans. Reginald H. and Ilse Fuller (Philadelphia: Fortress, 1980), *passim*.

29. For Jewish tradition on Abraham see Joachim Jeremias, *"Abraam,"* TDNT, 1:8-9; Samuel Sandmel, *Philo's Place in Judaism,* augmented ed. (New York: Ktav, 1971) 30-95; and Betz, pp. 139-140, with rich bibliography.

30. E.g., vv. 12-19 in 1 Cor. 15:1-33; cf. also 1 Cor. 2:6-16. Cf. A. Oepke, *Der Brief des Paulus an die Galater,* 2nd ed. (Berlin: Evangelische Verlagsanstalt, 1957) 71, 72.

31. Jewish interpreters understood "his faith" in Hab. 2:4 to mean the person's fidelity to monotheism, the fulfillment of the first commandment of the Decalog; cf. H. L. Strack and Paul Billerbeck, *Kommentar zum Neuen Testament aus Talmud und Midrasch* (Munich: C. H. Beck, 1954 = 1926), 3:542ff.

32. Paul's method of citing the OT may appear either extremely casual or even perverse when judged by modern standards of documentation. Measured by the scholarship of his own day, however, his use of the OT is honorable and persuasive. Cf. Betz, pp. 137-138, and E. Earle Ellis, *Paul's Use of the Old Testament* (Edinburgh: Oliver & Boyd, 1957).

33. Elsewhere the precise Greek term is used only in the phrase "redeem the time" (Eph. 5:16; Col. 4:5), the exact meaning of which is unclear.

34. The ancient evidence is given by Eduard Schweizer, *Lordship and Discipleship* (London: SCM Press, 1960) 22-31.

35. There is a rich collection of source material in Billerbeck 3:204-206. Hengel, 1:91, calls attention to the Book of Jubilees in this context.

36. On the suzerainty covenant see George E. Mendenhall, *Law and Covenant in Israel and the Ancient Near East* (Pittsburgh: The Biblical Colloquium, 1955) and Delbert R. Hillers, *Covenant: The History of a Biblical Idea* (Baltimore: Johns Hopkins, 1969), esp. pp. 169-188 for Qumran and NT indications.

37. He is mentioned once in the deutero-Pauline letters, 2 Tim. 3:8.

38. One problem does not affect the argument, but offers interesting insight into Paul's use of the OT. Paul states that the law came 430 years after the promise to Abraham. Exod. 12:40 (Hebrew) says that Israel was in Egypt for 430 years. Acts 7:6 and Gen. 15:13 both state that the stay in Egypt was 400 years. Paul apparently was following the Greek translation of Exod. 12:40 (the Septuagint), which stated that Israel was "in the land of Egypt and in the land of Canaan 430 years." Paul simply adopted the text before him.

39. C. K. Barrett, *From First Adam to Last* (New York: Charles Scribner's Sons, 1962) 46-67, has an excellent brief discussion of Moses in ancient Judaism and in Paul.

40. B. *Pesah* 54a (Billerbeck, 4:435).

41. Cf. George Foot Moore, *Judaism in the First Centuries of the Christian Era* (Cambridge: Harvard University Press, 1927), 1:263-280 and W. D. Davies, *Torah in the Messianic Age and/or the Age to Come* (Philadelphia: Society of Biblical Literature, 1952).

42. Cf. Josephus, *Ant.* 15.136: "We have learned the noblest of our doctrines and the holiest of our laws from the messengers sent by God" (trans. Ralph Marcus in *Josephus*, vol. 8, Loeb Classical Library [London: Heinemann; Cambridge: Harvard, 1963] 67).

43. See Betz, pp. 168-170, and Martin Dibelius, *Die Geisterwelt im Glauben des Paulus* (Göttingen: Vandenhoeck & Ruprecht, 1909) 23-28.

44. Heinrich Schlier, *Der Brief an die Galater*, 4th ed. (Göttingen: Vandenhoeck & Ruprecht, 1965) 162.

45. A. Lukyn Williams, *The Epistle of Paul to the Galatians* (Cambridge: University Press, 1914) 76.

46. Cf. Luther's *Lectures on Galatians, 1535*, in *Luther's Works*, vol. 26 (St. Louis: Concordia, 1963) 309-313, where the matter is found, though not the exact words.

47. A number of passages in the Greek of Philo speak of God giving external, objective evidence in a person; cf. *In Flacc.* 170; *De Abrahamo* 273; *Quis Rer. Div. Heres* 205-6; *De Mut. Nom.* 106. These references and their value are based on an unpublished paper by David M. Hay, "Faith as Divine Gift in Philo and Paul."

48. The literature on the *paidagōgos* is usually not easily available: The best treatments in commentaries are those by Oepke, pp. 86-99 (with copious references to ancient documents), and Betz, pp. 177-178 (good modern bibliography). Best handbook treatments are in Iwan von Müller, "Die griechischen Privataltertümer," *Die griechischen Privat- und Kriegsaltertümer*, 2nd ed. (Munich: C. H. Beck, 1893) 166-167; Wilhelm Adolph Becker, *Charikles*, 2nd ed. by Hermann Göll (Berlin: Verlag von S. Calvary, 1887), 2:46-50; Jérôme Carcopino, *Daily Life in Ancient Rome*, ed. Henry T. Rowell (New York: Bantam Books, 1971) 118f.; Walter Hatto Gross, "*Paidagōgos*," *Der Kleine Pauly* (Munich: Alfred Druckenmüller Verlag, 1972), 4:408.

49. The bibliography on Paul's view of the law is immense. Peter Stuhlmacher, " 'Das Ende des Getzes,' " *ZThK* 67 (1970): 14-39, stresses the significance of Paul's own conversion for his evaluation of the law. G. B. Caird, *Principalities and Powers* (Oxford: Clarendon Press, 1956) 41-53, stresses the tie between the law and demonic powers in Paul.

50. The noun *faith* occurs 142 times in Paul (including the occurrences in the deutero-Paulines: 8 in Ephesians, 5 in Colossians, and 33 in the Pastoral Epistles).

51. Cf. Rom. 13:14; Col. 3:12; Eph. 6:24; 1 Pet. 4:1; and the discussion in E. G. Selwyn, *The First Epistle of St. Peter*, 2nd ed. (London: Macmillan; New York: St. Martin's Press, 1969 = 1947) 388-400.

52. Cf. G.R. Beasley-Murray, *Baptism in the New Testament* (Grand Rapids: Wm. B. Eerdmans, 1973 = 1962) 146-151.

53. Betz, pp. 181-185.

54. Paul refers to it often (Rom. 1:16; 2:9; 14:6ff.; 1 Cor. 3:22f.) to argue that it no longer is valid.

55. Cited by Williams (see n. 45 above), 83.

56. The phrase "in Christ" is important in Paul. It occurs more than 60 times. In Galatians it occurs in 1:22; 2:4,17; 3:14,26,28; and 5:6. The old view that this phrase reflects a Hellenistic "Christ mysticism" is today largely given up; see W. D. Davies, *Paul and Rabbinic Judaism*, 2nd ed. (London: SPCK, 1955) 86-110. The terminology is discussed in almost every work on Pauline theology.

57. H. P. Hamann, *Galatians* (Adelaide: Lutheran Publishing House, 1976) 51-52, is correct when he says that these statements by Paul in v. 28 do "not involve a program of social revolution," but he is wrong in stating that the "concern of the apostle is purely religious." The apostle clearly holds that Christian convictions affect the everyday life of the Christian (cf. Rom. 12:1-2) in practical ways. While Paul was not a social reformer, his thoughts contain within them seeds that have matured into the harvest of social reform.

58. So the KJV; cf. Robert M. Grant, "Like Children," HTR 59 (1946): 71-73, and (surprisingly) W. L. Knox, *St. Paul and the Church of the Gentiles* (Cambridge: University Press, 1961 = 1939) 108-109.

59. The seminal study is Dibelius, *Geisterwelt* (see n. 45) 78-86, 227-230; he leans heavily on Hermann Diels, *Elementum* (Leipzig: B. G. Teubner, 1899), a work not well enough known in NT scholarship.

60. Diogenes Laertius 6.102 calls them "the twelve elemental spirits."

61. Cf. 2 Cor. 4:4, "the god of this age," Wis. 7:17ff.; 13:1-2; etc.; Bo Reicke, "The Law and This World according to Paul," JBL 70 (1951): 259-276; Oepke and Betz ad loc.

62. For the identification of the formula and its extent see Werner Kramer, *Christ, Lord, Son of God* (London: SCM Press, 1966) 111-115; Reginald H. Fuller, *The Foundations of New Testament Christology* (New York: Charles Scribner's Sons, 1965) 194-195, with n. 34 on pp. 200-201. Both stress the implications of preexistence. The most extensive discussion is that of James G. D. Dunn, *Christology in the Making* (Philadelphia: Westminster, 1980) 38-44. Dunne denies implications of preexistence while Klaus Wengst, *Christologische Formeln und Lieder des Urchristentums* (Gütersloh: Gerd Mohn, 1973) 58-60, denies the existence of the formula.

63. Cf. S. V. McCasland, "Abba, Father," JBL 72 (1953): 79-91; Joachim Jeremias, "Abba," *The Central Message of the New Testament* (London: SCM Press, 1965) 17-21; Hans Conzelmann, *An Outline of the Theology of the New Testament* (New York and Evanston: Harper & Row, 1969) 103.

64. Gal. 4:8-20 is not a "personal interlude," a sort of interruption in the argument, as Hamann suggests (p. 60). It is an integral part of the apologetic that motivates him throughout the letter.

65. Days = Sabbath and Day of Atonement; months = New Moon; seasons = Passover, Weeks, Tabernacles; years = New Year or Sabbatical; and Jubilee years as prescribed in the Torah.

66. E.g., Oepke, pp. 104-109.

67. Betz, pp. 220-221.

68. My analysis of structure is far from universally accepted. It is in determining the break between the theological argument and the paraenesis that commentators differ. Some find a break at 4:31.

69. First used on the Homeric poems, it was adopted by Alexandrian Jewish scholars (Philo, Aristobulus) and then came into the Christian church. See R. M. Grant, *The Letter and the Spirit* (New York: Macmillan, 1957); R. P. C. Hansen, *Allegory and Event* (Richmond, Va.: John Knox, 1959) 9-129.

70. C. K. Barrett, "The Allegory of Abraham, Sarah, and Hagar in the Argument of Galatians," in *Rechtfertigung: Festschrift für Ernst Käsemann* (Tübingen: J. C. B. Mohr; Göttingen: Vandenhoeck & Ruprecht, 1976) 1-16; his main point is on p. 6.

71. Betz, ad loc., has an exemplary discussion of the possibilities.

72. Paul betrays no concern over what some regard as a sharp contradiction to 3:15-18, where only one covenant is mentioned, the covenant of promise to which the law is an appendix, not a covenant in its own right. But if each passage is read in terms of Paul's goal, the conflict disappears. Paul is not giving a definitive name to the Sinai Torah, but using whatever is appropriate to a tradition or an illustration.

73. So, most recently, Betz, pp. 253-257, based also on his analysis of the structure of the letter as a rhetorical apologetic epistle. Duncan, p. 152, and Guthrie, p. 127, share this division. The question of the delimitation of the paraenetical section was thoroughly discussed by Otto Merk, "Der Beginn der Paränese im Galaterbrief," ZNW 60 (1969): 83-104. His argumentation convinces me that the break should be made at 5:13, though Paul introduces in 5:2-12 motifs that are significant in the paraenetic section.

74. See my "Freedom in Christ—Gift and Demand," *Concordia Theological Monthly* 40 (1969): 356-368, for a summary of Paul's view of

freedom. It includes a bibliography of literature to that date. Max Pohlenz, *Freedom in Greek Life and Thought* (New York: Humanities Press, 1966) 170-174, gives a good overview of the Greek ideas of freedom, and briefly treats Paul.

75. On yoke see Jer. 28:10; cf. K. H. Rengstorf, "*zygos* in the N.T.," TDNT 2:898-901; C. V. Wild, "Yoke," IDB, 4:924-925. Jews spoke of the "yoke of the Law."

76. WA, DB 7, 10, 1. 9f.

77. As Guthrie takes it; p. 131.

78. Suggestions include Peter, James, and even Barnabas.

79. The tentative suggestion of F. F. Bruce, *The Epistle to the Galatians: A Commentary on the Greek Text*, The New International Greek Testament Commentary (Grand Rapids: Eerdmans, 1982) 236. He also suggests the possibility of Paul's open attitude to Jewish-Christian circumcision.

80. Oepke, p. 123.

81. After 20 centuries of Christian piety we can scarcely recover the feelings of ancient Mediterranean people about crucifixion. Martin Hengel, *Crucifixion in the Ancient World and the Folly of the Message of the Cross* (Philadelphia: Fortress, 1977), details the feelings of revulsion against this "most cruel death."

82. The joke is almost paralleled in Phil. 3:2. There are excellent discussions of this verse in Lietzmann, pp. 38-39, Schlier, pp. 240-241, and above all in Hans F. von Campenhausen, "Ein witz des Apostels Paulus und die Anfänge des Christlichen Humors," *Aus der Frühzeit des Christentums: Studien zur Kirchengeschichte des ersten und zweiten Jahrhunderts* (Tübingen: J. C. B. Mohr, 1963) 102-108.

83. The formulation is that of Betz, p. 272.

84. See Eduard Schweizer, "*sarx*," TDNT, 7:125-135, esp. p. 133. Bruce, p. 240, describes the flesh as the "self-regarding element in human nature which has been corrupted at the source." See also the excellent discussions in Betz, p. 272, and Robert Jewett, *Paul's Anthropological Terms* (Leiden: E. J. Brill, 1971) 272-273.

85. In the OT there is no specific indication that Lev. 19:18 is regarded as the summation of the Law; moreover, in Lev. 19:18, the "neighbor" is another Israelite, not a human in general. Paul generalizes it to mean any human in need, as Jesus had done before him (Mark 12:29ff.; Luke 10:25-37); cf. Oepke, p. 131. See also Victor Paul Furnish, *The Love Command in the New Testament* (Nashville and New York: Abingdon, 1972), 95-111. Elsewhere in the NT see Matt. 5:43; 19:19; James 2:8. Cf. W. Gutbrod, "*nomos*," TDNT, 4:1075-1077.

86. On flesh and Spirit see Ernst Käsemann, "On Paul's Anthropology," *Perspectives on Paul* (Philadelphia: Fortress, 1971) 25-27; Jewett, pp. 67ff.; David John Lull, *The Spirit in Galatians* (Chico, Calif.: Scholars Press, 1980) 113ff.

87. The most helpful discussions are in Oepke, pp. 135-136; Schlier, pp. 248-250; and Betz, p. 280.

88. There is now a large bibliography on these catalogs. The fundamental study is that of Siegfried Wibbing, *Die Tugend- und Lasterkataloge im Neuen Testament* (Berlin: Alfred Töpelmann, 1959). Brief treatments are given by O. J. F. Seitz, "Lists, Ethical," IDB, 3:137-139 and D. Schroeder, "Lists, Ethical," IDB Supp., 546. William Barclay, *Flesh and Spirit* (London: SCM Press, 1962), gives a helpful interpretation of Gal. 5:19-23; see also the standard commentators.

89. E.g., Cicero, *Tusc* 4.9-33; Epict. II.16.45; Diog. Laert. VII.110-114; *Corpus Hermeticum* I.22f., 25; Wis. 14:22ff.; 4 Macc. 1:20ff.; 2:15; T. Jud. 16.

90. See Eduard Schweizer, "Traditional Ethical Patterns in the Pauline and Post-Pauline Letters and Their Development (Lists of Vices and House Tables)," *Text and Interpretation: Studies. . .Matthew Black* (Cambridge: Cambridge University Press, 1979) 195-201.

91. In the case of each vice or virtue I list the other occurrences in Paul, and additional references for some.

92. So Betz, pp. 284f., persuasively. Cf. Rudolf Schnackenburg, *Baptism in the Thought of St. Paul* (New York: Herder and Herder, 1964), 187-196. The seminal "Essay II" by Edward Gordon Selwyn, *The First Epistle of St. Peter*, 2nd ed. (London: Macmillan; New York: St. Martin's, 1947) 363-466, still deserves reading.

93. *Prophecy in Early Christianity and the Mediterranean World* (Grand Rapids: Eerdmans, 1983) 258.

94. 1 Cor. 13:4-8 is in a class by itself. The description of love's activities is formally different from a catalog, though conceptually there are many parallels. The closest parallels to this virtue list are found in the deutero-Pauline Ephesians (4:31).

95. Col. 3:14 lists it in close relationship with peace and thankfulness, a triad close to this in Galatians.

96. Bruce, p. 254, aptly calls attention to Aristotle, EN 2.1108a.

97. The term occurs 16 times in the Pauline corpus. It should be distinguished from *sin*, a term that Paul uses some 60 times, almost always in the singular. Sin is a power that lords it over humans (as in Gal. 3:22), while trespasses are infractions of specific directives (cf. Rom. 5:22, 23).

98. Some contemporary Jews, especially the Qumranites, did try to maintain the purity of their group by excluding sinners. Paul's concern is with the community as a whole. Where the community showed pride in sin (e.g., 1 Cor. 5:2), Paul is severe, demanding the exclusion of the sinner and the breaking of fellowship. This variation is a warning against hasty generalization from a solitary passage.

99. Betz, pp. 298-299, gives many citations. The expression is a standard motif in the discussion of friendship from Socrates to Paul; cf. G. Schrenk, *"baros,* etc.," TDNT, 1:555.

100. Similar sharp formations (*oxymora*) occur in Romans to underscore the absolute role of faith in justification, to the exclusion of the law: "Obedience of faith" (1:5) and "law of faith" (3:27). The phrase "living sacrifice" in Rom. 12:1 is on the surface nonsense, since it is of the essence that a sacrifice die or be destroyed; Paul uses it to stress that cult is no longer the locus of service to God, but the marketplace is the place for liturgy, for service to God.

101. C. H. Dodd, "ΕΝΝΟΜΟΣ ΧΡΙΣΤΟΥ," in *More New Testament Studies* (Grand Rapids: Eerdmans, 1968) 134-148, argues that Paul is thinking of specific sayings of Jesus that function as "precepts" or "ordinances," that is, as Torah. What the Lord "commanded" and "ordained" is the nucleus of Christian *halakah*. John G. Strehlan, "Burden-bearing and the Law of Christ: A Reexamination of Galatians 6:2," JBL 94 (1975): 266-276, argues that this verse introduces the theme of handling finances; it concludes with 6:6. Neither view is compelling.

102. It begins with the Delphic maxim "Know thyself," credited to one of the seven wise men, Chilon of Lacedemonia, in Stobaeus III.1.172.

103. Cf. Ronald F. Hock, *The Social Context of Paul's Ministry* (Philadelphia: Fortress, 1980).

104. J. Paul Sampley, *Pauline Partnership in Christ: Christian Community and Commitment in Light of Roman Law* (Philadelphia: Fortress, 1980), Sampley holds that Rom. 12:13 and 15:25-27 in context reflect this contractual arrangement (pp. 94-96); however, he disallows the relevance of Roman contractual law for interpreting Gal. 6:6 because of "the surely traditional formulation . . ." (p. 102, n. 35). But the stress in Gal. 6:1-10 on communal interrelationships (cf. 6:10) weakens his argument.

105. The RSV and NEB both treat 6:6 as an isolated, separate paragraph, thus implying it has no direct tie to what precedes or follows. The

Goodspeed translation and the 26th edition of the *Novum Testamentum Graece,* ed. Kurt Aland et al. (Stuttgart: Deutsche Bibelstiftung, 1979), both print 6:6-10 as a single paragraph. This rightly indicates that a conceptual thread runs through these verses.

106. Demosthenes, *Or.* 18.159, gives a striking example: "The one who offers the seed is responsible for the crop" (cited by Oepke, p. 154). See also Bruce, pp. 264-265.

107. In an age of concern for inclusive language one should note that *anthrōpos,* regularly translated "man" in the RSV, is equivalent to "everyone." Cf. Gal. 1:1, 10, 11, 12; 2:6, 16; 3:15; 5:3; 6:1. The noun *anthrōpos,* without change of form, can be used of a woman simply by using the feminine article, as in Lysias, *Or.* 1.24.

108. Oepke, p. 156.

109. Cf. G. Adolf Deissmann, *Light from the Ancient East,* trans. Lionel M. Strachan (New York: Harper & Brothers, n.d., preface of translator dated 1927) 106, n. 7. For illustrations of such a change of hand see document no. 8 (fig. 28) and document 9 (fig. 29) and the discussion on pp. 171-172. See also Gordon J. Bahr, "The Subscriptions in the Pauline Letters," JBL 87 (1968): 27-41, esp. pp. 34-35. Bahr holds that Paul's personal writing began at 5:2, not 6:11.

110. Theodor Zahn, *Der Brief des Paulus an die Galater* (Leipzig: A. Deichert, 1905) 277-278, argues that "large letters" refers to the entire book of Galatians. He bases his opinion on the interpretation of a majority of the early fathers, the difference of 6:11 from the other Pauline subscriptions, the use of the epistolary aorist, etc. Paul was so disturbed that he could not wait for a scribe, but wrote himself, uncomfortable as that was.

111. In Papyrus Tebtunis I.19.12 (114 B.C.), as cited by James H. Moulton and G. Milligan, *The Vocabulary of the Greek New Testament* (London: Hodder & Stoughton, 1949 = 1930) 264.

112. *Paul, the Law, and the Jewish People* (Philadelphia: Fortress, 1983) 191-192.

113. R. Bultmann, *Theology of the New Testament* (New York: Charles Scribner's Sons, 1951) 1:242.

114. See Martin Hengel, *Crucifixion* (Philadelphia: Fortress, 1977); the title of the German original, *mors turpissima crucis* ("the most cruel death of the cross"), is an accurate description of crucifixion from Rufinus' Latin translation of Origen's comments on Matt. 27:22ff.

115. H. Sasse, *"kosmos,"* TDNT 3:893; Bultmann, *New Testament Theology* 1:255-256.

116. For rich additional material see Peter Richardson, *Israel in the Apostolic Church* (Cambridge: University Press, 1969) 78-79.

117. Richardson, p. 79.
118. N. A. Dahl, "Der Name Israel: Zur Auslegung von Gal. 6:16," *Judaica* 6 (1950): 161-170; Betz, pp. 320-323; E. P. Sanders, *Paul, the Law, and the Jewish People,* 173-175.
119. Walter Bauer, *A Greek-English Lexicon of the New Testament,* trans. and adapted by W. F. Arndt and F. W. Gingrich, 2nd ed. by F. W. Gingrich and F. W. Danker (Chicago: University of Chicago Press, 1979) 768, s.v. *stigma* for rich documentation.

SELECTED BIBLIOGRAPHY OF
COMMENTARIES AVAILABLE IN ENGLISH

Betz, Hans Dieter. *Galatians: A Commentary on Paul's Letter to the Churches in Galatia.* Hermeneia. Philadelphia: Fortress, 1979. Critical, learned, judicious. Betz argues that the letter follows the rules of rhetoric for an apologetic discourse. The fundamental commentary and first reference for all advanced study of the book.

Bruce, F. F. *The Epistle of Paul to the Galatians: A Commentary on the Greek Text.* The New International Greek Testament Commentary. Grand Rapids: Eerdmans, 1982. A meticulous, sympathetic examination by an outstanding scholar.

Burton, Ernest de Witt. *A Critical and Exegetical Commentary on the Epistle to the Galatians.* The International Critical Commentary. Edinburgh: T. & T. Clark, 1921. A classic commentary. Careful attention to linguistic features. Prior to form criticism and so a bit dated. A major resource.

Cole, R. A. *The Epistle of Paul to the Galatians.* The Tyndale New Testament Commentaries. Grand Rapids: Eerdmans, 1965. A useful popular commentary that recognizes the ecumenical implications of the book.

Duncan, George S. *The Epistle of Paul to the Galatians.* The Moffat New Testament Commentary. New York and London: Harper and Brothers [1937]. Based on one of the first 20th-century translations of the New Testament, this popular commentary is more discursive than many—and a pleasure to read as a result.

Guthrie, Donald. *Galatians*. New Century Bible Commentary. London: Oliphants, 1973. Reprint, Grand Rapids: Eerdmans, 1981. An excellent commentary on the RSV. Informed, clear, well written.

Hamann, H. P. *Galatians*. Adelaide, Australia: Lutheran Publishing House, 1976. A fresh commentary. Highlights the distinctive value of the letter in spite of a somewhat concordistic approach to its relationship to Acts. Popular and clear.

Ramsay, Wm. M. *A Historical Commentary on St. Paul's Epistle to the Galatians*. New York: G. P. Putnam's Sons, 1900. Several reprints. Ramsay, classicist and archaeologist, was the premier proponent of the provincial or south Galatian theory. Useful historical materials on Asia Minor and Galatia.

There are many additional popular commentaries and each makes its own contribution. But no bibliography on Galatians would be complete if it did not mention, separately and in a class by itself, the contributions of Martin Luther: "Lectures on Galatians 1519," trans. Richard Jungkuntz, and "Lectures on Galatians 1535," trans. Jaroslav Pelikan (*Luther's Works*, vols. 26 and 27; St. Louis: Concordia Publishing House, 1963, 1964). The 1519 lectures are in vol. 27, pp. 151-410. The 1535 lectures occupy the whole of vol. 26 and the first 149 pages of vol. 27. Luther is no modern commentator, but comes to Galatians with the sense of Christian freedom, newly recovered, fresh in his mind. It gives his commentary an appealing immediacy that gets to the heart of Paul. He deserves constant attention.

ABOUT THE AUTHOR

Edgar Krentz earned his M. Div. from Concordia Seminary, St. Louis, and the Ph.D. in classical philology from Washington University. He has also studied at the American School of Classical Studies in Athens, Greece, and with Ernst Käsemann at Tübingen University. He has taught New Testament at Concordia Seminary and at Christ Seminary–Seminex in St. Louis. He now serves as Christ Seminary–Seminex Professor of New Testament and Chairperson of the Biblical Division at the Lutheran School of Theology at Chicago.

Dr. Krentz is the author of *Biblical Studies Today, The Historical-Critical Method, Easter* (Proclamation 3), and numerous articles and reviews. He serves as Associate Director of the Joint Expedition to Caesarea Maritima in Israel, and lectures frequently on archeology and biblical subjects.

PHILIPPIANS
John Koenig

INTRODUCTION

Philippians is unique among the letters of the Pauline corpus in showing us a congregation at harmony with its founding apostle. All of Paul's other extant epistles to churches which originated through his proclamation of the gospel are filled with polemics against the readers and statements of self-defense (Galatians, 1–2 Corinthians) or, at the very least, elaborate attempts to correct misunderstandings which have arisen about his teachings (1–2 Thessalonians).[1] But in Philippians one finds no hint of serious conflict—emotional, intellectual, or spiritual—between the apostle and his addressees. When Paul writes, "my brethren, whom I love and long for, my joy and my crown" (4:1), we have the feeling that he really means it. The church at Philippi could make a legitimate claim to being Paul's favorite (see the laudatory references to Philippian believers in Rom. 15:26; 2 Cor. 8:1-5; 11:9; and Phil. 4:15-16).

This does not mean that the Philippians were without problems. For example, they suffered from an anxiety-provoking conflict with local opponents (1:27-30), and a quarrel between two of their prominent members threatened to compromise their public mission (4:2-3). There is some evidence that unhealthy hierarchical structures were beginning to emerge in the congregation as a whole (2:2ff.). Finally, Paul foresees danger to the community from outside teachers who have recently visited or are soon to arrive (3:2-21). But nowhere in the discussion of these difficulties is there any suggestion that Paul and the Philippians do not see eye to eye on how to handle them. Evidence of ill will from any member of the congregation toward the apostle (or vice versa) is altogether lacking.

What does Paul tell a church when he is not contending with it or correcting it? For one thing, he celebrates his special relationship with these believers. The various forms of the Greek *chara* ("joy") and *chairō* ("rejoice") occur more frequently per page in Philippians than in any other New Testament document (see 1:4, 18, 25; 2:2, 17, 18, 28, 29; 3:1; 4:1, 4, 10). With almost every new thought Paul pauses either to blurt out his own joy or to encourage the Philippians in theirs. Second, Paul places high on his agenda the growth in faith of his readers. This is based above all on the unity and mutuality which Christ provides. In fact, Philippians is filled with the language of incorporation. The prepositional phrases "in Christ" and "in the Lord," with their equivalents, appear a total of 22 times in this short letter, the most notable of these in connection with the famous Christological hymn of 2:5ff.: "Have this mind among yourselves, which is yours in Christ Jesus, who, though he was in the form of God, did not count equality with God a thing to be grasped, but emptied himself. . . ." Words denoting "participation" and "communion" are likewise frequent (see p. 127 below and the commentary on 1:5-7), as are exhortations to a common mind (2:2-5; 3:15; 4:2).

From this pulsating unity in the sphere of Christ's lordship comes true growth. So Paul can write of the Philippians' "abounding" (1:9, 26) and of his own "straining forward to what lies ahead" (3:13) as a model for all believers. Collectively, the apostle's descriptions of and encouragements to growth in the epistle to Philippi might be termed "motions of maturity in Christ." Indeed, this is not a bad title for the entire letter, for in Paul's view it is precisely "those. . .who are mature" who see themselves still on the way, pressing forward "toward the goal for the prize of the upward call of God in Christ Jesus" (3:14-15).

The city of Philippi, named for the father of Alexander the Great, lay in Macedonia east of Thessalonica near the Aegean

Sea (in today's Greece just south of the Bulgarian border), roughly 200 air miles north-northeast of Athens. After the decisive victory of Antony and Octavian—the latter to become Caesar Augustus—over Brutus and Cassius (42 B.C.), Philippi was designated a Roman colony. This meant that portions of the city were deeded to retiring imperial legionaries and that Italian customs were widely practiced. These would include the speaking of Latin alongside Greek, the common language of the ancient world, and the prevalence of Roman law. Many native Greeks and Thracians also inhabited the city. A Jewish presence, too, is likely since Acts 16:13 refers to a "place of prayer" near the gates of Philippi where Paul and his party found women worshipers on the Sabbath. One of these was Lydia, known to Luke as the first Christian convert in Macedonia (16:14-15).

According to Acts, Paul's initial trip to Philippi, during his second missionary journey, marked the beginning of his ministry in Europe. It was a trying introduction to the West inasmuch as Paul and Silas suffered both beating and imprisonment from local authorities, illegally as things turned out (16:16-39; Paul's own recollection in 1 Thess. 2:2 of his having been "shamefully treated at Philippi" prior to his first residence in Thessalonica confirms the basic core of Luke's account). Yet some inhabitants of the city believed the apostle's message, and from them grew a church which eventually became dearer and more faithful to him than any other known to us. In our letter Paul writes to this congregation from prison not long after the Philippians have sent him a gift through their messenger Epaphroditus.

The place of origin most often proposed for Philippians is Rome. This location fits well with Paul's reflection on the possibility of his death (1:20-23; 2:17) at the hands of captors who include the praetorian guard (1:13). It also squares with the fact that Paul writes from a place where some Christians belong to "Caesar's household" (4:22). It has been pointed out, however, that both the praetorian guard and people associated with the imperial household would have lived in all the major provincial capitals, as well as in Rome. Thus, some scholars have proposed

Caesarea as the city from which Paul writes, because it is the only other imprisonment by Roman officials mentioned in Acts (apart from that which took place at Philippi itself). Moreover, Paul's references to Christian opponents in 1:15-17 and 3:2ff. could be characterizations of the conservative believers in Palestine who were suspicious of his work (Acts 21:17-22; see also Rom. 15:31b). Today, the remains of Roman Caesarea can be viewed on the Mediterranean shore of modern Israel, some 35 air miles north of Tel Aviv.

There is, however, a third city where the imprisonment assumed in Philippians might have taken place, namely, Ephesus, situated directly opposite Athens on the Aegean seacoast of ancient Asia Minor (today's Turkey). As the provincial capital of Asia, Ephesus would have accommodated a division of the praetorian guard, along with members of Caesar's household. There is no conclusive evidence that Paul ever suffered confinement in this city, although Acts tells us that a great controversy surrounding the apostle did erupt there, with the result that two of his co-workers from Macedonia were briefly held captive by a crowd (19:23-41). Later in Acts, Luke has Paul recalling "trials [in Ephesus] which befell me through the plots of the Jews" (20:19). More specifically, the apostle himself tells the Corinthians of a recent "affliction. . .in Asia" during which he "despaired of life" and felt he had "received the sentence of death" (2 Cor. 1:8-9). The word for "sentence" used here, *apokrima*, would be the usual one employed for official edicts of execution, and it may well refer to the threat of death presupposed in Phil. 1:19-26 and 2:17.

Another argument for the Ephesian origin of Philippians is the Asian capital's relative proximity to Philippi: approximately 275 air miles, as opposed to 830 from Caesarea to Philippi and 610 from Rome to Philippi. Moreover, travel in the first century from Philippi to Rome or Caesarea would have required considerable meanderings through difficult terrain and, in the case of Rome, a sea voyage. By contrast, trips between Philippi and Ephesus could be accomplished through a variety of land and sea legs, chosen on short notice with regard to the availability of ships and

124

changes in the weather. These logistical considerations are important because in Philippians Paul presupposes a number of transactions between himself and his readers. They include a visit from Epaphroditus to Paul in prison with greetings and gifts from Philippi (4:10-20); the letter Paul is sending back to Philippi with Epaphroditus (2:25); the apostle's hope to visit the Philippians himself "shortly" (2:24); his plan to send Timothy to them as soon as he learns his fate (2:23), coupled with his assumption that Timothy will return to him bearing news of the Philippians before he makes his own visit (2:19); a message by an unspecified carrier from Paul's place of imprisonment informing the Philippians that Epaphroditus had fallen ill while attending to Paul's needs (2:26)—or alternatively, a message *from* Philippi which alerted Epaphroditus to the fact that his friends back home had heard about his illness. This multitude of communications makes most sense if Paul is writing from a location relatively close to Philippi. And the chief candidate, all things considered, is Ephesus. Thus, if an Ephesian origin for Philippians cannot be established beyond doubt, it seems quite probable and will be accepted as fact in this commentary.

But there is one difficulty with trying to pin Philippians down to a single place of origin. In recent years, numerous scholars have become convinced that our canonical Philippians is not one letter at all but a compilation of two or three letters by Paul written to Philippi at different stages of his career and, perhaps, from different locations. One of the hypothetical letters isolated is 4:10-20, a section in which the apostle thanks his readers for their care and monetary aid, sent through Epaphroditus. These verses would seem to fit better at the beginning of Philippians, since Paul's response to the support from his friends is certainly one of the chief occasions for his writing. Yet he makes no specific reference to this gift in our canonical Philippians until 4:17f., almost the end of the letter. Moreover, 4:10-20 does not clearly presuppose an imprisonment. Hence, several scholars have concluded that it is a separate thank-you note composed by Paul at some time prior to his imprisonment. After Paul's death, when his letters were being collected and edited for circulation throughout the church, someone added this short, early letter to the end of a longer one, thus reversing the actual chronological sequence. Since we have good evidence that Paul's epistles were indeed subjected to later editing (see commentaries on 2 Corinthians 10–13 and Romans 16), we dare not dismiss this hypothesis as farfetched. Added support for attempts to discover multiple letters in our Philippians is provided by the fact that Polycarp, the bishop of Smyrna in Asia Minor who suffered martyrdom in A.D. 155, wrote to Philippi reminding believers there of the letters (plural) which Paul had sent them during his ministry (Pol. *Phil.* 3:2).

Nevertheless, the evidence marshalled for taking 4:10-20 as one of these letters is not finally persuasive. True, Paul does not make any *direct* reference to gifts sent from Philippi in chaps. 1–3 of our canonical letter. But he does mention the Philippians' "partnership in the gospel from the first day until now" (1:5; note the echo of this statement in 4:15). Furthermore, the apostle calls his readers "partakers with him of grace, both in his imprisonment and in the defense and confirmation of the gospel" (1:7). As we shall see in the commentary, both of these expressions contain financial overtones. Moreover, 4:14 probably *does* assume that Paul is in prison. There the apostle writes, "Yet it was kind of you to share my trouble." The word translated "trouble" is the Greek *thlipsis*, which not only occurs earlier in Philippians in a description of Paul's confinement ("thinking to *afflict* me in my imprisonment"; 1:17) but also denotes the trying experience in Asia which we have taken as a probable reference to the Ephesian incarceration that produced Philippians (2 Cor. 1:8ff.). In addition, the word for "share" in Phil. 4:14 (*synkoinōnēsantes*) is a verbal form of the noun "partakers" (*synkoinōnous*) in 1:7. On the whole, then, this data supports an organic connection between 1:5-7 and 4:10-20. That is, they are probably parts of the same letter. Paul's figurative compliments to the Philippians at the beginning turn into a straightforward thanksgiving at the end.

More difficult to assess is the evidence that 3:2—4:9 (others say 3:2—4:1 or 3:1b—4:1 or 3:2—4:3) constitutes part of a separate letter written to Philippi sometime later than the rest of our canonical epistle when Paul (a) is no longer a prisoner and (b) learns that some teachers whom he regards as dangerous are about to visit the congregation. This partition hypothesis rests largely on the observation that whereas chaps. 1, 2, and 4 indicate a reflective, almost relaxed attitude on the apostle's part, 3:2ff introduces a sudden, unprovoked blast, an intense polemic against a threat not obvious in the rest of the letter ("Look out for the dogs, look out for the evil-workers, look out for those who mutilate the flesh. For we are the true circumcision who worship God in spirit. . .").

There are problems with this hypothesis, however. In 3:1b, which is not regarded by most scholars as belonging to the fragment, Paul says: "To write the same things to you is not irksome to me, and is safe for you." What are "the same things?" According to most versions of the partition hypothises, they would be things contained in an earlier letter, namely, 1:1—2:30. But there is little in that section which one is likely to take as potentially repetitive to the Philippians or irksome to the apostle. The one possible candidate, rejoicing (1:4, 18; 2:18, 28-29), does not seem fitting. In fact, Paul's assertion that the "same things" are "safe" for the Philippians suggests that these things resemble preventative medicine: they are not tasty but necessary for health. Thus, 3:1b was probably meant to introduce the harsh words of 3:2. The word translated "finally" can mean "beyond that" or "as for the rest" and does not necessarily signal the end of a letter (see 1 Thess. 4:1; 2 Thess. 3:1). It is possible to understand "the same things" here as meaning "the same things I am asking Epaphroditus to communicate to you orally" (2:25-30).[2] But this speculation is not necessary since Paul notes in 3:18f. that he has often warned the Philippians about "enemies of the cross of Christ." Perhaps he did this personally or through other letters to Philippi now lost. (For references to earlier communications between Paul and Philippi, see 1:5; 4:15-16.) At any rate, the false teachers censured in 3:2-19 are not referred to in the rest of our canonical letter. The "opponents" sketched in 1:28 are of a different order, for the congregation knows them all too well and does not need to be given advance warning about them.

Even if one begins the hypothetical fragment with 3:1b itself, the case for its existence remains weak; for there are other points of correspondence between 1:1—3:1a and 3:1b—4:9 which strengthen the impression that our canonical Philippians is, after all, one complete epistle rather than sections of two or three letters spliced together. We have already noticed the *koinō-* root words for "sharing" which turn up in both 1:7 and 4:14. Additional variants of this word group appear throughout Philippians. Thus, Paul writes of the Philippians' "partnership in the gospel" with him (1:5; *koinōnia*), of their common "participation in the Spirit" (2:1; *koinōnia*), and of his own "share" in the sufferings of Christ (3:10; *koinōnia*), which he both holds up to the Philippians as a model in 3:15-17 and presumes to be already operative among them in 1:7 and 1:29-30. Near the end of his letter the apostle also commends his readers for being the only church to enter a "partnership" of giving and receiving with him (4:15; *koinōneō*, the verbal form of *koinōnia*).

Other expressions, most of which rarely appear in the New Testament as a whole but do occur in both 1:1—3:1 and 3:2—4:9, are the words for "gain" (1:21; 3:7-8), "strive together with" (1:27; 4:3), "better"/"surpassing" (2:3; 3:8; 4:7), and "set one's mind on" (1:7; 2:2, 5; 3:15, 19; 4:2, 10). In addition, Paul writes about "glorying in Christ" in both major sections of our canonical letter (1:26; 3:3). Although this linguistic evidence cannot add up to a proof for the unity of Philippians, it does combine with our observations regarding the purpose of 3:1 to push us in that direction. Therefore, the single-letter hypothesis will be adopted in this commentary.

While 3:2ff. does indeed disclose an odd change of mood, it should be pointed out that even in the earlier sections of Philippians Paul's state of mind is far from serene. In 1:21-23 he struggles with the future, his own life and death hanging in the balance

("For me to live is Christ, and to die is gain. . . I am hard pressed between the two"). Then, in vv. 24-25, he suddenly and unexpectedly reaches a point of equanimity, announcing his full confidence that he will live so that he can minister in Philippi once again. But just a few verses later, he writes as if this resolution had never occurred: "Even if I am to be poured as a libation upon the sacrificial offering of your faith, I am glad and rejoice with you all" (2:17). And the end is not yet. Following this speculation comes another 180° turn: "I trust in the Lord that shortly I myself shall come [to Philippi]" (2:24). These diverse statements provide clear evidence that the apostle is subject to erratic thoughts throughout the writing of Philippians. It may be that in 3:2ff. he has begun to contemplate his death once more and, fearing that he will not see the Philippians again, delivers an anxious warning against those who will try to seduce the congregation in his absence.

When was Philippians written? If we are correct in taking 2 Cor. 1:8-11 as a description of Paul's Ephesian imprisonment sent shortly after the apostle had gained his freedom, then Philippians must have been composed not much prior to this segment of the Corinthian correspondence. Many scholars also notice verbal and theological parallels between Philippians and Galatians, and the latter epistle in turn is frequently set within that phase of Paul's ministry which produced 2 Corinthians. Thus, Galatians, Philippians, and 2 Corinthians seem to form a triad in the apostle's career. It is notoriously difficult to assign actual dates to the various segments of Paul's life (see the commentary on *Romans*, pp. 14-15), but two major scholarly chronologies, based on quite different assumptions, allow for the year 55 as an educated guess.[3]

OUTLINE OF PHILIPPIANS

"Motions of Maturity in Christ"

I. The Greeting-Prayer (1:1-11)
    A. A Blessing from Paul and Timothy (1:1-2)
    B. Thanksgiving for the Philippians (1:3-8)
    C. A Prayer for Abounding in Righteousness (1:9-11)

II. The Apostle's Imprisonment for the Gospel (1:12-26)
    A. What Others Gain through Paul's Confinement (1:12-14)
    B. Christian Opponents of Paul (1:15-18)
    C. Paul's Reflections on His Life and Death (1:19-26)

III. The Community's Role in God's Saving Work (1:27—2:18)
    A. Apostle and Congregation as Suffering Witnesses for Christ (1:27-30)
    B. An Exhortation to Honor One Another in Christ (2:1-5)
    C. A Hymn Celebrating the Congregation's Share in Christ's Victory (2:6-11)
    D. God and the Philippians in the Working Out of Salvation (2:12-18)

IV. Travel Plans, in the Lord (2:19-30)
    A. Timothy's Visit and Paul's Hope to Follow Him (2:19-24)
    B. The Sending of Epaphroditus with the Present Letter (2:25-30)

COMMENTARY

■ The Greeting-Prayer (1:1-11)

A Blessing from Paul and Timothy (1:1-2)

Words mattered immensely in the ancient world, especially among people with Semitic backgrounds. Although Paul's opening sentences conform to certain stylistic rules for secular letter writing in the Greco-Roman period, the apostle alters these conventions so as to communicate something of God's saving presence to his readers precisely through his greeting. Paul and Timothy are **servants** of Christ writing to Christ's **saints** (literally, "holy ones," a favorite expression of Paul's for all believers). It is Christ who plunges apostles and people together into a reciprocal flow of service and joy. **Bishops and deacons** are mentioned only here in Paul's undisputed letters (see the commentary on 1–2 Timothy and Titus). They are not a group separate from the saints but do appear to exercise special tasks within the congregation. In the Greco-Roman world bishops were supervisors of various community activities and funds (both sacred and secular), while deacons were servants with special responsibilities for material goods, particularly the distribution of food. Paul may be using these terms here with reference to those Philippians who have regularly administered a financial aid program for him (see 1:5; 4:15ff.). In the latter part of the first century the terms *bishop* and *deacon* evolved into designations for the overall leader of a

Christian congregation and his assistants, but the appearance of both words in the plural here argues against reading that meaning into the Philippian situation. In this letter Paul's expressions for those whom he regards as leaders are "true yokefellow" (4:3), "fellow soldier" (2:25), and "fellow worker" (2:25; 4:4).

The climax of the apostle's salutation to the Philippians is a favorite benediction: **Grace to you and peace.** The first word, *charis,* would have sounded to Paul's Gentile readers much like the customary secular greeting *chaire* ("hail" or "hello"), but because of Paul's ministry among them the Philippians would have sensed God's advent through Christ in this wordplay and in the rich word **peace** which follows. Paul's blessing is more Jewish than Gentile, since **grace** probably stands for the Hebrew *hesed* (God's covenant-faithfulness) and **peace** for the great word of physical-spiritual wholeness, *shalom.* Timothy, Paul's loyal son in Christ, joins in the benediction. He is already well known to the Philippians and will be visiting them shortly (2:19-23). Unlike Paul, he has not been imprisoned. This fact suggests that the apostle was arrested as a ringleader, perhaps to make an example of him; there is no evidence for a general persecution of Christians at Ephesus.

Thanksgiving for the Philippians (1:3-8)

Formulas of thanksgiving like the one appearing here were common in secular letters of the first century and can be found in most of Paul's epistles. Yet this one distinguishes itself from the other Pauline thanksgivings by its great outpouring of affectionate feelings. Elsewhere the apostle tells his readers that he is grateful to God for their faith or gifts or loving service (Rom. 1:18ff.; 1 Cor. 1:4ff.; 1 Thess. 1:2ff.; Col. 1:3ff.). But only here and in Philemon 4 does Paul offer a prayer of gratitude for the remembrance of the readers themselves. Only here does he call attention to the joy he feels as he prays for them. These readers are special partners who have remained close to him throughout his ministry **from the first day until now,** i.e., from the time God acted through Paul's proclamation to bring the Philippian congregation into existence. Thus Paul holds the Philippians in his heart (v. 7) and yearns to see them again (v. 8). The first expression signals the apostle's unusual sense of intimacy with these people; the second, buttressed by an oath and an invocation of Christ's **affection,** reveals a longing for others on Paul's part which is unparalleled among his letters.

All of this warm language indicates that Paul feels confident about his relationship with the Philippian congregation. There is a steadiness about it not evident in his accounts of transactions with other groups of Christians. In all likelihood, this basic trust between apostle and readers has produced the extraordinary number of references to joy and rejoicing which occur in this letter (see the Introduction). Here is an obvious precedent for the close emotional attachments that sometimes develop between ministers and congregations today.

But the joyful mutuality between Paul and the Philippians is not based simply on their natural affection for one another. As a Jew, Paul knows that good feelings apart from acts of righteousness will drift away like smoke. His references to the Philippians' **partnership in the gospel** with him (v. 5) and their role as **partakers** with him **of grace, both in** his **imprisonment and in the defense and confirmation of the gospel** (v. 7) probably denote quite specific events of sharing in words, personal meetings or travels involving risk (see 2:25-27), and material goods, including the gift recently sent from Philippi. The Greek *koinōnia*, which appears here in the terms **partnership** and **partakers,** also shows up in 2 Cor. 8:4 where it describes the Philippians' generous contribution of money for the relief of poor Christians in Jerusalem.

Recent research has indicated that the various *koinōnia* words, especially as they appear in Phil. 1:5, 7; 2:1; 3:10; 4:14-15 and Philemon 6, 17 would have been heard by Paul's readers as embellishments upon the Roman contractual arrangement known as *societas* ("society"), which was practiced by numerous commercial and religious groups in the first century. Philippi, it will be recalled, was a Roman colony where Italian legal customs prevailed and many inhabitants spoke Latin as well as the common language of the ancient world, Greek. Thus, the *societas* would have been a part of everyday experience for the Philippian church. Probably at least some of its members belonged to business groups organized around the *societas* concept, the chief feature of which was a voluntary agreement to pay expenses for designated agents who acted on behalf of and in the best interests of the whole group. Both Paul and the Philippians appear to have interpreted their relationship with one another along these lines.[4] It is not that the partners reduced their mutuality in the gospel to business language, but rather that the terms of their common life were taken up and enriched in Christ. By infusing the notion of *societas* with their faith, the Philippians, poor as they were, created an effective structure for the support of Paul's ministry in other areas of the world (see 4:15-16; 2 Cor. 8:1-4; 9:1-4; 11:8-9; Acts 19:29; 20:1-6).

In Philippians **the gospel** is not only a verbal message. It is understood first of all as God's saving power within history (1:12; 4:3,15; see also Rom. 1:16) which reaches out to transform the whole world order (2:9-11; 3:21). Thus, **partnership in the gospel** (literally, "for the gospel"), of which **defense and confirmation** are one aspect, requires deeds of sharing in addition to words. God always initiates and completes such **good work** among humans (v. 6), but never apart from human effort. Paul will return to this thought in 2:12f.

A Prayer for Abounding in Righteousness (1:9-11)

The final goal of apostolic prayer and ministry as a whole is that **love may abound** (v. 9). Paul does not pray that the Philippians be kept safe in their status quo but that they move forward and grow in their gospel partnership so that **more and more** they may extend God's goodness to others. According to 1 Cor. 15:58—16:1f., "abounding in the work of the Lord" includes giving money to the poor. The **fruits of righteousness . . . through Jesus**

Christ (v. 11) with which the Philippians will be filled on the last day are probably not rewards but evidence that they have committed themselves again and again to the Christ who enables good works. For a description of how the Philippians once did this, see 2 Cor. 8:1-5. Here Paul may be recalling the phrase "fruit of the Spirit," which he uses in Gal. 5:22 and there defines as "love, joy, peace, patience, kindness, goodness, faithfulness, gentleness, self-control."

When the apostle prays that his readers might abound **with knowledge and all discernment** so that they can **approve what is excellent** (v. 10), he is thinking of a process in the Christian life by which one sees and acts in new ways. The words **knowledge** and **discernment** connote a deepened understanding of the blessings one has in Christ (compare Philemon 6) and a constant sensing of God's presence. This openness to the divine goodness prompts an approval or testing out by experience of what really matters (see Rom. 2:18, where exactly the same clause occurs, and Rom. 12:2, where Paul urges his readers to "be transformed by the renewal of your mind, that you may prove what is the will of God, what is good and acceptable and perfect"). The idea here is that perception and action are intimately related. Believers can dare to love more boldly as they discover new dimensions of God's love among them. And for Paul, those dimensions are always multiplying (1:21; 3:13f.; 4:12f.). The apostle's accent on abounding means that the words **pure and blameless for the day of Christ** in v. 10 (better: "sincere and blameless") refer not to a state of sinlessness but to Christ's final judgment that the Philippians have indeed responded to God's "upward call," with the "straining forward" (3:13f.) and "progress . . . in the faith" (1:25) which it inspires. Blamelessness results from launching out into the deep rather than from anchoring in safe harbors. Maturity in Christ means motion.

■ The Apostle's Imprisonment for the Gospel (1:12-26)

What Others Gain through Paul's Confinement (1:12-14)

Verses 12-26 are framed by a Greek noun which the RSV translates **advance** in v. 12 and **progress** in v. 25. The word was common in Greco-Roman philosophical circles, particularly among the Stoics, as a description of one's forward movement in the attaining of wisdom or virtue. Paul uses a verbal form of this word when he notes in Gal. 1:14 that prior to his conversion he himself had "advanced in Judaism" beyond many of his own age (see also Phil. 3:4-7, where the apostle writes of his "gain" through the observance of the Jewish law). In v. 12, however, it is the gospel which advances rather than Paul; and in v. 25 the reference is to the Philippians' **progress . . . in the faith.**

According to vv. 12-14, Paul's imprisonment has contributed to the forward movement of the gospel in two ways. First, **the whole praetorian guard** and **all the rest** have come to recognize that Paul is being held prisoner **for Christ.** That is, the soldiers and other officials who are accustomed to interrogate or punish persons charged with civil disobedience of various sorts have been enabled by Paul's witness to see that he is not a criminal but rather one who lives in the grasp of a new reality (a literal translation of v. 13 would be: "my chains have become plainly seen as being in Christ") that forces him to speak boldly, even at the risk of creating public disturbances. Paul does not claim that his captors have come to faith in Christ, but he clearly implies that they are now more favorably disposed toward the Lord he preaches than they previously were. According to the apostle, changes of attitude toward the gospel, even when they fall short of faith, should be seen as an "advancement" of God's cause. Second, the character of Paul's imprisonment, with its bold and effective witness to those who hold him prisoner, has encouraged most of the other believers in Ephesus to speak God's word more daringly, perhaps at risk to themselves. One gets the impression that just after Paul's arrest, gospel proclamation by the Ephesians became almost an underground affair. Fear paralyzed the believers until they began to see that, whatever the outcome of Paul's trial, Christ was moving powerfully in the apostle to open the hearts and minds of their fellow citizens. When it became clearer to believers and unbelievers alike that Paul's confinement was "in Christ," **most of the brethren** were **made confident in the Lord** (v. 14). The Ephesians shared in the resurrection power of Christ which Paul was receiving as a prisoner (see 3:10 and 2 Cor. 1:9, which probably refers to this imprisonment) and thus became effective witnesses themselves.

Paul is passing this news along to the Philippians because he knows that they too face opposition in their city and need encouragement to sustain their public "striving . . . for the faith of the gospel" (1:27-30). In vv. 12-14, as elsewhere in Philippians, human effort is seen to be harmoniously intertwined with the work of God. Although Paul's own witnessing and that of his brother-sister believers in Ephesus have served to **advance the gospel,** the predominantly impersonal language used here (**what has happened to me. . .it has become known. . .the brethren have been made confident**) shows that the apostle honors God in Christ as the real actor in, with, and under this human risk-taking.

Christian Opponents of Paul (1:15-18)

These verses reveal what we can also discover in many other New Testament sources: from earliest times in the church's history Christians did not simply love one another but also competed and split off from united communities into rival factions (denominations!). Here the apostle seems to be describing **some** of the Ephesian believers or Christian visitors to Ephesus (named as "brethren" in v. 14) who **preach Christ** from motives that are less than noble. The expressions **envy and rivalry** (v. 15) and **out of partisanship, not sincerely** (v. 17) indicate that Paul does not accuse his opponents of incorrect teaching per se but of attempts to hold up their own styles of gospel ministry as superior to his. We can imagine that these evangelists looked down upon Paul for "dishonoring" the gospel through the provoking of public controversies, and especially through his imprisonment as a troublemaker.

Perhaps these preachers were more subtle than he was in their presentation of the gospel, more convincing from a philosophical point of view. Perhaps their physical appearance was more winsome than Paul's. We can probably see them behind two reflections on ministry, written by the apostle to Corinth not long before and not long after his penning of Philippians:

> When I came to you brethren, I did not come proclaiming to you the testimony of God in lofty words of wisdom. For I decided to know nothing among you except Jesus Christ and him crucified; . . .and my speech and my message were not in plausible words of wisdom. . . (1 Cor. 2:1-4). For what we preach is not ourselves, but Jesus Christ as Lord, with ourselves as your servants for Jesus' sake. . . . But we have this treasure in earthen vessels. . . always carrying in the body the death of Jesus, so that the life of Jesus may also be manifested in our bodies (2 Cor. 4:5-10).

A more literal translation of v. 17 than that provided by the RSV would be: "thinking to raise up an affliction because of my chains." Certainly the affliction mentioned is partly the apostle's own (as in the RSV rendering). But it looks as if these competing preachers are also attempting to vex Christians who have sided with Paul because the latter believe that his imprisonment is indeed turning out **for the defense of the gospel.** The surprising climax to this section occurs in v. 18: **What then?** ("So what!"). The apostle's expansive state of mind allows him to take a long view of things. In the final analysis, he says, it does not really matter whether Christ is proclaimed **in pretense or in truth.** Human motives are important, but not ultimately important where the gospel is concerned. The gospel is advancing. God is winning, and that makes the apostle **rejoice.**

Paul's Reflections on His Life and Death (1:19-26)

Moreover, Paul has great confidence that his rejoicing will continue. With the **prayers** of the Philippians and the **help of the Spirit** to buoy him up (note once again the assumed mutuality of human and divine work), he knows that **this will turn out for** [his] **deliverance** (v. 19). The last clause is a direct quote from LXX Job 13:16 and is more accurately translated: "this, as far as I am concerned, will turn out for salvation." Many commentators take the statement as evidence that Paul now believes he will be released from prison. But the context surrounding this remark suggests that he may be playing on a scriptural motto that was probably familiar to his readers. At its deepest level, the "salvation" Paul expects is the same as the advancement or defense of the gospel (see 1:28 and 2:12 where the same word for "salvation" occurs with these connotations) in which his imprisonment plays such a vital role. That is why he can say in v. 20 that **Christ will be honored in my body, whether by life or by death.** Paul displays the gospel in the events of his life as well as through words (see especially Gal. 6:17; 2 Cor. 4:7-12; 6:3-10; 11:22-33; 12:1-10). What happens to him in the body, weal or woe, always provides an occasion for the manifesting of Christ's cross and resurrection power (see 3:10). Thus, Paul still reckons with the possibility of his own death; but the prayers of his readers and the lifeline (literally "supporting ligament") of the Holy Spirit will cause even this to take its place in God's progressing plan of salvation.

With vv. 21ff. the apostle begins to show his readers a struggle which he senses inside himself. If v. 19c represents a play on a biblical motto, v. 21 is probably an ironic variation on a common Greek saying. In Paul's day a number of pagan writers took the view that life was hard and that great gain was to be found in passing beyond this vale of tears, even if the next stage were oblivion.[5] Paul turns this pessimism on its head by asserting that present life **is Christ**—that is, the joy of his presence and power in the midst of suffering—while future life, life after death, **is gain** because it promises an even deeper relationship **with Christ.** Paul's expressions in vv. 22-23 suggest that he can actually **choose** between two alternatives, but a literal understanding of this volitional language probably does it an injustice. The main point is that the apostle feels torn between two attractive possibilities. At the moment, his **desire** is to rest from his labors **with Christ,** for that blessedness would be **far better** than the anxieties of the present. And yet it may not be the proper blessedness for him and the Philippians just now in God's eyes. One might paraphrase v. 22b as follows: "What I shall prefer, when the time finally comes, I cannot even tell." These are remarkable self-revelations from an authority figure. Open displays of vulnerability and indecision do not mix easily with conventional views of effective leadership, either in the first century or in our own day.

In vv. 24-25, having shared the confusion of his inner life with his readers, Paul does reach a point of resolution. Exactly how he learns that his presence **in the flesh** is **more necessary** for the Philippians we are not told. Nor does the text explain how Paul became convinced, on this basis, that he would be allowed to **remain and continue** with the Philippians. The transition from v. 23 to vv. 24-25 is a ragged one. Commentators speculate that Paul may have received a sudden prophetic illumination from God concerning the results of his trial (by analogy with Gal. 1:12; 2:2; see also Rom. 11:25). Or, alternatively, the apostle's "conviction grew out of a meditation on God's purpose" in his ministry as a whole.[6]

But regardless of how Paul came to this clarity of vision, what strikes the modern interpreter is its apparent independence from the weighing and measuring of political variables associated with his imprisonment. Paul develops no strategy for influencing his captors. He *knows* about his fate (compare v. 25 with v. 19) through a faith-insight into the progress of the gospel and his role within it. He sees that he must be present as a stimulus to the

Philippians' **progress and joy in the faith** (v. 25). This phrase echoes 1:2 where the same Greek word occurs to denote forward movement. **The faith** is both the Philippians' trust in God, with the abounding love which this will produce (1:9ff.), and also their proclamation of God's saving work to their neighbors (1:27). Thus, the Philippians' progress has a communal and even a cosmic dimension, as well as a personal one. For Paul, there is no individualistic sanctification. In v. 26 the familiar note of mutuality is struck yet another time. The Philippians will **glory in Christ Jesus** because of Paul's presence among them once again. The word for **coming** (the Greek *parousia*) may be an intended pun, for Paul uses it elsewhere as a technical term for Christ's second coming (1 Cor. 15:23; 1 Thess. 2:19; 3:13; 4:15; 5:23). The restoration of the apostle to his favorite congregation would then be a type and a preview of the Lord's visible return.

■ The Community's Role in God's Saving Work (1:27—2:18)

Apostle and Congregation as Suffering Witnesses for Christ (1:27-30)

In the last verses of chap. 1 Paul draws his readers back to present realities with some sober but encouraging words about the struggles they are all facing, struggles which by God's grace will produce a common witness to the gospel. Karl Barth has aptly translated the **only** of of v. 27 as "just one thing. . . ." [7] It is a gentle warning from Paul that the personal reunion which he and the Philippians long for dare not undercut the endurance they must presently show. The clause **let your manner of life be worthy** contains a Greek verb denoting the behavior of a good citizen, something Paul's readers would find especially meaningful in a Roman colony where the rights and duties of citizenship were extolled. The gospel demands no less than the best of pagan virtues. The apostle's metaphor of citizenship also suggests that

143

the gospel of Christ progresses in a communal manner. Later Paul will remind the Philippians that their "commonwealth is in heaven" (3:20), but here he wishes to stress that the heavenly community is already disclosing itself on earth through God's work in Christ among believers. Here **the gospel** is seen as roughly equivalent to Christ's present and expanding kingdom (see 2:9-11; 3:21b). For the sake of this gospel and its proclamation (**the faith of the gospel** probably refers to its verbal content) the Philippians must stand together as one, **striving side by side.**

In v. 28 **opponents** of Paul's readers are mentioned for the first time. There is no evidence that these people are Christians (contrast the false teachers described in 3:2ff.), and since they have power to frighten the Philippians, they must exert some influence on the local government. Presumably, conflict between them and the believers in Philippi is taking place as a more or less public debate about the gospel, perhaps over the issue of whether or not the church is a subversive *societas* (see the comments on 1:3-8). Paul's belief is that his readers' united and courageous exposition of **the faith** will function as a **clear omen** to the adversaries, of **destruction** for them but **salvation** for the Philippians. That is, the opponents will be led to see that they are standing in the way of God himself and that they would be wise to repent so as to share in the Philippians' good fortune. Here the words **destruction** and **salvation** refer primarily to future states which nevertheless reach out to imprint signs upon those who are destined to inherit them.

At v. 30 Paul states his conviction that no conversion of unbelievers can take place without cost to the Philippians. God will work through their suffering at the hands of the opponents to change the opponents. The Greek of v. 29a might be rendered: "For that which is for Christ's sake has been bestowed upon you by grace. . . ." The verb used is a form of the word *charis* (see 1:2). "That which is for Christ's sake" means both the ability of the Philippians to trust in Christ, which has been granted by God because of Christ, and the vocation to suffer in Christ's world-

144

redeeming mission. Both gift and task come to the Philippians "gracefully." A striking parallel to the vocation of suffering mentioned here occurs in 2 Cor. 12:9f. where the apostle, having heard Christ's word about the meaning of his thorn in the flesh, is moved to announce: "For the sake of Christ, then, I am content with weaknesses, insults, hardships, persecutions, calamities . . . ." Since Paul does not mention it, the Philippians have probably not yet suffered an imprisonment like his. But that may well happen. In any event, the apostle already understands his readers to be **engaged in the same conflict which you saw** (perhaps during Paul's imprisonment at Philippi; see Acts 16:19ff.) **and now hear to be mine** (v. 30). Separated by many miles, Paul and his readers draw near to one another in the advancement of the gospel.

An Exhortation to Honor One Another in Christ (2:1-5)

With 2:1-5 Paul elaborates upon the picture of unity he has begun to sketch in vv. 27 and 30. The apostle finds a common mind and a common voice absolutely fundamental for the effective proclamation of the gospel (the "this" of v. 28 refers to the Philippians' united witness, not their fearlessness, which is a fluctuating emotion). But such a communal sense must be achieved as well as enjoyed; hence the exhortations of vv. 1-5. This section forms part of a "mystery to ministry" pattern that occurs elsewhere in Paul's letters (1 Cor. 15:51—16:2; Rom. 11:25—12:8; 1 Thess. 4:13—5:22).[8] Typically, the apostle attempts to open his readers' minds and hearts to a grand, cosmic view of God's saving work. Here in Philippians that broad vista is represented by the Christ hymn which Paul quotes in vv. 6-11. His purpose in using this piece of early Christian worship is to remind, inspire, and invite his readers so that they will be empowered by their new apprehension of God's victory to proceed with their own day-by-day living of the gospel, confident that this same triumphant God is at work in them (2:12f.). In the present letter Paul modifies

145

his usual pattern by sandwiching the "great indicative" of vv. 6-11 in between two sets of imperatives (vv. 1-5 and 12-18).

So if there is any encouragement in Christ, the apostle writes in 2:1. He does not mean to cast doubt on the matter, for this **encouragement** and **incentive of love** and **participation** (*koinōnia*) **in the Spirit,** this **affection and sympathy** are precisely what he has been celebrating as already present throughout chap. 1. So the word **if** really means "because." Inasmuch as God's goodness lives among you, he says, therefore **complete my joy by being of the same mind** (v. 2). The urgings to unity here (**same . . . full accord . . . one mind**) do not envision a totalitarian goose step where everyone says and does exactly the same thing, for Paul advises even the badly splintered congregation at Corinth to affirm the rich "varieties of gifts . . . service . . . and working" in their midst (1 Cor. 12:4-6). The apostle's aim is to foster harmony: the shared attitude (for this is what **being of the same mind** means) that particular manifestations of the Spirit occur in each believer "for the common good" (1 Cor. 12:7).

In v. 3 certain barriers to this unity in diversity are listed, probably because Paul knows that some of them exist among the Philippians (4:2-3). Perhaps the modern experience that best exemplifies the **selfishness** and **conceit** cited here is that of divisive competition. In v. 3b Paul undercuts the drive to get ahead of one's neighbor by exhorting the Philippians to **count others better than yourselves.** This admonition should not be taken in an absolute sense; it is a method, an exercise to use when one feels or desires supremacy. For Paul, the ideal competition is to "outdo one another in showing honor" (Rom. 12:10). **Humility** hardly means being a doormat (Paul obviously was not!) but is instead the willed act of challenging one's own sense of giftedness when it threatens to divide the community of believers into "haves" and "have-nots," "insiders" and "outsiders" (see Rom. 12:3-8).

Neither here nor elsewhere does Paul argue for an absolute equality among believers (see, e.g., 1 Cor. 12:14-31), but he does push for a very broad vision of "self-interest" (v. 4). In fact, the word translated **interests** (a Greek pronoun that literally means "things") may well refer to personal gifts; for it is the value of the other which the selfish and conceited person most often tends to overlook, the notion that he or she needs to receive God's blessings through the hands of someone thought to be an inferior. Although Paul does not specifically employ the image of the church as Christ's body here, he clearly has that sort of organic interdependence in mind as he composes vv. 1-4. Similarly, in Gal. 6:2 he writes, "Bear one another's burdens and so fulfil the law of Christ." Finally, it is worth noting that the two chief traits of the spiritually mature person (*pneumatikos*) recorded in Paul's letters are a deep concern for the harmony of the local church and a humble recognition that one's own feelings of superiority may be striking at the heart of this harmony (1 Cor. 3:1-4; Gal. 6:1-3). In a healthy congregation the "strongest" know their own failings all too well and expect to learn from the "weakest." It is through this upside-down reciprocity that God works most powerfully (see 1 Cor. 1:26-31; 2 Cor. 13:1-10).

As if to clinch his argument for that unity in which even the most gifted must humble themselves, Paul introduces a passage which has come to be treasured as one of the most beautiful and powerful in all of Christian literature. **Have this mind among yourselves,** he begins. But then the Greek text of v. 5 becomes ambiguous; for what follows, literally, is: "which also [or indeed] in Christ Jesus." At least one verb must be supplied, and its character depends on whether one takes the hymn in vv. 6-11 as an example-setting device or as a panoramic view of salvation history. The second proposal is preferable because it accounts for more of the details in the hymn (vv. 10-11, for example).[9] Then the phrase **in Christ Jesus** would refer not to Jesus' personal disposition toward humility but, as it does quite frequently in Philippians (1:1, 13, 26; 2:1; 3:14; 4:7, 19, 21), to the new creation which believers discern and take part in when they are joined to Christ's lordship (see 2 Cor. 5:17). On this reading, 2:5b means something like: "which indeed is your new life in the realm of Christ Jesus."

A Hymn Celebrating the Congregation's Share in Christ's Victory (2:6-11)

This section has long been identified as a hymn because it fits into a definite stylistic category found elsewhere in the NT (see especially Col. 1:15-20; 1 Tim. 3:16; Heb. 1:3-4). Characteristically, NT hymns begin with the relative pronoun "who" and continue with clauses celebrating Christ's preexistence, incarnation, work of redemption, and resurrection-ascension. They also manifest a certain verse-like quality (as indicated by the strophic arrangements of vv. 6-11 found in TEV, NAB, and NIV). The writers of Colossians and Ephesians give us some insight into the origin of these hymns when they urge their readers to address one another in "psalms and hymns and spiritual songs" (Col. 3:16; Eph. 5:19; see also 1 Cor. 14:26). Early Christian worship abounded in spontaneous outpourings of poetic devotion, some of which were obviously recorded and repeated. Because Paul simply assumes, without explanation, that the words of vv. 6-11 will convey special meaning to his readers, most interpreters have concluded that the Philippians already knew this hymn—indeed, probably used it in their own worship. Whether Paul himself composed it, or one of the Philippians, or some other early Christian, we cannot determine.

A plausible case can, however, be made for the view that this hymn was sung at Baptisms, since the drama which it narrates is precisely that into which converts were incorporated when they passed under the waters. (Note the similarity of vv. 6-11 to Rom. 6:1-11, where Baptism is the point of focus.) Taking the hymn as part of a baptismal liturgy serves to clarify its use by Paul. The apostle would be "re-initiating" his readers, leading them to experience once again that great shift which occurred when they first became Christians, and then exploring the ethical consequences of this for the present situation. The power of the Philippian hymn consists in its ability to draw believers, through images and feelings, more deeply into the majesty of Christ, and thus to inspire behavior worthy of the Lord's cosmic goodness.

Two stanzas of a 19th-century hymn based on Phil. 2:6-11 may open a door to our deeper communion in this mystery with Paul and his first readers:

> *At the name of Jesus*
> *Ev'ry knee shall bow,*
> *Ev'ry tongue confess him*
> *King of glory now.*
> *'Tis the Father's pleasure*
> *We should call him Lord,*
> *Who from the beginning*
> *Was the mighty Word.*
>
> *In your hearts enthrone him;*
> *There let him subdue*
> *All that is not holy,*
> *All that is not true.*
> *Crown him as your captain*
> *In temptation's hour;*
> *Let his will enfold you*
> *In its light and power.*[10]

Several details within the Philippian hymn require comment. The phrases **in the form of God** and **equality with God** (v. 6) underline Christ's unique and exalted position prior to his incarnation. But they must be placed in tension with vv. 9-11 where it is clear that Christ always remains subordinate to God in the strict sense (as in 1 Cor. 15:27-28). A fourth-century doctrine of the Trinity has not yet developed in the New Testament. **The form of God** mentioned here is derivative. That is, it means the image or glory or power that comes from God through Christ to humans. Thus, in 2 Cor. 4:6 Paul writes that God "has shone in our hearts to give the light of the knowledge of the glory of God in the face of Christ." The **equality with God** which Christ enjoys is to be understood functionally: Christ is the perfect revelation of the divine. "He is the image of the invisible God, the first-born of all creation" (Col. 1:15). When the text states that Christ did not consider his equality with God **a thing to be grasped,** the intent is probably to contrast him with Lucifer, who did grab for such equality (Isa. 14:12-14), or also with Adam and Eve, who ate the forbidden fruit in order to "be like God" (Gen. 3:5f.).[11]

Christ, as God's true representation, knew that his sharing in divinity had come as a gift, with a call to service. Thus, he **emptied himself** to take on human flesh and then **humbled himself** even further, becoming **obedient unto death** (vv. 7-8). The clear implication here is that Christ had a choice in this matter; God did not compel him. The **form of a servant** (literally "slave," as in 1:1) probably refers not yet to Christ's humanity but rather to his voluntary enslavement under the principalities and powers which he later defeated (1 Cor. 2:8; Gal. 4:1-5). Here, as in the phrase **form of God** (where the same word *morphē* occurs), one ought to think of something other than total identity. **Form of a servant** means something other than "servant" pure and simple. This same reluctance to define Christ's "essence" appears in the expressions **likeness of men** and **found in human form** (*schēma*). Being **in the form of God,** Christ divested himself of divine privilege. Yet even as a man, he was never just a man. The composer of the hymn struggles to honor this uniqueness.

In v. 8b, however, there is no doubt about Jesus' full humanity: he **became obedient unto death, even death on a cross.** Because the last phrase does not fit with many scannings of the hymn into verses, it has often been taken as an interpolation by Paul himself (regardless of who authored the hymn as a whole) to accentuate his theology of the cross. This view makes sense in the light of Paul's reference one chapter later to Christians who "live as enemies of the cross of Christ" (3:18), that is, those who are not willing to share the humiliation of suffering for his sake. It may well be that at this point Paul has in mind the specifically Roman character of Christ's execution. Then he would be telling his readers in the Roman colony of Philippi that because their exalted Lord endured the most degrading form of imperial torture, they themselves can certainly undergo lesser persecutions at the hands of the authorities (see 1:28f.).

The triumphant word **therefore** introduces a final upward

swing in the salvation drama of the hymn (v. 9). Christ's obedience unto death in service to God brings forth a worldshaking response: God **highly exalted him and bestowed on him a name which is above every name.** The two words **highly exalted** are expressed by one verb in Greek; it occurs nowhere else in the New Testament and means "raise to the loftiest height." This unique language implies that Christ's status after the resurrection-ascension was even higher than his previous **equality with God.** So does the clause **bestowed on him the name,** where the verb used (the same as in 1:29a) carries with it the notion of grace-gift (*charis*). Again, this exalted state must be seen primarily in terms of Christ's work rather than his essence. The new height and the new name converge in the title *KYRIOS*, **Lord.** Now Jesus Christ rules the entire world for God in a way that he did not prior to his victory over death. Early Christian thought made much of Ps. 110:1 as a key to understanding Christ's exaltation ("The Lord says to my lord: 'Sit at my right hand, till I make your enemies your footstool' "); it is probably in the background here as well. For the kneeling of every creature, see Isa. 45:23 where the object of devotion is God, not Christ. The hymnist handles this transformation of meaning by asserting that Jesus' lordship exists for just one end: **to the glory of God the Father** (v. 11). The beings **in heaven and on earth and under the earth** are best understood as the entire created order, including angelic and demonic powers (see 1 Cor. 2:6-8; 15:24-28; Rom. 8:35-39; Col. 2:14-15).

During the last century a vast ocean of scholarly debate has formed around the question of which ancient thought patterns gave rise to this hymn,[12] for even if it is viewed as a charismatic outburst during worship, the hymn nevertheless makes use of idioms from its environment. Thus, questions such as the following are usually raised: Are the various images in the hymn based primarily on the OT, or do they derive from other sources? Indeed, were the earliest believers capable of producing such a high Christology without help from pagan myths? Theologically, the answers to these questions are not of ultimate concern, for

God can use any thought form he pleases to clothe his Word. It will be remembered, for example, that certain elements in the various OT expositions of creation are borrowed from pagan neighbors in the ancient Near East and "baptized." Moreover, surprising shifts of consciousness occur in the history of religions. It is not the case that each new thought develops smoothly and rationally out of previous convictions.

Nevertheless, current scholarship inclines toward the view that "raw material" for all the major thoughts and images in our Philippian hymn already existed in first-century Judaism. OT precedents for some of the hymnic language have been pointed out above (see the discussion of 2:6,9,10). In addition, it may be noted that the expression **form of God** in v. 6 could well be a variation on Jewish speculation about (*a*) the glories of the first man Adam prior to his life on earth (as in the Alexandrian Jewish writer Philo) or (*b*) the personified figure of Wisdom, who aided God in the work of creation (Proverbs 8) and then, as "a spotless mirror of the working of God and an image of his goodness" (Wis. 7:26), descended to earth to dwell with Israel in the form of the Torah (Sirach 24).[13] Because Paul elsewhere plays upon connections between Christ and Adam on the one hand (Rom. 5:12-21; 1 Cor. 15:42-50) and between Christ and Wisdom on the other (1 Cor. 1:24; 10:4), it makes good sense to posit these two categories of speculation as background material for Phil. 2:6-11.

Given the experimental nature of early Christologies, the image systems of Adam and Wisdom can be seen as complementary source materials rather than mutually exclusive ones. We need not be surprised that poetic structures like the Philippian hymn combine them. Indeed, additional image systems may be present, since commentators have also offered reasonable arguments for the influence of Daniel's "son of man" and Isaiah's suffering servant on parts of our hymn.[14] Furthermore, a Jewish scholar, working from fragments unearthed at Qumran, has discovered that the mysterious king Melchizedek (Gen. 14:18; Ps. 110:4) came to be regarded by some first-century Jews as preexistent and divine. From such modes of thought early Christians seem to have adopted Melchizedek as a model for interpreting Jesus' heavenly identity (see Hebrews 5–7).[15] Perhaps this figure too has shaped portions of our hymn. In summary, current scholarship continues to show that the Judaism of Jesus' day was a very rich and diverse amalgam, full of resources for the kind of pictures displayed in Phil. 2:6-11. Yet the historical person of Jesus was required to set in motion the actual composition of the hymn.

Have all the events narrated in this hymn already come to pass? From one point of view, the answer is yes. Gifted with prophetic insight, the hymnist gazes upon the last day when Christ reigns without opposition. In his vision the years fall away and God's triumph looms forth as altogether present (compare the Apocalypse of John and such visionary sections of Ephesians as 1:3; 2:6; 3:10,18). Neither Paul nor the composer of the Philippians hymn (if they are different people) would think of these realities as far away in time or space. On the other hand, Paul is no romantic escapist. He lives very much in the present world order where he sees Christ contending with the powers of this age:

> Then [at a time still in the future] comes the end, when he [Christ] delivers the kingdom to God the Father after destroying every rule and every authority and power. For he must reign until he has put all his enemies under his feet (1 Cor. 15:24-25).

This Pauline conviction must be set in tension with the triumphal words of Phil. 2:9-11. Yes, Christ reigns even now as sovereign Lord of the universe. Nevertheless, as we now experience it, his rule remains incomplete because the divine will is not fully "done on earth as it is in heaven." Believers must continue to "await a Savior" who, at his visible coming, will transform their "lowly body to be like his glorious body, by the power which enables him even to subject all things to himself" (Phil. 3:21). Both the "already" and the "not yet" of Christ's rule shape Paul's admonitions to the believers at Philippi.

God and the Philippians in the Working Out of Salvation (2:12-18)

It might seem, with the crescendo of v. 11 still echoing in his readers' ears, that Paul has settled once and for all the question of who brings about the world's redemption. It is God in Christ alone! But then comes an unsettling paradox: **Therefore, my beloved. . .work out your own salvation** (v. 12). This cannot mean that the Philippians are to earn their place with God, for such a teaching would run contrary to Paul's clarion declarations of justification by grace through faith (see, within Philippians itself, 1:6, 29, and especially 3:9). In fact, the word **salvation** as it occurs here is a corporate notion denoting the Philippians' life together in God's unfolding plan (1:28). Working out this salvation would mean a collective living out by believers of their share in the great drama just narrated. As Christ took on human form to redeem the world, so those who are in Christ at Philippi must incarnate God's will through actions that specifically befit the redemption of their city (see 2:14-15). That is the meaning of the word **own**: the salvation in your corner of the world. This language recalls Luther's insight that believers are to be little Christs for others. Paul is not writing here about works of the law through which one attempts to establish merit before God but about the outworking of salvation, which is the advancement of the gospel (1:12) or, alternatively, the Philippians' progress and joy in the faith (1:25). Working out this salvation means laboring in the gospel (4:3) and abounding in the work of the Lord (1 Cor. 15:58; see also Phil. 1:9). Salvation, then, is understood as a process still very much in motion (compare 1 Cor. 1:18; 15:2; 2 Cor. 2:15). It both catches us up and pushes us forward (3:12).

But it also requires our effort! There is a very real sense in which believers act as co-workers with God (2 Cor. 6:1) who must make decisions, take risks, overcome inertia, and persist in obedience—often when no clarity or motivating power seems to be present. Like Christ, who chose his incarnation and sustained his obedience even unto death, so believers, both individually and in groups, must sometimes take things into their own hands as if everything depended upon them. Thus, they will venture forth **with fear and trembling.** This is the way Paul first entered Corinth with his foolish gospel of the crucified Christ (1 Cor. 2:1-3). This is the way, in Kierkegaard's reconstruction of Gen. 22:1ff., Abraham trudged up Mount Moriah to sacrifice his only son (see *Fear and Trembling;* 1845).

However, there are probably other sides to this **fear and trembling.** The phrase also occurs in 2 Cor. 7:15-16, where Paul praises his readers on behalf of his colleague Titus, who "remembers the obedience of you all, and the fear and trembling with which you received him." The material surrounding this passage indicates that here the reference is not to anxiety in the face of a monumental task, but to a respectful obedience, having to do especially with the building of trust between Paul, his emissaries, and the Corinthian congregation. Similarly, in Philippians Paul may well be alluding to the mutual honoring of one another which he has just urged his readers to practice (2:1-5).[16] Furthermore, because Paul has just related the inspiring story of redemption in the Christ hymn, he probably expects his word **fear** to convey a note of wonder, as it does in Rom. 11:20, where he instructs his Gentile readers in the mystery of their election. "So do not be proud," the apostle writes concerning God's choice of them over the majority in Israel, "but stand in awe [literally, 'fear']." Christians must tremble at the tasks set before them, but their fear includes a sense of grateful astonishment that they and their efforts are actually being taken up into God's great purpose.

This thought is expanded in v. 13 where Paul states the other side of his paradox: **for God is at work in you.** The same God who acts in Christ for the world's redemption dwells among the Philippians (the accent with regard to God's presence is on community, as in 1 Thess. 2:13 and 1 Cor. 3:16, but an indwelling of individuals is not excluded) to aid them in giving their redemption concrete shape where they are. This God is a very present help in time of trouble, and he will strengthen the wills of the Philippians so that they can choose his excellent paths (1:9-10). He will not forsake the "good work" he has begun among them (1:6) but will continue to provide the resources they need to accomplish what he desires. William Hulme offers an illuminating interpretation of this passage in his book *Your Potential Under God:*

> God's work within us is obviously *His* activity, while working out our own salvation is *our* activity. God's activity is not supplemented by our passivity. Rather God's activity inspires and makes possible our response, our activity. He works *within* us so that he can work *with* us. . . .[17]

Do all things without grumbling or questioning (v. 14). Here Paul speaks to some difficulties his readers may presently face in maintaining their community spirit through the inevitable vexations of everyday life. God wills for them to persist in their working out of salvation so that their church may shine out as a beacon to guide the majority of humankind back to his grace (v. 15). Again, salvation is pictured as a community venture for the sake of the gospel. Thus, the Philippians must hold fast to this **word of life** (compare 1 Thess. 2:13). In v. 16 Paul injects his personal hopes for the Philippians' future. How their work fares on the day of Christ (see 1 Cor. 3:10-15; 2 Cor. 5:10) is of great concern to him. He himself will be judged, in part, by their faithfulness. Paul never views himself simply as an evangelist but always as a pastor responsible for the present welfare and continued growth of his congregations.

In v. 17 the recurrent possibility of the apostle's death breaks out into the open once again. The resolution reached in 1:25-26 is not a final one after all. All human insights, even prophetic and apostolic ones, are imperfect visions seen "in a mirror dimly" (1 Cor. 13:9, 12). Paul may still be **poured as a libation** (drink offering) and thus never visit the Philippians again in the flesh. The **sacrificial offering of your faith** probably refers to the readers' generous support of Paul during his imprisonment. The thought of this faithful act fills him with joy, and he encourages his readers to join him, no matter what happens (v. 18). In the Lord, their gift will not be wasted, for if Paul suffers martyrdom, it will become the ceremonial foundation for his libation, "a fragrant offering, a sacrifice acceptable and pleasing to God" (4:18).

■ Travel Plans, in the Lord (2:19-30)

Timothy's Visit and Paul's Hope to Follow Him (2:19-24)

Thoughts of his unique relationship with the Philippians prompt Paul to formulate plans for renewed contact with them. **I hope in the Lord Jesus** (v. 19). This is Paul's ever-present contingency. He hopes to send Timothy, and there is a real emotional investment in this hope since he longs for the quick return of this co-worker with cheering news from Philippi. But always, the apostle's future is primarily a hope conditioned by the Lord's plan. If Paul cannot send Timothy as he wishes, the Lord will show him a better way, perhaps that way of being with Christ which is "far better" (1:23). Timothy's single-minded service, both to the Philippians and alongside Paul in the gospel, is praised in vv. 20-22. The phrase **no one like him** (v. 20) stands for an unusual Greek word which could mean "equal to me in soul" or "equally interested with me in your affairs." Either way, it represents an extravagant compliment. In fact, this unqualified vote of confidence for an associate is not paralleled anywhere else in the undisputed Pauline letters. Its occurrence in the epistle to Philippi signifies once again the intimacy Paul enjoys with his readers, an intimacy regularly and effectively mediated by his loyal **son. . .in the gospel** (v. 22). The words **in the gospel** are literally "for the gospel" (as in 1:5). They serve to underline the importance of human activity in the advancement of God's cause. When Paul complains about **all** the people, except Timothy, who **look after their own interests, not those of Jesus Christ** (v. 21), it is hard to know just whom he has in mind. Earlier in the letter he reports that most of the Ephesians "have been made confident in the Lord" for a more courageous proclamation of the gospel (1:14), so they are probably not the objects of his criticism—unless he thinks they have paid too little attention to his own needs as a prisoner. On the other hand, if Paul means to draw adverse comparisons between Timothy and some of his other co-workers (Titus? Silas? Luke?), he must be experiencing frustrations with particular aspects of their work which he does not reveal here or elsewhere in his letters. On any reading, his statement seems a harsh judgment and suggests that not even apostles were free from the tendency to overgeneralize.

According to Paul's plan, Timothy will be sent **soon** (v. 19), but not until the apostle has some definite word about his fate: **how it will go with me** (v. 23). This juxtaposition of scenarios indicates that Paul expects his case to be settled in the near future, one way or the other. If the apostle should be condemned to die, Timothy would probably go to Philippi with the account of his martyrdom. Pressure from the impending decision perhaps accounts for the notable reversals of mood which occur in this letter (see, in addition to 2:20-21, 1:23-25 together with 2:17, and especially 3:1-2). In v. 24 the apostle once again expresses confidence **in the Lord** that he will **shortly** be free to visit his favorite congregation. It must be emphasized that Paul's trust resides in Christ as a living and active person, not as a heavenly guarantee of his private desire. Nevertheless, *at this point* the apostle feels strongly that the mind of Christ does envision a continuing ministry for him (as in 1:25 where the same verb is used to express special awareness of the divine plan). Paul declares his preferences, his hopes, and his confidences, but his actual plans must remain subject to the Lord's will.

The Sending of Epaphroditus with the Present Letter (2:25-30)

Liberal praise from Paul goes not only to Timothy but also to Epaphroditus, messenger from Philippi and intended bearer of the letter Paul is composing. He is first mentioned here, even though his health was a matter of concern not only to the apostle but also to the Philippians who had received news of his sickness (v. 26). Probably Epaphroditus fell ill in Ephesus or on the way there. What the Philippians did not know until now was that he had nearly died while attending Paul (vv. 26-27). Few details of this story are given, but Epaphroditus' own return to Philippi would presumably fill in the gaps, probably before Paul's letter was read aloud. The fact that Paul has decided to send his epistle now, instead of waiting to pass on more definite information about the outcome of his trial, testifies once again to his very deep connection with his readers. It was Epaphroditus' personal need to rejoin his own people (v. 26), along with their care for him and Paul's desire to communicate his love and thanks to the Philippians, that combined to produce this letter. The apostle felt he could not wait to share his thoughts, despite the uncertainty of his situation.

In introducing Epaphroditus, Paul first names him as his own associate: **my brother and fellow worker and fellow soldier** (v. 25). **Brother** is a common NT term for "believer," although the possessive pronoun stresses Paul's closeness to Epaphroditus in a humanly fraternal way. **Fellow workers** are a group of men and women, most of them resident in particular congregations, with whom the apostle has passed some time (often as a guest) in the course of his ministry. Paul's several references to these people give the impression that they offered him financial or moral support when he needed it most (see Rom. 16:3,9,21; Phil. 4:3; 1 Thess. 3:2; Philemon 1,24). However, since Timothy, Priscilla, and Aquila bear this title, we may guess that fellow workers also joined with Paul in the actual proclamation of the gospel. Only Epaphroditus and Archippus (Philemon 2) are designated as Paul's **fellow soldiers.** Probably the reference is to special battles for the gospel which they have fought together. In Epaphroditus' case his illness (literally "weakness," the same word Paul uses for his own thorn in the flesh in 2 Cor. 12:9f.) may be that battle. In v. 30 Paul characterizes this malady as something that has transpired **for the work of Christ.**

Once the apostle has described Epaphroditus' faithfulness to him, he turns to honor the Philippians by naming Epaphroditus as their emissary: **your messenger and minister to my need.** In Greek the two nouns are *apostolos* ("one who is sent," the same

word Paul often uses—but not in this letter—to designate his
own vocation) and *leitourgos* ("servant concerned with offerings
to God," as in the English word *liturgist*). Epaphroditus not only
acts as a good courier but also, through the gifts from Philippi
that he delivers to Paul and through his own presence with the
apostle, he takes on the role of a priest who offers up a sacrifice
to God for the advancement of the gospel (compare 2:17; 2:30,
where the word rendered "service" is the Greek *leitourgia;* 4:18;
and Rom. 15:16, where Paul sees himself as a *leitourgos* for the
gospel).

Although Epaphroditus' ministry with Paul brought him close
to death, God revived him and thus spared the apostle a great
disappointment (**lest I should have sorrow upon sorrow;** v. 23).
This second, underlying sorrow must refer to the constant pain
of imprisonment, coupled with a certain mourning on Paul's part
over the fact that he has been let down by people he trusted
(2:21). Epaphroditus' death would not only have deprived him
of living contact with his favorite congregation; it would also have
robbed the Philippians of a beloved brother. But now in vv. 28-
29 the apostle can urge his readers to rejoice over Epaphroditus'
recovery and imminent reunion with them. Their emissary will
come home to them as an inspiring example of service to the
Lord. The clause **that I may be less anxious** (v. 28) is a further
indication that Paul's emotional life takes many turns during the
composition of this letter. The apostle's current anxiety may be
a fear that if Epaphroditus continues to stay with him in prison,
his illness will flare up again. As much as Paul delights in this
man's presence, he finds it **necessary** (v. 25) to send him back.

■ Warnings and Longings (3:1-21)

Judaizing Teachers and Paul's Experience of Christ (3:1-11)

The RSV prints 3:1 as a separate paragraph for, as it stands,
the verse is difficult to connect with either 2:30 or 3:2. The word
finally seems to indicate the completion of something; but the

Greek may also be translated "furthermore" or "as for the rest" (1 Cor. 1:16; 2 Thess. 3:1), which means that the first clause of 3:1 could refer either backward or forward. The second clause, **to write the same things to you** . . . (3:1b), sounds strange here because it is not immediately clear what these **same things** are. Nevertheless, a good case can be made for the view that Paul is reminding the Philippians of previous warnings he has issued to them, either orally or in letters now lost to us (see 3:18f. and the discussion of whether Philippians is a single letter, pp. 124ff. above). Thus, Paul's thought takes a new turn between 3:1a and 3:1b; the former belongs with 2:30 and the latter introduces the harsh alarm to be sounded in 3:2ff. For reflections on the plausibility of such a sharp mood swing within a single letter, see pp. 126f.

Those whom the Philippians must beware of (presumably because they will not *look* like dangerous teachers) are denounced as **dogs . . . evil-workers . . . and those who mutilate the flesh** (3:2). The epithet **dogs** was sometimes used by Jews as a derisive name for unclean Gentiles (Mark 7:24-30). But it was also a title of honor adopted by itinerant pagan philosophers called Cynics (from the Greek *kynas,* "dogs," which occurs here) who eschewed the entanglements of everyday life to pursue simple virtues. The apostle's usage is obviously polemical and may include both meanings, although the context favors the first (see 3:4ff.). For Paul, the claim of these people to cultic purity or superior virtue is hollow. They themselves are **dogs** in the worst sense of that word. In 2 Cor. 11:13 the apostle exposes some wandering Jewish Christian opponents as "deceitful workmen," using a Greek expression very similar to the **evil-workers** that appears here. The last clause of 3:2 translates literally as "look out for the mutilation." It may refer either to people who advocate circumcision for Gentile Christians or, if Paul is uncertain whether these opponents will actually do that (in 2 Corinthians circumcision is not an issue), to the rite of circumcision itself as a logical conclusion to the opponents' teaching. Like the term **dogs**, the reference to "mutilation" is full of sarcasm.

In v. 3, again taking the Greek literally, Paul asserts, **we are the circumcision.** The word **true** may be supplied from the context, but that must be done cautiously because it is not Paul's intention here to contrast Jews as a whole with Christians as a whole, in order to assert that the latter have replaced the former as God's true people. The following verses bear out this judgment. Paul is arguing only against *Christians* (probably Jewish, but not necessarily so) who claim that observance of the Jewish law is necessary to establish one's righteousness before God (3:9). These people may think of themselves as **the true circumcision,** in contrast to Jews who do not believe; but Paul's point is that *no* Christian, Jew or Gentile, can receive righteousness through means other than faith (3:9). Heritage (vv. 4-5) and personal obedience (vv. 5-6) do not count for that purpose. Thus, the word **circumcision,** as used in v. 3, is meant ironically, perhaps in quotation marks, and functions to deflate the opponents' proud self-designation. For Paul, neither circumcision nor uncircumcision matters (Gal. 3:28; 6:15) but only that worship of God which is in the Spirit and glories (literally "boasts") in Jesus Christ rather than **in the flesh,** i.e., what one is by physical lineage or proselyte adoption and what one does to achieve virtue. For a more extensive version of Paul's wrestlings with the relationship between Israel and the church, see Romans 9–11.

With v. 4 Paul begins a polemical autobiography that is designed to show that while he once met the legal standards extolled by the false teachers even better than they now do, the Christ who laid hold of him so outshone his (real!) achievements that he had no choice but to abandon all boasts. Beginning at v. 5, Paul recites his impressive credentials. Born a diaspora Jew in Greek-speaking Tarsus, he was nevertheless reared in a family that took care to observe all the ordinances of the Jewish law. Indeed, Paul identifies himself as **a Hebrew born of Hebrews,** which probably means that the holy language was spoken in his family, an exceptional practice even among Jews living in Palestine, where most people knew only Aramaic. The apostle also cites his religious denomination: **as to the law a Pharisee.** Even

in Palestine only a tiny percentage of the Jewish population actually belonged to the Pharisaic party. The first-century Jewish
historian Josephus reports that they numbered about 6000. As
for Paul's claim here, it is the only self-reference in extant ancient
literature to membership in pre-70 Pharisaism by a Hellenistic
Jew. This does not mean that Paul was unique, but he was exceptional in the Judaism of his day (see Gal. 1:14). Within his
own community at Tarsus and even in Palestine he would have
been seen as a man of the far right, a rigoristic protector of cultic
purity. It was probably this zeal that led Paul to persecute the
church (v. 6), where the high walls of distinction between Jew
and Gentile, pure and impure, were beginning to break down.
Thus, the apostle's characterization of himself as a persecutor lies
just between two explicit references to his careful observance of
the Jewish law (**as to the law a Pharisee . . . as to righteousness
under the law blameless**). This blamelessness does not mean that
Paul thought he was without sin—no Jew held such a view—but
that he had been extraordinarily faithful in keeping the letter of
God's commandments, probably by observing pious traditions
that went beyond the written laws of the Pentateuch.

But all this **gain** Paul began to consider as **loss for the sake of
Christ** (v. 7). The last phrase is better translated "because of
Christ" since Christ is here described as that new reality which
turned Paul's worldview on its head. The word **indeed** (v. 8) is
a very strong expression in Greek and conveys the thought that
Paul's first transforming encounter with Christ has now become
his daily rule of life. He continues to **count everything as loss
because of the surpassing worth of knowing Christ Jesus** (v. 8).
One must get the sequence straight here. Neither in his conversion nor in his subsequent life was Paul so overwhelmed by
his sin or guilt or disdain for the world that he found himself
compelled to seek a gracious God (contrast Luther). According
to his own story, he felt altogether confident about his righteousness until he met Christ; it was **the surpassing worth of knowing
Christ** which put his accomplishments under a shadow. And now
this pattern of reversal shapes his whole life as a believer. He

knows real triumphs and defeats (e.g., 2 Cor. 6:4-10; 11:23-32; Rom. 15:17-19), and he feels these things to their depths. But then, again and again, Christ comes to reveal that he himself is the great truth to be known. So Paul utters the words **my Lord** and beholds the world with new eyes (see 2 Cor. 5:16f. and Gal. 6:14f., where Paul links knowledge of Christ with the perception of a "new creation").

This **knowing** of **Christ Jesus my Lord** is a knowing by faith which moves beyond all rational or sense apprehensions (2 Cor. 4:6, 18; 5:7, 16f.); it is also intensely personal (1 Cor. 6:13-17; Gal. 2:20). But it is not, for that reason, private or noncommunal. In fact, Paul's entire letter to Philippi stands as a witness to the way Christ reveals himself through human relationships in the church. Apostle and congregation live in Christ together (1:5-8, 29-30); by their mutual recognition of one another (2:1-5) the Lord makes himself known (see 1 Cor. 11:27-32; 12:1-31). So the knowing of Christ is a continuing series of events, each of which grips and changes the believer. When Paul writes **I have suffered the loss of all things** (past tense), he probably has in mind something like this thought, expressed near the end of his letter to the Galatians: "But far be it from me to glory except in the cross of our Lord Jesus Christ, by which the world has been crucified to me and I to the world" (6:14). A once-for-all event, perhaps his conversion or Baptism, has killed the power of the world's standards for success in his life. And yet this victory must take on new form day by day. Paul must continue to **count them as refuse** (the Greek word means "excrement" or "garbage"). That is, he must repeatedly affirm, by faith, that Christ's worth far surpasses all conventional achievements—to such an extent that, by comparison, they belong in the trash heap.

That daily decision (compare Luther's "daily dying") represents the only way Paul can **gain Christ** (v. 8) **and be found in him** (v. 9). These are eschatological (end-time) references indicating that the journey of faith is not over. The apostle must persist in Christ so that he can grasp Christ with finality, so that his own righteousness, **based on law,** will not deceive him and deprive him

of **the righteousness from God** (v. 9). Because of human pride
there is always danger that the lesser good will be chosen over
the greater one, that believers will sell their inheritance for a
mess of pottage. The phrase **through faith in Christ** is more accurately rendered "through the faithfulness of Christ" and would
then stand for Christ's obedience to God's plan as narrated in the
hymn (2:6-11). The human response of trusting in this work of
Christ is designated by the clause **that depends on faith.**

In v. 10 the constant motion of the Christian life is accented
once again: **that I may know him.** This hope connects with the
phrase **in order that** (v. 8) and stands in tension with the **knowing
Christ** mentioned there. But a resolution of the two is not difficult. Paul knows Christ already, knows him intimately. And yet,
he must also proceed, through the ordinary events of his days,
to know his Lord in new ways. It is this continuing discovery of
Christ that will issue, ultimately, in Paul's attaining (which means
"reaching," not "achieving") **the resurrection from the dead** (v.
11). The phrase **if possible** casts no doubt on God's faithfulness
but does allow for a human (even apostolic) falling away, as in 1
Cor. 9:24-27. There may be an implied polemic here against a
teaching of the opponents that perfection in grace can be guar-
anteed (see 3:12-16), perhaps by the sealing of circumcision.

The rich pastures of v. 10 require additional exploration. Sentence structure and philology suggest the following literal translation: "to know him, that is, both the power of his resurrection
and the communion (*koinōnia*) of his sufferings, being conformed
to his death." In other words, power and suffering constitute the
two aspects of knowing Christ. But this suffering receives further
definition. It is not just ordinary hurt or illness but the ongoing
experience of being molded together with Christ's death. This
conformation "qualifies" one for the future resurrection (v. 11).
Here Paul's thought spins itself out in a "chiastic" structure:

(a) The power of Christ's resurrection

(b) Christ's sufferings

To know him: (b) Christ's death

(a) The general resurrection

The chief point is that all these things belong together. Paul has learned his theology of the cross over and over, so that it has become the very hallmark of his ministry. Through fear and trembling (1 Cor. 2:1-5; Phil. 2:12f.), through illness and weakness (2 Cor. 12:1-10), through threat of death and the real death of cherished securities (2 Cor. 1:8-10) God's resurrection power in Christ emerges for the restoration of individuals and the advancement of the gospel.

Here is the Christ hymn again, spelled out in somewhat different language. Christ humbled himself; laying aside divine privilege, he became a human servant and obeyed God even unto death. By God's grace his apparent defeat actually won the final victory and brought about a new dominion for him (2:6-11). But now, according to Paul, these events are compressed and replayed in the believer's life. The dying and resurrection power of Christ are actually present with the believer in such a way that the first becomes an occasion for the second:

> We are . . . always carrying in the body the death of Jesus, so that the life of Jesus may also be manifest in our bodies. For while we live we are always being given up to death for Jesus' sake, so that the life of Jesus may be manifested in our mortal flesh (2 Cor. 4:10-11).

It is important at this point to observe that in both Philippians and 2 Corinthians Paul is arguing, fighting against the presumed teaching of his opponents that God's power comes simply, apart from the sharing of Christ's sufferings. Modern interpreters will want to guard against the erroneous views that Paul had no use for power at all (see 4:13 and 2 Cor. 12:11-12; 13:1-4), or that he insisted on particular quantities of suffering as proof for the legitimacy of one's faith (see 2 Cor. 10:12), or that he felt the power of God must always come wrapped in a painful experience. Moreover, the difficult question of how to distinguish between suffering with Christ and suffering which is altogether senseless or self-inflicted cannot be answered from these verses alone, although Paul's use of the word *koinōnia* and its compounds in

Philippians as a whole strongly suggests that for him the sufferings of Christ are those that serve to build up communities (see 1:29f.).

The Apostle's Straining Forward as a Model for the Philippians (3:12-16)

In vv. 12-14 the apostle bends over backwards to insist that he himself, who could beat the opponents at their own game (vv. 5-6), must continue to travel the life-in-death road. Only in the future can he enjoy a completed resurrection life (v. 11). Until then, he writes, **I press on to make it my own** (v. 12). The central image, which Paul develops further in vv. 13-14, is that of an athlete, perhaps on a marathon run. Persistent motion and steady effort are the key qualities required. But how does this race differ from the fruitless striving to earn one's own righteousness which Paul so roundly denounces in v. 9? The answer, once again, lies in the person of Christ who has **made** the runner **his own** (v. 12) and then draws him forward toward himself with the **upward call of God** (v. 14). Wordplays in v. 12 lend visual humor to these thoughts. Paul has not yet **obtained** (*lambanō* in Greek) the general resurrection, but he presses on to **make it** his **own** (*katalambanō*) because Christ has first reached out to possess him (*katalambanō*). The second verb often means "grasp" or "seize," and these translations both fit the context nicely. The "Hound of Heaven"[18] has hunted Paul down and caught him on his way to persecute (*diōkein;* v. 6) the church in Damascus. Seized by Christ, Paul is turned around and set off on another pursuit (**press on** translates *diōkein* in vv. 12 and 14). Christ's ownership of him means not confinement but freedom to venture forward, to seek life's true prize with confidence that the Alpha and Omega of all things is embracing him. The active and passive features of this picture hang together paradoxically. Paul presses on and strains forward **because** he is continually grasped and led.[19]

Robert Bridges' text for J. S. Bach's famous chorale arrangement of "Jesu, Joy of Man's Desiring" (Cantata No. 147) depicts

a spiritual ascent that is more Platonic than Pauline. Yet, together
with Bach's hypnotic melody, the words help us feel the elation
and exaltation of the race in Christ Paul is describing:

> *Jesu, joy of man's desiring,*
> *Holy wisdom, love most bright,*
> *Drawn by Thee, our souls, aspiring,*
> *Soar to uncreated light.*

> *Word of God, our flesh that fashioned,*
> *With the fire of life impassioned,*
> *Striving still to truth unknown,*
> *Soaring, dying round Thy throne.*[20]

In vv. 13-14 Paul cites two main features of this race. First, it
requires **forgetting what lies behind** (the triumphs that lead to
pride as well as the defeats which lead to despair) and **straining
forward to what lies ahead** (i.e., to the Christ who is always
revealing himself in new forms of resurrection power through
suffering). This is the imperative, the call for human seeking and
striving. Second, the race in Christ offers an enticement: **the prize
of the upward call of God.** Here Paul may be thinking of a custom
practiced at the Olympian games whereby the name of the victor
was called out as a gesture of honor just prior to his crowning
with the laurel wreath.[21] This is the indicative, the promise that
in Christ God will finally commend the believing runner for his
or her efforts throughout the race. Here the forgotten past will
be recovered and taken up into the work of the Lord. It is this
hope that draws the apostle forward.

With v. 15 Paul makes explicit what he has been implying all
along in this section: **Let those who are mature be thus minded.**
The apostle's life is not idiosyncratic but exemplary, for what he
goes through typifies the life of each mature believer. The word
here translated **mature** (*teleios*) is related to the verb "be perfect"
in v. 12 and probably reflects a slogan used by the false teachers.
They consider themselves full-grown in the faith because they
think they have reached the highest plateaus of spiritual understanding and virtue. But Paul, using their own nomenclature,

charges that they have missed the center of life in Christ. To be mature really means recognizing that one has not yet arrived at perfection (v. 12). A grown-up believer is one who pushes forward in the conviction that God is always calling from the future (v. 14). Maturity consists of both knowing Christ and coming to know Christ at the same time (vv. 8, 10). And always this knowledge reaches believers through the cross: together with the power of his resurrection comes the communion in his sufferings (3:10; see also 1:29 and 1 Cor. 2:1-10 where Paul has previously used the word *mature* to describe those who receive the power of God in the cross of Christ).

Is the apostle discoursing on progress in vv. 12-15? From one perspective, the answer must be yes, because Paul does believe that a certain mind-set (3:15; note the same Greek word in 2:2, 5) is required for maturity and that not all Christians have attained it (1 Cor. 3:1). But, on the other hand, the mind-set which characterizes maturity is the very opposite of boastfulness (2:3-5; 3:3, 12). Thus, it resists cataloging signs of progress in favor of living the present fully and **straining forward** toward God's future. There is a sense, of course, in which this forward thrust always comes bound together with a blossoming of love and faith (1:9, 25), but never so as to stimulate pride over against God. Rather, the result will be a more solid commitment to the sufficiency of Christ (3:3), to that power through suffering which forms and re-forms itself like the designs of a kaleidoscope in the lives of believers.

When Paul writes **if in anything you are otherwise minded, God will reveal it to you** (v. 15), he is probably referring to a course correction within the borders of maturity, for he numbers himself both among those who are already mature (v. 15a) and among those who must "live up to" (NIV) the maturity they have attained in their attitudes (v. 16). The content of God's revelation will always be a variation on the theology of the cross. In a passage describing the very imprisonment from which Philippians originated, Paul relates his own experience of divine correction: "Why, we felt that we had received the sentence of death; but that was to make us rely not on ourselves but on God who raises the dead" (2 Cor. 1:9; see also Rom. 4:17; 1 Cor. 1:26-31).

False Glory and the Coming Glory in Christ (3:17-21)

The theme of "apostle as model" continues with v. 17: **join in imitating me.** Both in rabbinic Judaism and in Hellenistic popular philosophy teachers were expected to offer their own lives as examples. Paul employs this convention for the congregations he has founded (see 1 Cor. 4:15-17; 11:1) but here with a special twist, since he has just explained in vv. 7-14 that he is anything but a finished product. Only his "motions of maturity in Christ" need to be imitated, above all, his resolution to know Christ's power by sharing his sufferings, "becoming like him in his death" (v. 10). There are other believers, too, whom the readers should **mark** as examples along with Paul. These probably include not only the apostle's close associates, like Timothy (1 Cor. 4:17), but also Epaphroditus (2:29-30) and other friends within the Philippian congregation (4:2-3).

In contrast to these good examples of life in Christ stand the **many** who **live as enemies of the cross of Christ** (v. 18). They are probably Christians because Paul writes about them **with tears** and has previously warned the Philippians of their errors. But are they the same false teachers described in 3:2ff.? At first glance, there would seem to be little correspondence between the two groups, for these **enemies** make **their god . . . the belly, and they glory in their shame, with minds set on earthly things** (v. 19). That is, their behavior appears to be crudely immoral as opposed to that of the "dogs," who advocate obedience to the Jewish law and speak of their own perfection (vv. 9, 12, 15). But such a distinction between 3:2ff. and 3:18ff. is overdrawn, since v. 19 probably refers not to physical excess but to religious experience. The word here translated **belly** also means "inmost parts" or "heart" (see Prov. 20:27; John 7:38) and could stand for the seat of human emotion. Then the sense would be that these Christians put ultimate faith in how they feel, thus making their belly into a god.

In line with this hypothesis is the clause about shame, which translates literally into "the glory of whom is their shame." The issue here is the character and location of true glory, for in vv. 20-21 Paul is concerned to emphasize that the present bodies of believers are not yet glorified and will become so only when the Lord Jesus returns from heaven to transform them. This looks very much like a polemic against people who claim already to have achieved some perfection in their physical natures (see 2 Cor. 4:5-12; 5:11-13; 10:9-12; 12:1-10, where Paul is battling a similar false teaching). The **shame** of the opponents then becomes the lowliness of their bodies (v. 21) which they mistakenly treat as God's heavenly glory resident in them. Here, as in many of his other polemical statements, Paul writes with irony. The phrase **with minds set on earthly things** stands in contrast to the mind-set of the mature believer (2:2,5; 3:15) and refers not to lust or gluttony but to a premature, and therefore false, glorification of earthly existence. On this hypothesis, the opponents want nothing but power and glory; therefore, they deny the presence of the cross in their daily lives (by means of willful illusion?) and become its enemies.

For Paul, however, the true **commonwealth is in heaven** (v. 20). The word for **commonwealth,** *politeuma* in Greek, shows that the apostle is playing on the Philippians' status as members of a Roman colony. His point is that their real home, both somatically and spiritually, has yet to come. Paul does not devalue ordinary physical life here but simply states that it requires more redemption than the enemies suppose. Jesus must still return from heaven to establish God's kingdom completely upon earth. This will bring a radical transformation of existence for believers, for then—but only then—they will share Christ's glory in a bodily way (see also Rom. 8:17-23; 1 Cor. 15:42-53). Until that day of the Lord (1:6; 2:16) they can know his resurrection power solely through the medium of their **lowly body,** that is, by partaking of Christ's suffering and death along with his continuing victory over those forces that oppose God. The expression **to be like** (v. 21) is the adjectival form of the participle "becoming like him" (v.

10) and probably represents an intentional allusion by Paul to that conformation.

The clause **by the power which enables him even to subject all things to himself** should be read alongside 1 Cor. 15:24-28, where Christ is also portrayed as God's viceroy, charged with subjecting "every rule and every authority and power" to himself for the sake of the Father. In 1 Corinthians it is clear that God provides the force for this subjugating activity (15:27) and that it is a finished event from the divine perspective "in heaven" (as in Phil. 2:9-11) but must nevertheless be worked out on earth by Christ. In both thought and terminology 2:9-11; 3:20-21; and 1 Cor. 15:24-28 are strikingly consistent with regard to the already/not yet dimensions of salvation. Christ is presently the **Lord** who labors for the world's redemption. He will return as **Savior** (the only occurrence of this word in Paul's undisputed epistles!) to complete his rule with a dramatic transformation of believers. For now, the Philippians must join their laboring Lord in the working out of salvation (2:12), sharing the same energy of God which empowers him (compare the variants of the Greek word *energein* in 2:13 and 3:21).

■ Appeals for Reconciliation, Prayer, and High-Mindedness (4:1-9)

A Dispute to Be Settled (4:1-3)

The compassionate address of v. 1 provides a transition from the grandeur of Christ's cosmic work to the continuing reality of human struggle. In fact, the two are related. As the Philippians are to **stand firm . . . in the Lord,** that is, join with him in subjecting the principalities and powers (compare 1 Cor. 15:24-28, 58), so also two leading members of the congregation are to work toward a common mind **in the Lord** (v. 2; see also 2:2-3). The redemption being wrought by Christ extends simultaneously to the world as a whole and to two alienated individuals. Paul does not chide these prominent women for their disagreement but honors them, along with Clement, as **fellow workers** (v. 3). Several other women associates of Paul are mentioned in Romans 16. The identity of the **true yokefellow** who is asked to provide special help in settling this dispute remains a mystery. It could be Epaphroditus, the bearer of the letter. The **book of life** is a term from Jewish apocalyptic literature (see Luke 10:20; Rev. 3:5; 20:15) which denotes God's foreknowledge of the people he is saving. Whether the disharmony between **Euodia and Syntyche** concerns a large or a small matter, it compromises the congregation's witness to its neighbors. The resolution of this difficulty will mark a step forward in the progress of the gospel.

The Peace Which Passes All Understanding (4:4-7)

Paul may be still thinking of the two women when he urges all his readers to **rejoice in the Lord** (v. 4). This is the third time in four verses that he employs the familiar phrase of incorporation. In the sphere of Christ's reign joy overcomes all pain, though this is a joy which must be recalled and embraced and expressed to one another. It is no simple giddiness that washes over believers like a wave but rather a deep treasure which needs to be sought and claimed. Hence Paul's double use of the imperative: **again I will say, Rejoice.** The word translated **forbearance** could also mean "gentleness" or "kindness" and may well refer again to the settling of the dispute (compare Gal. 6:1). If it becomes known in Philippi that two feuding members of the church have been reconciled by amiable means, this in itself will demonstrate to **all men** the power of the gospel. **The Lord is at hand.** Here is an affirmation of faith that Christ will soon return from heaven to set all things right (3:20f.). But it is also an assurance that the Lord is already present with Paul's readers as they risk living out the gospel in Philippi. Even now believers are laboring "in Christ," with God himself working in and among them (2:12f.).

The apostle urges his readers to **have no anxiety** (v. 6), but since he himself expresses considerable agitation in this very letter (1:23; 2:21, 27; 3:2ff.), he cannot mean that believers must never allow themselves to get wrought up about anything. Instead, the counsel here would be to overcome the inevitable turbulences of life by offering them up to God. As in Philemon 4-6, petitions are seen to be interwoven **with thanksgiving.** The speaking of gratitude in worship both arouses joy and shapes **supplication** (compare 1 Thess. 5:16-18; Col. 3:15-17; Eph. 5:19-20). As they pray, and regardless of their immediate emotional state, the Philippians can be sure that **the peace of God** (see 1:2) will keep watch over their feelings and thoughts so as to ground them **in Christ Jesus** (v. 7). This peace is something more than a sense of tranquility, for it **passes all understanding** and can even coexist with inner turmoil (see Gal. 5:16-17, 22). Anyone who has prayed through an early morning anxiety attack will know what the apostle means.

The True Goals (4:8-9)

In v. 8 the word **finally** can also be translated "And as for the rest." It does not necessarily signal the end of a letter (see the Introduction above). Paul's exhortation to **think about** (better: "keep reckoning with") the lofty realities cited here shows that he does not despise pagan language for virtue or striving toward it. Rather, he wants his readers to equal the best behavior of their pagan neighbors. In Christ, however, the **true,** the **honorable,** the **just,** etc., take on new dimensions. With faith, more of what the nations long for is discerned and more is enacted (see 1:9-11). The specific content of this "baptized" virtue is alluded to in v. 9: **what you have learned and received and heard and seen in me.** Here Paul probably has in mind oral and written traditions about Jesus, as well as the Philippians' personal acquaintance with him through visits and letters. The real, historical lives of Christ and his apostles give solid shape to the otherwise abstract ethical ideals of v. 8. Christians know these concepts of goodness made flesh in the person of their Lord. The second part of v. 9 echoes 2:12f.: **do** [these things]; **and the God of peace will be with you.**

■ Closing Words of Gratitude and Affection (4:10-23)

Paul's Thanks and Benediction on His Partners (4:10-20)

Paul follows his own advice about rejoicing **in the Lord** (see 4:4) by recalling the Philippians' recent gift to him in prison (v. 10). Apparently it has been some time since he received their support (earlier gifts from Philippi are mentioned in 4:16 and 2 Cor. 11:9), even though they alone had **entered into partnership** (or *societas*) with him for this purpose when the congregation came into being (4:15; see above on 1:5-7). But Paul is careful not to chide; stating at first that his readers **have revived** their **concern** for him, he then corrects himself so as to praise them for their constancy. It was just that they **had no opportunity.** This expression could mean that Paul was not in one place long enough for the Philippians to catch up with him! Or perhaps their poverty sometimes prevented them from following through on their covenant with the apostle (see 2 Cor. 8:2). At any rate, it is likely that Paul has lived on "short rations" during the recent past. Even though he insists that he does not **complain of** need or **want** (v. 11), his subsequent words reveal that he has had to learn this virtue, an admission which looks like new information for the Philippians. Perhaps the apostle is alluding to trials suffered during this very imprisonment (". . . that was to make us rely not on ourselves but on God who raises the dead"; 2 Cor. 1:9).

The word translated **content** is a popular Stoic term for "self-sufficient." With Paul, however, this sufficiency applies only to the self which has been strengthened by communion with Christ (2 Cor. 3:4-5). The apostle uses this word to highlight the inexhaustible resources available to him, whether his outward circumstances are characterized by abundance or by poverty (v. 12). The clause here rendered **I have learned the secret of facing** is only one word in Greek. It is a technical term (occurring just this once in the NT) for initiation into a mystery religion. Paul's choice of language lends weight to the view that he is talking about some recent growth in his life, some threshold lately passed in his constant "straining forward to what lies ahead" (3:13). As he presses on toward the goal, he nevertheless knows a place of peace within himself from which he can work out his salvation (2:12) under every condition. Indeed, he **can do all things** necessary for the faithful practice of his vocation **in** the Christ **who strengthens** him (v. 13). It is worthy of note by western Christians that Paul considers the facing of **plenty** and **abundance** to be just as much a **secret** as the facing of **hunger** and **want**.

With v. 14 the apostle shifts from this reflection-exhortation (vv. 11-13) back again to his gratitude for the Philippians' gift. The verb translated **share** is a compound form of *koinōnein*, a stem common to the Greek words for **partnership** (1:5; 4:15), "partakers" (1:7), "participation" (2:1) and "fellowship" (3:10; NIV). This letter contains a virtual explosion of terminology for sharing, probably because the apostle's relationship with his readers is unique: **no church entered into partnership with me in giving and receiving except you** (v. 15). For notes regarding the contractual nature of this arrangement see the commentary on 1:5-7 above. In many respects the phrase **giving and receiving** provides a beautiful summary of life in Christ, although the reciprocity involved is too fluid and complex to be captured in any single description of it. Here, apparently, the Philippians have promised to furnish some regular form of financial support for Paul's ministry. In return, they will receive guidance from him in the knowledge that they are acting through him for the advancement of the gospel. But the give and take between apostle and congregation can never be limited to this form of the transaction. Paul and his readers together are mutual "partakers of grace" and of suffering with Christ (1:7; 3:10; 4:14). Thus, at any moment, they will all be both **giving and receiving** the riches of the gospel. Indeed, the apostle himself expects to gain spiritual blessings from those he visits (Rom. 1:11-12).

Paul elaborates on this deeper view of reciprocity in vv. 16-20. The word **help** does not occur as such in the Greek text of

v. 16. Literally, it reads: "once and twice you sent to me for my need" (*chreia*, the same word that appears in 2:25 and 4:19). This term can mean "request" as well as "need" and perhaps stands for both at once.[22] On one level, it certainly refers here to money or some other form of material support. But in v. 17 the gift that meets Paul's need is characterized as **fruit which increases to your credit,** that is, as a natural outgrowth of the Philippians' love, as the righteousness which comes from Christ and for which the Philippians will be called to account on the day of Christ (see 1:9-11). The material gift which Paul's readers have sent is actually a part of their transaction with God. It is **a fragrant offering, a sacrifice acceptable and pleasing to God** (v. 18). Paul can mix this liturgical language with commercial terminology (**your credit. I have received full payment, and more**) because for him the physical and the spiritual always come intertwined. Every human exchange takes place in the presence of God and is therefore a three-way partnership. The word **more** probably means Epaphroditus' personal presence as a minister to Paul in the Philippians' name (2:25). Thus, in v. 18 the apostle refers to **gifts** (plural) sent through Epaphroditus; these would include greetings, prayers, news, and other nonmonetary types of support.

Verse 19 takes the form of a promise. Whatever **need** the Philippians themselves have, spiritual or material, **God will supply** (literally "fulfill") it **according to his riches.** Writing to the Corinthians not long after his release from prison in Ephesus, Paul narrates an incident involving "the churches of Macedonia"—Philippi being one of these—where this promise has found a concrete fulfillment: ". . . in a severe test of affliction, their abundance of joy and their extreme poverty have overflowed in a wealth of liberality on their part" (2 Cor. 8:2; see 8:1-5 as a whole). Here too God is seen as that endless source of wealth which enables all giving and receiving by believers (see esp. 2 Cor. 8:9; 9:6-15). It is this divine magnanimity which inspires a closing burst of praise from the apostle: **To our God and Father be glory for ever and ever. Amen** (v. 20).

Greetings and the Grace of Christ (4:21-23)

Once more the foundational experience of incorporation becomes prominent, for all believers at Philippi hear themselves greeted **in Christ Jesus** (v. 21). The theme of unity in the Lord is further heightened when Paul notes that this greeting comes not only from him but also from those **who are with** him in prison and indeed, from **all the saints** in Ephesus, **especially those of Caesar's household** (v. 22). Here is the earliest extant evidence for the gospel's penetration into the imperial retinue. Whether these Christians were members of the emperor's family or freedmen or slaves is not revealed. In any event, the point is made: no level of society will remain untouched by Christ. And through their relationship with Paul the Philippians will continue to share in this progress of the gospel. The final **grace** in Paul's letter (v. 23), which corresponds to the opening greeting (1:2), serves as an eloquent summary of all that has been said. This blessing on the human **spirit** of the Philippians (see Rom. 8:15-16) is both already present and still to come. The Greek text is identical with the last verse in Philemon.

NOTES

1. Romans and Philemon are written to churches which Paul has not yet visited (see Rom. 1:8-15 and the Introduction to Philemon below). This is also true of Colossians (see 2:1), and in any case the authorship of this letter is disputed. Likewise, Ephesians and the Pastoral Epistles (1–2 Timothy and Titus) are thought to have been written by someone other than Paul himself.
2. V. P. Furnish, "The Place and Purpose of Phil. III," NTS 10 (1963-65): 80-88.
3. R. Jewett, *A Chronology of Paul's Life* (Philadelphia: Fortress, 1979); see pp. 95-104 and the foldout table inside the rear cover. W. G. Kümmel, *Introduction to the New* Testament, rev. ed., trans. H. C. Kee (Nashville: Abingdon, 1975) 332. Kümmel actually offers a spectrum of probable dates, 55 being the "mean" number.
4. J. P. Sampley, *Pauline Partnership in Christ: Christian Community and Commitment in Light of Roman Law* (Philadelphia: Fortress, 1980); see esp. pp. 51-77.
5. W. D. Palmer, " 'To Die Is Gain' (Philippians 1:21)," *Novum Testamentum* 17 (1975): 203-218; see esp. pp. 208-215.
6. R. P. Martin, *Philippians* (Grand Rapids: Eerdmans, 1980) 79.
7. *The Epistle to the Philippians,* trans. J. W. Leitch (Richmond: John Knox, 1962) 44.
8. J. Koenig, "From Mystery to Ministry: Paul as Interpreter of Charismatic Gifts," *Union Seminary Quarterly Review* 33 (1978): 167-174.
9. E. Käsemann, "A Critical Analysis of Philippians 2:5-11," in *God and Christ, Journal for Theology and Church,* vol. 5, ed. by R. W. Funk (New York: Harper & Row, 1969) 83ff.
10. *Lutheran Book of Worship* 179, stanzas 1,5. The text is by Caroline M. Noel (1817-1877) and the tune by R. Vaughan Williams (1872-1958).

11. F. W. Beare, *A Commentary on the Epistle to the Philippians* (New York: Harper & Row, 1959) 79-80.
12. The diverse conclusions are nicely summarized in R. P. Martin, *Carmen Christi: Philippians 2:5-11 in Recent Interpretation and in the Setting of Early Christian Worship* (Cambridge: Cambridge University Press, 1967).
13. M. Hengel, *The Son of God*, trans. J. Bowden (Philadelphia: Fortress, 1976) 1, 69-76.
14. M. A. Getty, R.S.M., *Philippians and Philemon* (Wilmington: Michael Glazier, 1980) 29-31.
15. D. Flusser, "Jesus in the Context of History," in *The Crucible of Christianity*, ed. A. Toynbee (New York and Cleveland: World Publishing Co., 1969) 229-230.
16. Getty, p. 37.
17. W. Hulme, *Your Potential under God: Resources for Growth* (Minneapolis: Augsburg, 1978) 22.
18. See Francis Thompson's poem by this title in *The Oxford Book of Christian Verse*, ed. Lord David Cecil (Oxford: Clarendon Press, 1951).
19. I owe these insights to Sr. Marilyn Robinson, O.S.U. They are found in her unpublished paper, "Transformation and Ethics in Philippians 3:8-15," 1978 (submitted to the graduate school of St. John's University, Collegeville, Minn., in partial fulfillment of the requirements for the degree of Master of Arts in Theology).
20. See the *Church Anthem Book*, ed. H. Walford Davies and H. G. Ley (Oxford: Clarendon Press, 1959) 195.
21. Martin, p. 139.
22. Sampley, p. 55.

SELECTED BIBLIOGRAPHY OF
COMMENTARIES AVAILABLE IN ENGLISH

Barth, K. *The Epistle to the Philippians*. Tr. by J. W. Leitch. Richmond: John Knox, 1962 (originally published in 1927). An engaging treatment by a great theologian. This work stresses the meaning of the text for today. Barth sees Philippians in the context of Paul's work as a whole and often cites interpretations of the epistle by Luther and Calvin.

Beare, F. W. *A Commentary on the Epistle to the Philippians*. New York: Harper and Row, 1959. Based on the RSV text with frequent references to the Greek. Beare argues for the partition of our canonical epistle into three separate letters.

Collange, J. F. *The Epistle of Saint Paul to the Philippians*. Translated by A. W. Heathcotes. London: Epworth Press, 1979. A French work first published in 1973, this is probably the most detailed treatment of Philippians currently available in English. Collange finds three letters in our canonical epistle but differs from Beare in the definition of their contents.

Getty, M. A. *Philippians and Philemon*. New Testament Message 14. Wilmington: Michael Glazier, Inc., 1980. This is a biblical-theological commentary from a Roman Catholic perspective. Based on the RSV text, it contains few references to the nuances of the Greek.

Houlden, J. L. *Paul's Letters from Prison: Philippians, Colossians, Philemon, and Ephesians*. Philadelphia: Westminster,

1977. A recent work which carefully assesses and employs current scholarship on Philippians. Houlden takes the epistle as a unity.

Lightfoot, J. B. *Saint Paul's Epistle to the Philippians.* Grand Rapids: Zondervan, 1953 (based on the 12th edition, originally published in 1888). A classic treatment by the British scholar-bishop, based on the Greek text. Attention to philology and syntax is the major strength of this commentary.

Martin, R. P. *Philippians. New Century Bible Commentary.* Revised edition. Grand Rapids: Eerdmans, 1980. A solid and thorough work by a leading evangelical scholar. Based on the RSV text with many references to the Greek and to current scholarship. This is probably the best overall commentary on Philippians available in English.

PHILEMON
John Koenig

INTRODUCTION

Christian artists through the centuries have not exactly flocked to the letter called Philemon for inspiration. Nevertheless, in San Francisco's Grace Cathedral observant visitors can discover a remarkable tableau depicting the events of our epistle. At the top of a large stained-glass window on the northern wall of the nave stands the OT prophet Amos, thundering his oracles of Yahweh against the oppressive practices of Israel's rich landowners. Just below Amos, in much smaller scale, is a double scene: on the left, a man writes from his prison cell; on the right, a younger man delivers a letter to a third figure, well dressed and seated on a dais. The caption reads: "Paul returns Onesimus to Philemon." Underneath this vignette, to the left, one notices a portrait of the evangelical leader William Wilberforce, famous for his legislative role in repealing the English laws of slavery during the first third of the 19th century. Below him, exhorting his audience from a pulpit, is Walter Rauschenbusch, chief architect of the thinking and practice which we now call "the Social Gospel." Clearly, the artist responsible for this window sees our epistle to Philemon within the long tradition of Judeo-Christian attempts to achieve justice. The commentary below will bear out the accuracy of this vision.

Yet in Philemon Paul's efforts toward equity do not take the form of direct words from the Lord (see, e.g., the hesitant "perhaps" of v. 15). Nor does the apostle write from the perspective of one who is trying to change the Roman laws of slavery.[1] Nowhere does he comment on the social effects of the gospel for all humanity. This epistle is a personal note to a Christian slaveholder on behalf of a fugitive known to both author and addressee. In Paul's view, the justice to be achieved *in this case* will best come about through a friendly and even playful[2] argument with his "beloved fellow worker" Philemon (v. 1). In other words, our epistle takes on the character of a "graceful persuasion to justice," and this is perhaps its most descriptive title overall. Paul presumes that he and Philemon (and now the slave Onesimus as well, v. 10) are linked together with Christ in a living tether. Through their partnership (vv. 6, 17), which is sustained and constantly renewed by the Lord, Paul anticipates breakthroughs in social relationships.

No thinking person can maintain that this approach should provide the sole model for all struggles toward justice today. And yet it is often the case that groups and individuals on both sides of our current controversies (not to mention wars!) identify in a more than passing manner with the Christian faith. When this factor is at work, it may be that one way to break through the dividing walls of hostility is something akin to the ironic humor which comes naturally to Paul's argument in his letter to Philemon. Such a humor trusts that the other, the adversary, is at heart one who longs to do the good because he or she has been grasped by the goodness of God in Christ (vv. 6, 14).

The composition of our epistle is often thought to have occurred at the same time and place as that of Colossians, since the latter contains a list of co-workers attending Paul in prison (4:7-18) which corresponds very closely to Philemon 23-24.[3] However, even if Colossians is taken as a genuine Pauline letter, there are significant differences between the situations presupposed in the two letters. In Colossians, Epaphras is not called a prisoner, but in Philemon 23 he is. On the other hand, Col. 4:10 identifies Aristarchus as a prisoner, but this is not so in Philemon 24. "Jesus who is called Justus" greets the readers of Colossians (4:11), but he is not present at the writing of Philemon, nor is Tychicus, the bearer of Colossians (4:7-8). This last bit of data tells us a good deal, because in Colossians Tychicus is being sent on his mission along with Onesimus, "the faithful and beloved brother who is one of yourselves" (4:9), that is, one who comes from the Lycus Valley region of Phrygia in which Colossae is located. If the trip described in Col. 4:7-9 were identical with the returning of the runaway slave Onesimus to his master in Colossae, Tychicus would probably have been mentioned in our epistle.

Another piece of information that disturbs the time/place link between Philemon and Colossians is the fact that Paul nowhere suggests in the longer epistle that he is planning to visit his readers. But in Philemon 22 he writes, ". . . prepare a guest room for me, for I am hoping through your prayers to be granted to you." Even if Philemon lived in Laodicea or Hierapolis rather than Colossae itself (see Col. 4:13-16), Paul would be likely to include the Colossians in any visit to the area inasmuch as their city formed a triangle with the other two, no side of which was longer than 20 miles. Why would he not announce this to the Colossians themselves?[4]

On the whole, the evidence suggests that Colossians and Philemon originated from somewhat different situations, though perhaps from the same place. If this is so, Onesimus' freedom to travel as a messenger (assumed in Col. 4:9) leads us to the further conclusion that Colossians was written sometime after Philemon when Onesimus' master had returned him to Paul for service in the gospel (see Philemon 13 and the commentary on v. 21).[5]

From which imprisonment of the apostle does Philemon stem? It is impossible to be certain, but three observations support the view that Paul wrote to Onesimus' master from Ephesus during the same confinement that produced Philippians:

1. The Colossae/Hierapolis/Laodicea triangle is only about 100 air miles east of Ephesus. As a fugitive slave Onesimus would find it relatively easy to reach the provincial capital (contrast Rome, from which Philemon is usually thought to have originated when it is closely joined with Colossians).

2. There are many close parallels, in style as well as content, between Philippians and Philemon—more than between Colossians and Philemon. See the commentaries on Phil. 1:2, 5-7, 10; 2:25; 4:23 and Philemon 1, 4–7, 9, 10, 13, 22. This overlapping of thought suggests, though it does not prove, that the two epistles were written at about the same time.

3. It is not clear why Paul would ask Philemon to prepare a guest room for him (v. 22)—that is, make ready for his presence in the near future—if he were writing from some place far away, e.g., Rome. On the other hand, Paul's plan to visit the Philippians "shortly" after his release (Phil. 2:24) would not change substantially if he later decided to make a quick trip to the Lycus Valley and back before heading northwest to Macedonia.

These observations suggest that Philemon was composed after Philippians in the course of Paul's Ephesian imprisonment. By then, the apostle was happily reunited with a number of co-workers (Philemon 23-24) whose loyalty he had previously doubted (Phil. 2:19-21; at the writing of Philippians only Timothy and Epaphroditus are present). Moreover, as he sends off his epistle to Philemon, Paul displays no further anxiety regarding the outcome of his confinement (contrast Phil. 1:19-26; 2:17, 23 with Philemon 22). In short, the scenario proposed here is: Philippians followed by Philemon followed (sometime after Onesimus' return to Paul) by Colossians. All three letters (if Colossians is really by Paul) probably originated from the apostle's cell in Ephesus between 55 and 56.[6] Col. 2:1 suggests that Paul has not yet visited the Lycus Valley, and since Colossians as a whole contains no travel plans, he may have decided not to follow through on his previously announced visit to Philemon (v. 22).

As noted above, the reference to Onesimus' origin in the Lycus Valley (Col. 4:9) makes it probable that Philemon too lived in this region. But where? The hint of an answer emerges in Col. 4:15-17:

> Give my greetings to the brethren at Laodicea, and to Nympha and the church in her house. And when this letter [Colossians] has been

read among you, have it read also in the church of the Laodiceans; and see that you read also the letter from Laodicea. And say to Archippus, "See that you fulfill the ministry which you received in the Lord."

The most natural reading of this passage yields the view that Archippus is not a Colossian but a prominent member of the Laodicean church.[7] But Archippus is also greeted by name in Philemon 2, along with Apphia, Philemon himself, and the church in his house. Thus Archippus may be a member of Philemon's family. In any case, he lives in the same town, and this of course would mean that Philemon too is a Laodicean. But here one must admit that the evidence proves scanty at every point and does not allow for hard-line hypotheses.

No less speculative, but worth pondering, is the view that the Onesimus of our epistle later became the bishop of Ephesus known to Ignatius and praised by him in his letter to the Ephesians (1:3; 6:2), usually dated about A.D. 115. One advantage of this thesis is that it helps account for the preservation and eventual canonization of an otherwise obscure personal note. However that may be, we are fortunate indeed to have this little giant of a book in the treasure house of our Scriptures.

OUTLINE OF PHILEMON

"A Graceful Persuasion to Justice"

  I. Greetings from a Partner in Prison (1-3)
 II. Thanksgiving for Philemon's Hospitality to the Saints (4-7)
III. A Petition Philemon Will Find Hard to Refuse (8-14)
 IV. How Philemon's Partnership in Christ with Paul and Onesimus Can Result in Justice (15-20)
  V. The Sealing of the Agreement—Plus a Final Request (21-22)
 VI. Greetings from Paul's Companions and a Blessing on Philemon's House (23-25)

COMMENTARY

■ Greetings from a Partner in Prison (1-3)

Paul hails Philemon with an unusual self-designation: **prisoner for Christ Jesus.** Although the apostle elsewhere mentions his chains (Phil. 1:7, 13-17; Col. 4:18), it is only here and in v. 9, among the undisputed letters, that he actually refers to himself as a **prisoner.** Paul's use of this title—and this title alone—at the beginning of his letter is probably an expression of solidarity with the slave Onesimus. The latter is also a man in bondage and, since his conversion, he too suffers his confinement for Christ (v. 10; see also 1 Cor. 7:20-24). Along with Paul, Timothy greets Philemon at this point rather than at the end of the letter (see vv. 23-24), which perhaps indicates that he knows Philemon personally. In any event, Paul himself has experienced close personal contact with his addressee. Not only does he call him **beloved fellow worker,** a term which always denotes a laboring together for the gospel in a particular location (see the commentary on Phil. 2:25); he also refers to a time when he helped Philemon through a period of great crisis, perhaps as his father in the faith (v. 19).

Apphia is greeted as a **sister** believer (v. 2); she may be Philemon's wife. **Archippus,** too, could be a member of Philemon's immediate family, perhaps a son. Since he is named as a **fellow soldier** (see Phil. 2:25, the only other use of this term by Paul), it is clear that he also has a personal relationship with Paul. For observations on the reference to Archippus in Col. 4:17, see the Introduction above. Finally, the **church** that meets in Philemon's house receives an apostolic greeting. In v. 2 and throughout the body of this letter the second person pronoun (**you, your**) is singular. Because Philemon's name appears first in the list of people greeted, he must be the individual Paul has in view. Yet in his opening and closing blessings (vv. 3 and 25), both of them introduced by the foundational word **grace,** Paul employs the plural **you** so as to address the church. Plural forms also appear in the prayer request of v. 22. Thus, a certain tension characterizes this personal letter. The bulk of it is directed to Philemon himself, but the beginning and the end suggest that the epistle as a whole was to be read before the assembled church. As a result, Philemon would enjoy no absolute privacy for pondering the apostle's instructions to him. The **grace. . .and peace** benediction in v. 3 is identical with that of Phil. 1:2 (and other Pauline letters, but not Col. 1:2). See the commentary on Philippians for a fuller exposition.

■ Thanksgiving for Philemon's Hospitality to the Saints (4-7)

With v. 4 the apostle introduces a prayer of gratitude to God for the person and work of his addressee. Variations on the thanksgiving formula appear frequently in Paul's letters, but only here is one of them applied to an individual believer. In terms of both vocabulary and word order this thanksgiving stands closer to Phil. 1:3-4 than to any other passage in the apostolic corpus. By singling Philemon out from his local church (in the presence of that church), Paul accords him a high honor. Philemon's special vocation as a believer is his **love and faith** toward **all the saints** (v. 5), probably expressed in his gracious reception of travelers. The adjective **all** indicates that Philemon has not been prejudicial about his hospitality but has welcomed everyone who comes in the Lord's name. This little adjective performs heavy duty, for with it Paul is already prefiguring the request he will make on behalf of the runaway slave Onesimus (v. 17). The **love and faith** Philemon practices are offered first to **the Lord Jesus** (compare 2 Cor. 8:1-5). This is what gives them power and direction. As applied to people, the word **faith** may be translated "faithfulness"; or it may denote the "faith working through love" to which Paul refers in Gal. 5:6.

In v. 6 the words **and I pray** do not actually appear in the Greek text. The syntax indicates that it is Paul's thankful remembrance of Philemon before God (v. 4) which is expected to yield the desired results. Typically, Paul sees thanksgiving itself as an effective form of petition (compare Phil. 4:6; 1 Thess. 5:16-18; Col. 3:16). Verse 6 as a whole is difficult to translate, but a literal rendering would be something like the following: "I thank my God (v. 4). . .in order that the sharing (*koinōnia*) of your faith might become active, with a knowledge of all the good in our midst which is for Christ." The idea here is the same as that expressed in Phil. 1:9 (where the identical expression *en epignōsei*, "with knowledge," occurs), namely, that a new perception of God's goodness in Christ will draw believers toward practical incarnations of the divine will which are appropriate to their own time and place. Paul has something quite specific in mind as he writes this to Philemon. He will shortly ask his fellow worker to confirm his reputation for love toward **all the saints** (v. 5) by enacting **all the good** for Christ latent in the current situation. The word *koinōnia* in v. 6 would call forth a host of images for Philemon having to do with various commercial and religious contracts. On this first century notion of *societas*, see the commentary on Phil. 1:5-7. The sharing which Philemon is asked to do would be understood by him as a responsibility to the whole Christian community. Paul expands on this idea in v. 17 by using the word "partner" (*koinōnos*, i.e., fellow member of our *societas*).

With v. 7 Paul again compliments Philemon, thereby grounding further the request he is about to make. The apostle himself has **derived much joy and comfort** from Philemon's hospitality.

Whether he has actually enjoyed it himself we cannot tell. The point here is that he has heard from those whose **hearts. . .have been refreshed** through their contact with Philemon. His graciousness is no superficial one, for it meets the inner needs of the saints as well as their physical ones. Later in this epistle Paul will play upon the word for "hearts" (*splanchna*) in his unfolding plan to win over Philemon (see vv. 12, 20).

■ A Petition Philemon Will Find Hard to Refuse (8-14)

If it is not plain to Philemon already, the word **accordingly** signals him that Paul has been leading up to a request. One wonders if Onesimus, the bearer of this letter, has said anything yet on his own behalf and whether he is present to hear his master read the communiqué he has delivered. In any event, the atmosphere must have been charged! Would v. 8 not sound quite heavy-handed to Philemon? Paul claims the right to **command** his fellow worker, and this in front of the very congregation he hosts. Indeed, the clause **what is required** seems to imply that Paul knows exactly what form Philemon's behavior should take. But the words used actually mean "what is fitting" and thus allow for some flexibility in the matter. Moreover, vv. 4-7 might have produced such warm feelings in Philemon that he would hear v. 8 as something of a mock threat from an old friend. In either case, v. 9 represents an attempt to build on the love Philemon has shown (vv. 5, 7) through an **appeal** (*parakalō*, which corresponds to the "comfort," *paraklēsis*, of v. 7 that Paul has received from Philemon's love; note the similar connection between these two Greek words in Phil. 2:1 and 4:2). Still, even this **appeal** packs a great deal of power, for it issues from no less than an **ambassador** (compare 2 Cor. 5:20) **and now a prisoner also for Christ Jesus** (see v. 1). Paul's unique work and suffering carry an authority which can never be taken lightly.

In v. 10 the apostle makes his appeal explicit for the first time.

He writes this letter on behalf of **Onesimus.** The father-child relationship sketched here refers to Paul's role as one through whom Onesimus first came to faith—or perhaps came back to faith after a lapse. Timothy is similarly described as Paul's child. . .in the gospel" (Phil. 2:22; 1 Cor. 4:17). Although Acts 16:1 notes that Timothy was already a disciple when he met Paul, it was the apostle who led him to his vocation as an evangelist. In 1 Cor. 4:14 Paul calls all the Corinthians his children because they became believers through his proclamation. On the other hand, Paul's fatherly work among the Thessalonians is seen to be that of nurturing those who believe already (1 Thess. 2:11). The point in v. 10 is that Onesimus now enjoys a special relationship with the apostle which calls into question his status in the household of Philemon. One feels the edge on this verse, a paraphrase of which might read: "Your slave, friend Philemon, has become **my child.**" Whether Onesimus sought Paul out to find refuge or whether he simply stumbled upon him during his confinement at Ephesus is impossible to tell. Paul himself attaches no weight to the sequence of events that led up to their meeting.

From v. 11 we learn that Onesimus had not been an ideal slave from Philemon's point of view. **Formerly he was useless to you** (see also v. 18). The word for **useless** (*achrēstos*) is a play on the meaning of the name **Onesimus** in Greek, i.e., "useful." Now, following his conversion (or re-conversion), Onesimus has grown into his name; he has become useful and ready to serve. Since Paul considers him **useful** to Philemon, the meaning must be that he is no longer anxious to flee but has declared himself ready and willing to resume his status as a slave. Legally, of course, he had no choice; but Paul's point is that Onesimus now understands even his slavery as an opportunity for freedom in the Lord (see 1 Cor. 7:21-24). Here the apostle merely hints at Onesimus' usefulness to himself, preferring to spell this out more fully in v. 13.

In the intervening sentence (v. 12) Paul inserts a testimony to his own obedience, combined with a comic twist. As the apostle tells it, he not only returns Onesimus to his rightful owner (he is bound by law to do so) but also sends him back **to you,** i.e., to Philemon his personal friend. As Philemon's fellow worker, the apostle makes him a present: a renewed slave, a willing and useful slave. Of course (Paul adds parenthetically) this gift costs him a lot, for he is **sending** back his **very heart!** By now, Philemon has probably begun to catch the drift of Paul's argument. The apostle portrays himself as one who more than obeys the law. Indeed, he is doing Philemon a big favor, at tremendous sacrifice to himself. Perhaps a chuckle breaks out from the assembled congregation at this point, perhaps from Philemon himself. The word for heart is *splanchna,* and now it stands not only for what Philemon refreshes in the saints (v. 7) but also for Paul's inner self and for the object of his affections, Onesimus. The apostle will play this card once again (v. 20). Unlike the Stoics, Paul often exposes his emotional life to full view. He seldom attempts to convince his readers of anything without telling them how he feels about it.

The apostle expands upon his relationship with Onesimus in v. 13 without letting up on the comic pressure. This man could have been such a great help to him in his imprisonment. In fact, he could have served Paul **on your behalf,** that is, with the same loving care that Philemon himself was famous for and would surely want to offer Paul if only he had the chance. The phrase **imprisonment for the gospel** recalls Phil. 1:7, 12-17 and underlines the vital role in Christ's mission which Onesimus (and Philemon through him) might have played by staying with Paul. Of course this lament is really functioning as an enticement, a possibility for the future which still exists, contingent upon Philemon's permission.

With v. 14 Paul's decision to return Onesimus becomes an overpolite (and therefore ironic) expression of respect for Philemon's position as a Christian property owner: **I preferred to do nothing without your consent in order that your goodness might not be by compulsion but of your own free will.** The phrase **your goodness** refers back to v. 6 and thus encourages Philemon's personal enactment of God's gracious will *in this situation.* Eph. 2:10 provides an instructive parallel: "For we are his workmanship, created in Christ Jesus for good works, which God prepared beforehand that we should walk in them."

Is Paul aware of the pressure he is placing on Philemon in vv. 8-14? Is there any sense at all in which Philemon retains freedom of will? These questions are impossible to answer, since we dare not simply impose 20th-century psychological standards on a 1st-century situation. What we can do, however, is to note the striking consistency in Paul's approach throughout this letter. He tries very hard, through a variety of arguments, to persuade rather than to command. As he proceeds, however, his arguments become progressively more humorous; and this trend must have been apparent to Philemon. The paradox of our letter is that it comes across as simultaneously lighthearted and heavy-handed.

■ How Philemon's Partnership in Christ with Paul and Onesimus Can Result in Justice (15-20)

Another common thread running through this epistle is Paul's concern to show Philemon how the current situation can blossom into a fuller life in Christ for all parties. As the apostle sees it, the doing of true justice will benefit everyone. In vv. 15-16 Paul speculates about God's providence in the present series of events. The little word **perhaps** shows that he does not really know why all of this has happened; he has no revelation from the Lord about it. And yet believers are permitted (in some ways compelled) to search for God's working in their lives. Hence this apostolic argument proceeds from the use of imagination. The words **have him back for ever** (v. 15) contain a certain tension. On one level, they indicate that Philemon is receiving just payment in the return of his runaway slave. But on a deeper level, he is also entering into a new and eternal relationship with Onesimus which transcends everything that has happened between them up to now. Here Philemon's ownership of Onesimus recedes from the picture, because now that Onesimus has become an obedient believer, his status as **beloved brother** far overshadows his status as **slave** (v. 16). Although Paul stops short of requesting that Philemon manumit his slave, i.e., declare him a freedman under the law, the phrase **both in the flesh and in the Lord** makes it clear that a greater socioeconomic equity between Philemon and Onesimus must follow. From now on, their life together cannot be just a matter of "spiritual" equality before God. Here the new creation in Christ breaks through into the earthly arena of "private" property. (See 1 Cor. 11:11-12 and Gal. 3:27f., where the transformation of life in the flesh is not mentioned but must be presupposed.) Nevertheless, brothers Philemon and Onesimus themselves are left to determine what shape this reordering will take. The apostle pictures Onesimus' arrival as a gain for Philemon (**how much more to you**), an opportunity for him to enjoy an enriched and enlarged body of Christ in his own house church.

With v. 17 the apostle shifts back again to his own relationship with Onesimus. This runaway slave will come as an apostolic legate, indeed, as though he were the apostle himself. Regarding Paul's partnership with Philemon in a *societas*, see the commentary on v. 6 above and on Phil. 1:5-7. If Philemon takes his **partner** role seriously, he will be responsible for welcoming Onesimus just as graciously as he would welcome Paul, with at least as much love as he lavishes on "all the saints" (vv. 5-7). Presumably, Paul also considers Philemon to be *his* partner, which means that the apostle is willing to declare his solidarity with this slave owner, as well as with Onesimus. Paul never writes Philemon off as a benighted oppressor but instead appeals to his highest instincts, including his sense of humor. It is the triad of Paul, Onesimus, and Philemon which must create justice in Christ together. Each must do his part.

In v. 18 Paul expresses empathy with the **wronged** Philemon. The word literally means "has dealt [you] an injustice." Perhaps Philemon thought of himself as a benevolent slave owner and felt that Onesimus had no cause to flee (see the observations on first-century slavery in the Introduction, n. 1). The hypothetical **if he has wronged. . .or owes** probably envisages a real situation of legal grievance on Philemon's part, though it is difficult to tell whether Onesimus has simply been an inefficient worker (see the "useless" of v. 11) or whether he has absconded with some of Philemon's property, or both.

In any case, Paul boldly steps forward to pay the bill, writing a promissory note in his very own hand (v. 19). The word for **repay** is exactly the one current in first-century business circles for IOUs. Philemon could have used his letter from Paul to demand his due in a court of law. Did this offer strike Philemon as a joke? The bravado of Paul's language certainly implies such an intention. It is just possible that the apostle could have requested money from his Macedonian friends to make this restitution, but it was not his usual practice to ask for funds (see Phil. 4:10-18). As an indigent tentmaker in prison, he was hardly a man of great means. On another level, however, Paul's comic ploy must be seen as quite serious and even practical. He promises to redress an injustice committed against Philemon (probably an emotional one since it is distinguished from the owing) and then proves, with a mock disclaimer, that he is really capable of doing just that: **to say nothing of your owing me even your own self** (v. 19). The reference here is probably to Paul's role as Philemon's spiritual advisor or father in the faith. If Philemon insists on legal justice, Paul is ready to remind him of a higher law, not operative in the courts ("Bear one another's burden and so fulfil the law of Christ"; Gal. 6:2). By the standards of this law, Philemon is deeply in debt to Paul, even after the emotional and financial bill run up by Onesimus has been settled from the apostle's account.

So now, having dealt with Philemon's grievance, Paul can come forth with his appeal on even firmer ground: **Yes, brother, I want some benefit from you in the Lord** (v. 20). This language too is spiced with play. The single word in Greek which has been translated **I want some benefit** is *onaimēn*, the very verb from which Onesimus' name is derived! Philemon would surely have recognized this. The phrase **in the Lord** reinforces the higher law concept of v. 19 and reminds us that Paul makes no sharp distinction between spiritual communion with Christ and the problems of everyday life. When the apostle asks Philemon to **refresh**

my heart in Christ, he uses the word *splanchna* a third and final time. Now it alludes both to Philemon's reputation for refreshing the hearts of the saints (v. 7) and to Paul's fatherly identification with Onesimus (v. 12). The wordplay ties everything together. In the end, Philemon is simply being asked to practice his own special vocation as host.

■ The Sealing of the Agreement—Plus a Final Request (21-22)

In v. 21 Paul announces himself **confident** of Philemon's **obedience.** This is probably obedience to the Lord, as Philemon has now come to understand it, and not just compliance with Paul's instructions (see v. 8). Indeed, even at the end of this letter, it is not altogether clear what Philemon should do, beyond receiving Onesimus graciously as a brother in Christ and "in the flesh" (v. 16). Exactly how the relationship between these two men will change is not spelled out. Paul trusts that the Lord will guide their ways. Nevertheless, he does insert a declaration of faith **(knowing that you will do even more than I say)** which would inevitably stoke up his fellow worker's sense of responsibility. This **more** would almost certainly remind Philemon of Paul's wish that Onesimus could be present in Ephesus to serve him during his imprisonment (v. 13). Col. 4:7-9 offers good evidence that Philemon did assent to what Paul hints at. But whether Onesimus rejoined Paul as a slave under orders or as a freedman we cannot tell.

With v. 22 Paul makes a final request: **Prepare a guest room for me.** As in Phil. 2:24, he expects his release to come soon, with the result that he will be able to resume his traveling ministry. If v. 21 represents a realistic hope that Onesimus will return to Paul while he is still in Ephesus, then v. 22 need not be taken as a threat that the apostle wants to visit Philemon just to check up on him. Probably the chief object of the visit is simply to renew this important friendship in Christ and to exchange the love that cannot be communicated by letter. By placing himself in the intercessory hands of the whole congregation (the pronouns **your** and **you** are plural), Paul makes the assumption that Philemon and his brother-sister believers will want him to come. The apostle believes firmly that the prayers of the saints will help to end his imprisonment (see also Phil. 1:19 and especially 2 Cor. 1:11 where, following his release from this Ephesian confinement, Paul refers to his freedom as a "blessing granted us in answer to many prayers").

■ Greetings from Paul's Companions and a Blessing on Philemon's House (23-25)

Paul conveys greetings to Philemon (here the **you** is singular again) from several apostolic **fellow workers.** They are also fellow workers with Philemon (v. 1) and hence wish to encourage him in his special task. The individuals named are not introduced in detail, so Philemon probably knows who they are even if he has not met them all personally. **Epaphras, my fellow prisoner** (the title also appears in Rom. 16:7 and Col. 4:10), almost certainly would be acquainted with Philemon because he not only founded the Colossian congregation but also worked among believers in the neighboring towns of Hierapolis and Laodicea (Col. 1:7; 4:13). See the Introduction above on the relationship between Colossians and our letter to Philemon.

Mark (v. 24) seems to be something of a bridge figure between Peter and Paul in the early church's memory (see 1 Peter 5:13). Whatever the dispute was between him and Paul (Acts 15:36-39 does not supply much information), it must have been resolved by this time. In Col. 4:10 Mark is identified as "the cousin of Barnabas." At one point in Paul's career (but apparently not during the writing of Philemon) **Aristarchus** was the apostle's "fellow prisoner"; he was also a man "of the circumcision," i.e., a Jewish Christian (Col. 4:10-11). According to Acts, he came from Thessalonica, traveled with Paul on his last trip to Jerusalem, and is the only believer mentioned by name to have accompanied him on his voyage to Italy (19:29; 20:4; 27:2). For other references to **Demas,** see Col. 4:14 and 2 Tim. 4:11. **Luke** appears in these same two passages; in the former he is surnamed "the beloved physician."

Paul ends his letter as he begins it (see v. 3), with a blessing on the church in Philemon's house. Both linguistically and theologically **grace** lies at the heart of this small but paradigmatic transaction in the early days of the Christian movement.

NOTES

1. S. Bartchy's comprehensive work on slavery in the first century (*Mallon Chrēsai: First Century Slavery and the Interpretation of 1 Corinthians 7:21* [SBL Diss. 11; Missoula, Mont.: Scholars Press, 1973]) shows that no significant efforts were made by groups within or on the fringes of the imperial government to abolish the institution, although laws governing the treatment and manumission of slaves were becoming generally more humane. The only people who consistently refused to practice slavery as a group were the Essenes. Some owners acted with kindness toward their slaves and helped them to gain their freedom; others were incredibly cruel. Slaves held by Jewish owners seem to have been well treated. But one regular practice prevailed everywhere. No owner freed a slave unless it was to the owner's advantage. This could be defined in economic, moral, or other terms, but by law it was the owner's privilege to do the defining (see esp. pp. 54-110).
2. My insights regarding this aspect of the epistle have been aided and supplemented by those of E. Shanahan in her paper, "One in Christ: Polyvalent Reference and Word-Play in Philemon," delivered at the May 1981 meeting of the Delaware Valley Society of Biblical Literature.
3. J. Knox has argued not only that Philemon was composed at the same time as Colossians, but also that the Archippus of Col. 4:17 and Philemon 2 was the intended recipient of the letter called Philemon. In Knox's view, it was he who owned the slave Onesimus. See *Philemon among the Letters of Paul* (Chicago: University of Chicago Press, 1935) 25-34. For a critique of this hypothesis consult C.F.D. Moule, *The Epistles to the Colossians and Philemon* (Cambridge: Cambridge University Press) 14-18, and the commentary below on Philemon 1-2.
4. Some scholars would identify "the letter from Laodicea" which the Colossians are to read (Col. 4:16) with our Philemon and thus answer

our question with the thesis that the Colossians would learn about Paul's travel plans from reading Philemon. But this is a very indirect way of communicating and not characteristic of the apostle. Nor does Paul elsewhere send travel plans orally, via messengers; so it ought not be assumed that Tychicus would reveal these (Col. 4:7).

5. P. Stuhlmacher, having concluded with E. Lohse and others that Colossians is deutero-Pauline, argues that precisely because the letter comes from a circle of Paul's disciples not long after his death, it is likely to give us accurate information concerning the lives of the apostle's co-workers. Thus, Col. 4:9 provides strong evidence that Onesimus did become known in the early church as a missionary helper of Paul. And this in turn suggests that Philemon must have released him from household service. See *Der Brief an Philemon, Evangelisch-Katholischer Kommentar zum Neuen Testament* (Zurich: Benziger Verlag, 1975) 53f.

6. R. Jewett, *A Chronology of Paul's Life* (Philadelphia: Fortress, 1979); see the foldout table inside the rear cover. Jewett, however, takes Colossians and Philemon together and hypothesizes another Ephesian imprisonment, early in 55, for the writing of Philippians.

7. We do not have enough information to determine what Archippus' special ministry was. There is no real foundation for J. Knox's view (n. 3 above) that Archippus was the intended recipient of the letter we call Philemon (see the commentary on vv. 1-2) and that Col. 4:17 therefore served to remind him of his responsibility for the gracious reception and/or manumission of Onesimus.

SELECTED BIBLIOGRAPHY OF
COMMENTARIES AVAILABLE IN ENGLISH

Getty, M.A. *Philippians and Philemon*. New Testament Message
14. Wilmington: Michael Glazier, Inc., 1980. This is a biblical-
theological commentary from a Roman Catholic perspective.
Based on the RSV text, it contains few references to the nuances
of the Greek.

Houlden, J.L. *Paul's Letters from Prison: Philippians, Colossians, Philemon, and Ephesians*. Philadelphia: Westminster,
1977. Written by an Anglican scholar who accepts all four epistles as Pauline, this work provides helpful evaluations of recent
critical scholarship as it impinges upon our letter.

Knox, J. *Philemon among the Letters of Paul*. Chicago: University
of Chicago Press, 1935. This is a classic work which still provides many valuable insights, particularly with regard to the
place of Philemon in Paul's ministry as a whole. Nevertheless,
Knox's major hypothesis, that Archippus is the real recipient
of our canonical letter, has not won many adherents.

Lohse, E. *A Commentary on the Epistles to the Colossians and
to Philemon*. Hermeneia. Translated by W. R. Poehlmann and
R. J. Karris. Philadelphia: Fortress, 1971. Lohse's work, first
published in German in 1968 and based on the Greek text, is
probably the most thorough treatment of our epistle available
in English, especially on the issue of its connection with Colossians, which the author takes as deutero-Pauline.

Martin, R.P. *Colossians and Philemon.* New Century Bible. London: Oliphants, 1974. This treatment, by an evangelical scholar, is based on the RSV text but includes numerous references to the Greek and to current critical scholarship. Martin posits a common origin from Ephesus for Colossians (seen as a genuine Pauline letter) and Philemon.

Moule, C.F.D. *The Epistles to the Colossians and to Philemon.* The Cambridge Greek Testament Commentary. Cambridge: Cambridge University Press, 1968. Moule writes with great clarity and circumspection; he concludes that Paul is the author of Colossians and that he wrote Philemon at about the same time, probably from Rome.

ABOUT THE AUTHOR

John Koenig received his B.D. from Concordia Seminary, St. Louis, and his Th.D. from Union Seminary in New York. He is an ordained minister of the Lutheran Church in America. Prior to assuming his current position as professor of New Testament at the General Seminary of the Episcopal Church in New York City, he taught at Princeton and Union Seminaries. Among his publications are *Charismata: God's Gifts for God's People; Jews and Christians in Dialogue: New Testament Foundations;* and *New Testament Hospitality.*

I THESSALONIANS
Donald H. Juel

INTRODUCTION

Paul's first letter to the church at Thessalonica is not classified as one of his major epistles. In the relatively brief letter, Paul attacked no heresies and penned few lines destined to alter the course of church history. More than half the letter is devoted to thanksgiving, allowing Paul the opportunity to express his concern and appreciation to God for the new congregation in Macedonia. The letter is important because it allows us to glimpse a side of Paul's ministry easily missed in his major letters. All of Paul's life was not devoted to attacking errorists or to defending himself. In the pages of this letter we encounter a pastor deeply concerned for his parishioners, grateful to learn that they had survived the first wave of hostility, thankful to God the gospel had achieved such results. Like Philippians, 1 Thessalonians is permeated with joy and gratitude.

A prominent feature of the letter is Paul's use of the expression "as you know." No fewer than 10 times he refers to matters Christians at Thessalonica can be expected to know. The letter is more a reminder than a source of new information. Paul addresses men and women who were already believers. He writes not to convert them but to offer encouragement and to help the congregation understand what was implied in their initial confession of faith. He could assume the Thessalonians knew the gospel; what they needed was help in understanding how it related to their lives and courage to keep doing what they knew to be right (4:1).

■ The Thessalonian Ministry (Acts 17:1-10)

The church at Thessalonica was founded by Paul on his so-called second missionary journey, shortly after he had established a congregation at Philippi. Paul enjoyed considerable success in his Macedonian ministry, though he encountered fierce resistance. He speaks of having been "shamefully treated at Philippi" and of preaching in Thessalonica "in the face of great opposition" (1 Thess. 2:2). Nevertheless, two thriving churches were established.

According to Acts, Paul came to Thessalonica after having been imprisoned in Philippi. He began his work, as is typical in Acts, by seeking to convert Jews in the local synagogue (Acts 17:2-4). A minor uprising among local Jews brought his work to an abrupt end after only three weeks. Paul then traveled to Beroea and from there to Athens, leaving behind Silas and Timothy with instructions to join him "as soon as possible" (Acts 17:15). According to Acts, they rejoined Paul in Corinth (18:5).

There are some difficulties squaring the information in Acts with details Paul provides in 1 Thessalonians. According to 3:1-5, Timothy accompanied Paul to Athens and was then sent back to Thessalonica to determine how the congregation was faring. Upon Timothy's return (to Corinth), Paul learned that the congregation had survived the adversity, and he dashed off a letter. Though the sequence of Paul's movements is correct, the author of Acts apparently did not possess information about the travels of Paul's companions.

It is likewise difficult to imagine that Paul stayed in Thessalonica only three weeks. The following details from 1 Thessalonians do not fit:

1. Paul reminds the congregation that he worked "night and day" while in Thessalonica so as not to burden them (2:9).[1] We should probably understand his remark literally. The life of a craftsman—Paul was a leatherworker—required long hours and allowed little free time. It seems unlikely Paul would have had

sufficient time within a period of three weeks to establish a congregation in the city while working to support himself.

2. In Phil. 4:16 Paul refers to at least two occasions on which the congregation sent financial assistance during the Thessalonian ministry. The details surely presuppose a longer ministry than a few weeks.

3. In 1:6-9 Paul praises the congregation for having become an example not only for believers in Macedonia and Achaia, but everywhere. If Paul wrote not long after his departure from Thessalonica, as seems to be the case, we must infer a more lengthy ministry to allow time for a reputation to have developed and spread.

4. Paul uses intimate terms to describe his relationship to the Thessalonians ("nurse" in 2:7, "father" in 2:11), and he notes that the church came to view him as an example (1:6). The language may be conventional (see below), but it seems to presuppose a greater sense of familiarity than a few weeks would allow.

5. In 5:2 Paul refers to those who "labor among you and are over you in the Lord and admonish you." The references need not imply an elaborate ecclesiastical structure, but they do presume a rudimentary organization within the congregation.

Taken together, the evidence points to a longer stay than three weeks. The temporal reference in Acts may be attributed to the author's tendency to compress events into a brief span of time, as well as to sketchy information.[2] Estimates of the length of Paul's stay must rely on educated guesswork, but a few months seems more likely than a few weeks. Robert Jewett estimates that Paul remained in the city for between three and four months.[3]

There is also some difficulty accepting the accuracy of Luke's description of Paul's ministry to the Jewish community in Thessalonica:

1. In Galatians 2 Paul suggests that at least for the period following the apostolic conference his sphere of responsibility is the non-Jewish world (Gal. 2:7-8). In Romans 11, Paul insists that though he does not preach to Jews, he is nevertheless interested in their ultimate salvation (11:13-15). He is confident that at least

indirectly his mission to Gentiles will make an impact on the Jewish community. Such comments are difficult to square with Luke's portrait of Paul in Acts, regularly beginning his work in local synagogues.

2. In referring to persecutions suffered by the Thessalonians, Paul draws a parallel between what the churches of Judea have suffered at the hands of "the Jews" and what the Thessalonians have suffered at the hands of their "countrymen" (2:14-16). In this case, it is unlikely that "Jews" here means simply "Judeans," residents of Judea. In the other, the most natural interpretation of "countrymen" would be that they are not Jews.

3. No trace of Jewish culture or of a synagogue has yet been unearthed in Thessalonica. That may be coincidental. There is little to suggest, however, that the city was a center of Jewish activity with a vigorous synagogue life, as Acts suggests. The description of Paul's Thessalonian ministry in Acts may owe more to the theology of Acts than to historical information.[4]

The author of Acts knew of Paul's travels through Macedonia and of a mission in Thessalonica. The mission followed closely the successful establishment of a church in Philippi and preceded Paul's visit to Athens and then to Corinth, where he remained for a year and a half. His information seems to have been limited to such bare details. We can be relatively certain that Paul's letter to the young church was written soon after his arrival in Corinth, probably in A.D. 50-51, upon Timothy's return from Thessalonica. About little more can we be certain.

■ The Nature of the Letter

There seems little doubt that our 1 Thessalonians was written by Paul and that it represents a unified composition. Partition theories have been few and singularly unconvincing. The letter divides neatly into two parts. Chaps. 1–3 include information about Paul's experiences in Thessalonica and about the circumstances attending the letter's composition. Chaps. 4–5 include advice from Paul to the church. The letter contains no extended argument, as do Romans and Galatians, and Paul's advice is far more conventional than in 1 Corinthians, where he deals with everything from marriage to shopping for meat.

Communication in antiquity was a social enterprise, governed by convention. That is particularly true of written correspondence. Even at the most popular level, letter writing was highly formalized. At a more sophisticated level there were rhetorical handbooks for those in public life, offering advice about what sorts of letters were appropriate for particular occasions. Knowledge of letter structure and of epistolary conventions can provide helpful clues for those of us who must read ancient letters as outsiders.[5]

Certain features of Paul's letter are regular occurrences in Greek letters and in Paul's other correspondence. Chaps. 1–3, for example, comprise an extended "thanksgiving" in which the writer indicates something of his relationship to the recipients, says something about the reasons for the letter, and introduces the letter's theme. Chaps. 4–5 can be classified as paraenesis (exhortation). The chapters are introduced, as is customary in Paul's letters, by a technical use of the verb *parakalō*, variously translated as "I appeal" or "I exhort."

A significant interpretive issue is the relationship between chaps. 1–3 and 4–5. What is the focus of the letter? If chaps. 1–3 are the center, the goal of the letter would be to maintain good relations with the congregation. The somewhat defensive comments in chap. 2 might suggest that Paul wrote to head off criticism of which he had become aware. We would have to explain the purpose of the extended thanksgiving with all its personal information about Paul and the congregation.

Knowledge of epistolographic conventions is particularly helpful in determining the focus of the letter. Abraham Malherbe has offered convincing evidence that the heart of the letter is the final two chapters and that the letter should be understood as "paraenetic" (exhortative). We may briefly summarize some of his arguments as follows:[6]

1. In letters of exhortation it was customary to include material familiar to the recipient(s). The letter was intended not primarily to provide new information but to serve as a reminder. Our problem, Seneca argued, is not that we are ignorant of what is right but that we do not do it. Reminders focus our attention on what we ought to do. Paraenetic letters thus make frequent use of "as you know."

2. Moralists regularly employed models for people to imitate, describing ideal behavior of their model in antithetical style (e.g., 1 Thess. 2:5-7, "For we never used either words of flattery . . . nor did we seek glory . . . But we were gentle among you . . ."). Paul's description of his ministry need not imply that he was defending himself against charges. Rather, he spoke of his behavior as exemplary (which the church already recognized—1:6) in preparation for specific advice to the congregation. Paul expects his treatment of the congregation to be mirrored in the way they treat one another (see below).

3. Good relations between sender and recipient provided a sound basis for moral advice. Paul's efforts to remind the congregation of their close ties to him and to maintain those ties are appropriate to the overall purpose of the letter. Paul's letter was a means of overcoming a separation, serving as a substitute for his presence.

4. Much of Paul's imagery parallels descriptions of the ideal philosopher among his contemporaries (see the commentary for specifics), thus locating his ministry in a particular social context and within paraenetic tradition.

We may thus understand Paul's letter as an exhortation, the main focus of which is the two concluding chapters. The opening chapters lay a foundation for the advice Paul will give the congregation. There is little evidence that Paul wrote to defend himself against charges, as in his Galatian and Corinthian correspondence. Relations with the Thessalonian congregation were sound. Knowing that convention dictates the structure of Paul's letter as well as his use of particular imagery and even certain moral topics, we may find certain questions to be of particular interest. We may wish to know, for example, what distinguished Paul's ministry as an apostle of Christ from that of contemporary moral philosophers and what distinguished his ethical admonitions from those of his contemporaries. Is his advice about doing "what you know is right" grounded in the gospel he preached, and if so, in what ways? Knowledge of epistolographic conventions in antiquity does not exhaust interpretation, but it can provide some direction.

■ Paul and "the Jews"

One final matter requires brief comment. In this letter, the first that we have from Paul, are bitterly anti-Jewish remarks:

> For you, brethren, became imitators of the churches of God which are in Judea; for you suffered the same things from your own countrymen as they did from the Jews, who killed both the Lord Jesus and the prophets, and drove us out, and displease God and oppose all men by hindering us from speaking to the Gentiles that they may be saved—so as always to fill up the measure of their sins. But God's wrath has come upon them at last! (2:14-16).

Apart from questions about their general appropriateness as expressions of Christian sentiment, his words contradict rather directly other statements he made, notably in Romans 9–11:

> I want you to understand this mystery, brethren: a hardening has come upon part of Israel, until the full number of the Gentiles come in, and so all Israel will be saved. . . . As regards the gospel they are enemies of God, for your sake; but as regards election they are beloved for the sake of their forefathers. For the gift and the call of God are irrevocable (Rom. 11:25-29).

There is no doubt about the authenticity of either letter or of the respective passages. Likewise, there is no way to fit both statements into a systematic whole. Neither will it suffice to dismiss one or the other by appeal to the situational character of

Paul's letters, as if there were no coherence in Paul's theology. The statements are contradictory. Paul was capable of contradicting himself, but this matter requires further comment since it is so close to the heart of Paul's theology. God's electing grace and the future of Israel are closely related to the gospel.

There seems little alternative but to speak of a development of Paul's thought on this matter. Such a notion poses difficulties. Most of Paul's career as a missionary lay behind him before he wrote even the first of his letters. His conversion may be dated around A.D. 33; his first letter was not written until 50 or 51, the last no later than 60. It is difficult to believe he had not worked out a theology before he wrote to the Thessalonians.

A shift in Paul's thinking is still the most likely explanation. Paul's career changed after the apostolic conference in 49. The conference, called to think through the problem of Jew-Gentile relations within Christian congregations, brought the problem to the fore rather than settling it. Prior to the conference there were apparently no agreed-upon guidelines regarding social interaction within congregations. The conference was a first step toward some regularization of Jew-Gentile relations, representing the initiative of Jewish Christians suddenly aware of their precarious position in a church flooded with Gentile converts. Paul's account of his conflict with Peter and Barnabas in Antioch (Galatians 2) indicates that church leaders were by no means of the same mind about the implications of the council. Paul was very much on his own in the Antiochene church when he insisted that the gospel demanded open fellowship at meals between Jewish and non-Jewish Christians. By the time he wrote to the Romans, he recognized that the unity of the church was hanging precariously in the balance, and that efforts to reconcile the Jewish elements within the Christian family would require extraordinary effort and would entail personal danger (Rom. 15:30-33). Paul was right. The efforts cost him his life.

It is likely that events forced Paul to think through the question of "the Jews" more carefully during the last decade of his ministry as the Jewish-Christian contingent became more forceful. His preoccupation with his collection for Jerusalem is evidence of his concern (see the Romans commentary on 15:30-33). Further, Paul recognized that the validity of his ministry depended not simply upon his reception among Gentiles but among Jewish believers increasingly suspicious of his gospel. Paul never solved the problem of Israel's unbelief, but his reflections in Romans 9–11 represent a more mature statement on the matter than his impassioned remarks in 1 Thessalonians. These verses cannot be deleted from the canon, but they ought not to be the basis of systematic reflection on relations between Christians and Jews in the contemporary setting.

OUTLINE OF 1 THESSALONIANS

  I. Greeting (1:1)
 II. Thanksgiving (1:2—3:13)
    A. "Your Faith in God Has Gone Forth Everywhere" (1:2-10)
    B. Paul Defends His Actions and Motives (2:1-12)
    C. Performance under Pressure (2:13-16)
    D. Timothy's Mission on Paul's Behalf (2:17—3:13)
III. Exhortation (4:1—5:22)
    A. Sexual Ethics (4:3-8)
    B. Love of the Brethren (4:9-12)
    C. "Those Who Are Asleep" (4:13-18)
    D. Times and Seasons (5:1-11)
    E. Concluding Admonitions (5:12-22)
IV. Prayer and Benediction (5:23-28)

COMMENTARY

■ Greeting (1:1)

As in all Greek letters, the sender's name comes first, then the recipient's, followed by a brief salutation. Here Paul uses no official designation; he introduces himself simply as **Paul,** suggesting that he has no need to assert his authority. In contrast, he opens his letter to the Romans, the Galatians, and both letters to the Corinthians with the official "apostle." In those letters it was necessary to say the word.

Timothy and **Silvanus** (Silas in Acts) were Paul's co-workers who frequently served as emissaries. Their names are the most frequently mentioned of Paul's companions. Both played an active role in the ministry in Greece.

On Paul's greeting, see the commentary on Philippians.

■ Thanksgiving (1:2—3:13)

The portion of the letter introduced by the verb **give thanks** is known as the thanksgiving. It is a regular feature of Paul's letters—and of other letters in antiquity.[7] One function of the thanksgiving is to offer some sense of the relationship that exists between sender and recipient. There is no thanksgiving in Galatians, evidence of the strained relations between Paul and the Galatian congregations. Virtually two-thirds of Paul's letter to the

Thessalonians is devoted to the thanksgiving. The unusually lengthy section indicates that the congregation was dear to Paul and that relations were in good order. The tone of the letter is appropriately noncombative. The good news Paul had received from Timothy, coupled with his experience in Thessalonica, could be expressed properly only by such an outpouring of gratitude to God.

"Your Faith in God Has Gone Forth Everywhere" (1:2-10)

Verse 2 might be rendered more aptly than in the RSV: "We find an occasion for thanking God whenever we remember you in our prayers, because we recall before our God and Father your work of faith."[8] The opening lines follow a definite pattern from which Paul seldom deviates. The regularity of the thanksgiving formula cannot obscure the depth of feeling, however. Paul is grateful to God for his church. Though he thanks God, the whole statement is addressed to the congregation (you) and serves as a compliment. Gratitude to God is appropriate, however, since whatever has occurred in Thessalonica is due to the working of his Spirit.

Specifically, Paul recalls with gratitude their **work of faith and labor of love and steadfastness of hope.** It is unlikely that Paul is referring to any particular demonstration of faith, love, or hope apart from the general performance of the congregation under pressure. Note the use of the triad **faith, hope,** and **love** (1 Corinthians 13).

Paul's reason for gratitude is even more precisely specified in v. 4: **he has chosen you** (lit. "because we know . . . your election"). The existence of the congregation, its survival, and its vibrant faith testify to the efficacy of God's electing grace. Hope is anchored in God's eternal will.

Paul recalls fondly that his gospel **came to you not only in word, but also in power and in the Holy Spirit and with full conviction.** Paul offers no apology for his preaching. Acts' portrait of Paul as a great orator is probably an exaggeration (see 2 Cor. 11:6), but his preaching was effective. The reason, Paul insists, is that it was accompanied by powerful signs of God's presence. The image of Paul as weak and ineffectual is an exaggeration in the other direction. Things happened when Paul preached. In Galatians he lists healings and prophecies as accompanying signs (Gal. 3:1-5); in 1 Corinthians 12–14 he refers to inspired speech. Acts' image of Paul as a great miracle worker is not a mere figment of someone's imagination.

And you became imitators of us, Paul reminds the church. Such comments may cause us embarrassment; they did not cause Paul any. He refers to himself as a model to be imitated in 1 and 2 Corinthians and in Galatians. He often finds it difficult to distinguish between himself and his gospel. Paul did not use his doctrine of justification as an excuse for his life. He sought to embody his gospel. The particular feature of his ministry to which he appeals here is his suffering for Christ. The Thessalonians emulated Paul—and the Lord—in that they **received the word in much affliction,** which must mean they suffered for their faith.

In emulating Paul, the congregation has now become an example to others—not only in Greece but **everywhere.** Paul may be engaging in hyperbole when he says that in view of what others have heard about the church **we need not say anything.** Clearly, however, the experience of the congregation serves to advance the gospel; it is part of the **word of the Lord** that has **sounded forth.** The story of how pagans in Thessalonica turned from worship of **idols to serve a living and true God** inspires others to do the same.

Decades ago, form critics insisted upon distinguishing between traditions about Jesus, which proved useful in preaching and teaching and could thus be traced to the beginning of the Christian movement, and traditions about the apostles, which had no place in church life until later (implying that stories about heroes of the faith represent a corruption of the pure kerygma). In light of Paul's comments, such a view is unlikely. Stories about Paul and his churches played a central role in Paul's missionary preaching. The "word of God" was never a naked word about heavenly realities, nor even a word about Jesus alone. It was from the outset an embodied word, bound up with the life and experiences of the first believers.[9]

Paul's distinction between idol worship and serving **a living and true God** is reminiscent of the language of Hellenized Judaism. Conversion to Judaism meant acknowledging the one true God. The specifically Christian elements follow: God is known as the one who raised Jesus from the dead. The good news is about that crucified and risen Lord who will return from heaven to **deliver** God's children **from the wrath to come.** The concluding sentences have a confessional ring and probably derive from pre-Pauline tradition.

Paul Defends His Actions and Motives (2:1-12)

This section is not a digression but an expansion upon earlier comments ("what kind of men we proved to be among you" [1:5]; "what a welcome we had among you" [1:9]). Paul reminds the congregation of what they already know, recalling the sometimes painful experiences that attended the founding of the congregation.

These verses have an apologetic cast, suggesting to some commentators that Paul is defending himself against specific charges leveled against him. More likely, the statements are traditional features of a paraenetic letter, establishing the credentials of one who will later offer advice. The use of contrasts (I was not this . . . but that) and a remarkable number of precise terms appear in descriptions of philosopher-preachers in the writings of Paul's contemporaries. Like street preachers who pointed to their willingness to endure the abuse of an audience as an indication of their commitment to the truth and of their interest in others, Paul refers to his **courage** to preach **the gospel in the face of great opposition.** Dio Chrysostom, Stoic philosopher turned Cynic preacher, said that a true philosopher must speak out of purity of mind and be guileless; **our appeal does not spring from error or uncleanness, nor is it made with guile,** said Paul. Dio insisted that a real philosopher, as opposed to a charlatan, preaches not for glory or personal gain; **for we never used either words of flattery, as you know, or a cloak for greed . . . nor did we seek glory from men,** insisted Paul. Paul's comment that he was **gentle as a nurse** is used by Dio to speak of orator-philosophers who know when to be harsh and when gentle in their care of souls.[10]

The passage, in short, sounds like a traditional self-commendation offered by philosopher-preachers in preparation for advice. In an epistolary setting, the comments solidify relations between Paul and the congregation to prepare for what follows. The Thessalonians already viewed Paul as someone to emulate. He wants them to know that their judgment is sound and that he has confidence in their ability to distinguish frauds from the true apostle.

In one respect, Paul does not need to argue his case before a human court. He has been **approved by God to be entrusted with the gospel.** Paul admits that were he God, he would never have chosen someone like himself ("I am the least of the apostles, unfit to be called an apostle" [1 Cor. 15:9]). But God made the choice, commissioning Paul as an apostle. His sole concern is **to please God who tests our hearts,** not people who can be deceived by appearances.

Yet that is not the whole story. The mere presence of such apologetic statements implies that it is important what people think. That Paul could be bold and forthright is clear; that he irritated and offended some, often intentionally, is likewise apparent. People must be offended for the right reasons, however. If the gospel is a scandal, an audience must be confronted by the real scandal, not by some minor stumbling block. It is important to Paul that his church—and others—know that his motives are pure and that he is trustworthy. If apostles can serve as examples to advance the gospel, they can also serve as unnecessary impediments.

Paul's imagery betrays the intensity of feeling for his congregation. He was **gentle, like a nurse,** he insists—a contrast to some philosopher-preachers who boasted of their bold attacks on their audiences. He did not even claim his due as an apostle. He

worked night and day so as not to be a **burden.** The **labor and toil** refer not to his preaching but to the manual labor that was part of his trade as a leatherworker. Paul shared everything with the congregation, even himself (v. 8). He was as solicitous of them as a **nurse** for **her** own **children** or as a **father** for his offspring. The family imagery is particularly striking. The use of intimate terms like "father" or "brother" or "sister" to speak of fellow members of a community was unusual. In fact, pagan critics of Christianity viewed the movement as antisocial and as a threat to families. In a sense it was. The NT offers graphic evidence of what faith involved. For some, becoming a believer meant leaving spouse, children, and parents (1 Cor. 7:12-16; John 9; Mark 10:29; 13:12-13). The imagery also indicates the extent to which the church served as a primary social group for believers, as Jesus promised:

> Truly, I say to you, there is no one who has left house or brothers or sisters or mother or father or children or lands, for my sake and for the gospel, who will not receive a hundredfold now in this time, houses and brothers and sisters and mothers and children and lands, with persecutions . . . (Mark 10:29-30).

Congregations provided a home for many who had none, as well as a new family for those who had to leave their own. The imagery was potent because it described the way things were. Another reason for its aptness was that congregations were organized as house churches, meeting in homes. Separation of life into the sacred and the secular was not as easy as for us, for whom religion has to do with church buildings and Sunday relationships, distinct from the "real world."

As an apostle, Paul was like a father to his congregations. He was called not only to preach **the gospel,** i.e., to announce salvation so as to lead people to conversion and Baptism, but to **exhort, encourage,** and **charge** his congregation **to lead a life** [literally, "walk"] **worthy of God, who calls you into his own kingdom and glory.** As their pastor, Paul is interested in what follows conversion. He recalls his experiences with the church and the tradition in which they have been instructed in order to draw out the implications of the gospel for discipleship. The phrase is reminiscent of Eph. 4:1, which introduces three chapters devoted to the implications of God's call for "walking."

The **glory** and **kingdom** to which God calls the Thessalonians is still future. The present is not the time for glorification, but for walking "in newness of life" (Rom. 6:4).

Performance under Pressure (2:13-16)

Paul renews the thanksgiving in v. 13, stating an additional reason for his gratitude to God: **you accepted** the word of God **not as the word of men but as the word of God.** "Faith comes through hearing," Paul writes in Rom. 10:17; before anyone can hear, there must be a preacher. The words by which Paul shared the gospel, however, were not cast in a special language. They were liable to misunderstanding. Some mistook them for mere words or as indications that Paul was in error. By the same words, however—the ordinary human words from Paul's mouth—the Thessalonians were converted. For them, ordinary language became the word of God. There is no way to guarantee that the preached word will be heard as gospel. Only God can make that happen; this is why Paul offers thanks to God that the Thessalonians heard and believed.

As evidence that God is at work in his preaching, Paul points to the conduct of the congregation. They have behaved in a manner appropriate to the gospel, having become **imitators of the churches of God in Christ Jesus which are in Judea** as well as of Paul and the Lord. Their willingness to endure persecution for the sake of the gospel is reminiscent of the experience of Judean churches—and thus a confirmation that God is indeed at work in their midst.

The statements that follow are unparalleled in Paul's writings. **The Jews** are indicted for having **killed both the Lord Jesus and the prophets** and for hindering Paul's mission **to the Gentiles.** The accusation that Israel killed the prophets is not unique to

Paul or the NT. Though there are scarcely any biblical references to the execution of prophets, by the first century, traditions had formed about the rejection and murder of prophets in ancient Israel. Isaiah was allegedly sawn in two.[11] To make sense of their unpopularity with the establishment, other sectarians had placed themselves in the line of the prophets the leaders had resisted (see Stephen's speech in Acts 7 for a classic example). In that line Paul places Jesus, himself, the Judean churches, and now the Thessalonians. Persecution is not a sign of disqualification. Suffering for the truth can be a badge to be worn with honor, a sign of fidelity in a world too easily swayed by mere opinion and popularity. God's saints have always been in the minority.

The danger of such a position should be obvious. Absolute confidence in the truth of one's position in the face of opposition from virtually everyone can be the most noble or the most destructive expression of religious commitment. The line between dogged faithfulness and outright fanaticism is thin. Jonestown stands as eloquent testimony to the demonic power of misplaced certainty. In most cases, the public forum is a more likely place to arrive at truth than the dark recesses of private opinion. Intolerance that feels no obligation to argue its case can become terribly destructive.

Yet the alternative to a rigid sectarianism is not an open mind and tolerance of all options. For Paul, truth had to do with particulars—with someone named Jesus. He could agree with Jews that truth must be squared with the Scriptures, but he recognized that to be understood properly, the Scriptures must be read in light of the cross. There are no external tests by which to measure the truth of the gospel. To Paul, the experience of the Thessalonians offered evidence that God was at work; others saw the gospel as destructive and openly opposed its adherents. Paul was unwilling to let success be the ultimate criterion of truth. Jesus, after all, had been rejected by all those who should have been best equipped to adjudicate the truth. Like others who had been gifted with the eyes of faith, Paul knew that truth could be known only to faith. There is no escape from the awful tension. Unpopularity by itself is hardly an adequate measure of fidelity to the truth. Nevertheless, the faithful can expect to be at odds with a world that prefers its own standards to the message of the cross.

Paul indicts **the Jews** for resisting his ministry to the Gentiles. His letters give ample testimony to the problems caused by his advocacy of a law-free mission to non-Jews who, he insisted, became children of Abraham by faith alone. Paul believed that the principle of God's free grace for Gentiles, completely apart from the Torah, was worth defending no matter what the risks. It was advocacy of that view that led to his eventual arrest and death.

Like Luke and Matthew, Paul operates with a view that there is some predetermined **measure of sins** that is to be **filled up** before appropriate punishment is meted out (see Matt. 23:29-36 and Luke 11:47-51). Precisely what Paul meant by **wrath has come upon them** is unclear. The aorist (*ephthasen*, "has come") seems to point to a past event. To what could Paul be referring? On the other hand, **God's wrath** is eschatological language, as is the verb (see the use in Luke 11:20, "The Kingdom of God has come upon you"). Is the past tense the equivalent of the Hebrew "prophetic perfect," i.e., a past tense used where a future is meant, to express the certainty of the coming event? That seems most likely. Paul seems convinced that a final line has been crossed and that unbelieving Jews will now be subject to the judgment of God—"finally" (or "for ever").

The passage is a difficult one. It is unclear why Paul would choose **the churches in Judea** and **the Jews** as exemplary for the Thessalonians. In his letters Paul makes little reference to congregational life in Judea and has less to say about events within the Jewish community. Had Paul suffered some outrage at the hands of the Jewish community in Corinth, where he was writing the letter, that motivated such remarks? Even if there was particular motivation, the comments do not square with what Paul says elsewhere, particularly in Romans 9–11.

233

Several things should be noted about the passage before dismissing it as an unfortunate outburst. First, Paul's use of **the Jews** is not paralleled by a term like "the Christians." Congregations in Judea included primarily circumcised believers. Only in one passage does Paul use *Israel* to refer to the church of Jews and Gentiles, and even that passage is disputed (see the commentary on Gal. 6:16). In Romans, *Israel* remains an entity distinct from the congregations of believers in Jesus, with a destiny still to be fulfilled. Paul's language is not unlike that used by Qumran sectarians to speak of fellow Israelites whom they regarded as "children of darkness." At the most, Paul's comments about **the Jews** are a reference to Israelites who have not accepted the gospel, not an outright rejection of "Jews" as a people. After all, Paul was himself born a Jew. Toward the end of his career, he insisted that he could not write off his "kinsmen by race," for whose sake he would suffer damnation if it would bring them to faith (Rom. 9:1-5).

Paul comes closest of any NT author to understanding congregations who confessed Jesus as Messiah as a new religious entity, distinct from Israel under the law. In a moment of passion, he penned words to the Thessalonians about unbelievers within the Jewish community who had opposed Jesus and his followers— words that are unacceptable for contemporary Christians and that proved to be inadequate even for Paul. The words clearly indicate, however, that for Paul and the unbelieving Jewish community, faith in Jesus as Israel's Messiah was not an obvious move for those who knew the Scriptures. There was something scandalous about Paul's message of a crucified Christ, a scandal he had no intention of obscuring (1 Corinthians 1). And if belief in Jesus was not the obvious goal of God's election of Israel in the eyes of the Jewish community, for Paul faith in Christ was not one religious possibility among others, an alternate track to life under the Torah. The God of Abraham had raised Jesus from the dead—and nothing could ever be the same, neither one's understanding of God nor of the way of life appropriate to those who had been called to a new hope.

Timothy's Mission on Paul's Behalf (2:17—3:13)

Paul offers further testimony to his feelings for the Thessalonians, drawing again on family imagery. Paul, the nurse and father, is now made an orphan by his absence from the congregation.

Knowing of their plight he was unable to go. **Satan hindered us** is all that he says. Perhaps he is referring to his thorn in the flesh, Satan's means of harassment (2 Cor. 12:7), a physical problem that prevented travel. Or perhaps Paul is referring to some external circumstance that made a visit impossible, such as opposition from officials (Acts 17). The use of **us** may suggest that the problem involved Paul and his co-workers, though Timothy is free to visit. Paul did not have to specify the reason in his letter, since the letter carrier could fill in any blanks. Whatever the cause, Paul was unable to make a visit, and his letter and emissary served as a surrogate.

The congregation was dear to Paul. They are his **hope** and **joy** and **crown of boasting.** Paul's "boast," as in Romans, has little to do with accomplishments which he can hold before God as a source of merit. He boasts in God. Yet he does not belittle his work as an apostle. The congregation exists as testimony to God's grace and the power of the gospel channeled through Paul's ministry. God's grace toward Paul has not been in vain (1 Cor. 15:10). Further, the remarks reveal that the congregation is his raison d'être, the point of his life. His role as apostle is tied to those to whom he is sent. Paul's reference to **our Lord Jesus at his coming** as the occasion for his boast in the congregation is further evidence that Paul understood himself as a pastor, not simply as an evangelist. His task was to stand by his churches and to present them blameless to Christ at his return.

When Paul could no longer stand the suspense, he sent Timothy to learn how the congregation was faring, and **to establish you in your faith and to exhort you.** The words are an apt summary of the purpose of the letter itself. **We told you beforehand** what to expect, Paul reminds the church. Simply knowing what is to happen is not enough, however. Frequent reminders of God's promises and encouragement from fellow believers are necessary sustenance.

With the reference to Timothy's return and his favorable report about the situation in Thessalonica, Paul bursts into thanksgiving once again. Paul has been **comforted.** The Greek word is *parakalein*, "to console" (the Fourth Gospel calls the Holy Spirit the Paraclete, comforter). Paul sent Timothy with his letter to exhort and console the congregation (3:2); in return, they have comforted Paul. Whatever personal distress Paul suffers is tolerable in the knowledge that his churches are surviving, whose well-being is constantly on his mind (2 Cor. 11:28-29).

For the third time Paul offers thanks to God for the church, now finally concluding the thanksgiving with the customary statement of purpose: he prays **that we may see you face to face and supply what is lacking in your faith** (cf. Rom. 1:11-12). For now his letter must suffice.

The prayer in vv. 11-13 is a formal conclusion of the thanksgiving. Paul's petition is that the faithful **may increase and abound in love to one another and to all . . . as we do to you.** Already connections between Paul's comments about his relations with the Thessalonians and his admonitions to them become apparent. Paul's behavior toward them is to be exemplary. He will have more to say on love of the brethren in the following chapter. Interesting here is his insistence that Christians ought to abound in love not only to one another but to outsiders as well. The words are reminiscent of those of Jesus. The goal of such behavior is to be **unblamable in holiness . . . at the coming of our Lord Jesus with all his saints.** Paul does not conceive such holiness as a state to be attained. He prays that their hearts may be **established,** made firm. At the conclusion of the letter he prays that God may keep them "sound and blameless" (5:23). Sanctity is a gift from God, given at Baptism. It is a gift for living, however, to be expressed in relations among believers and between believers and others. It matters how Christians live their lives. Believers are to live more fully as God's children, to appropriate the freedom that is already theirs, to abound in the love born of God's love—until the coming of our Lord Jesus.

The use of **saints** in this verse is unusual; see below on 4:13-18.

■ Exhortation (4:1—5:22)

With 4:1 Paul opens a new section in the letter, marked by the use of the verb *parakalō* (here translated **we exhort**). RSV translators may not have recognized the verb as a technical term and thus translated it in several different ways in Paul's letters. Translation should be uniform. Like "I give thanks," the words "I appeal to you" introduce a particular section of the letter in which Paul makes a request. The verb occurs regularly in diplomatic and royal correspondence when a superior, writing in his official capacity, chooses to make a request rather than issue a command (Paul's distinction between "commanding" and "requesting" in Philemon 8-10 perfectly reflects the distinction). As an apostle, Paul has the authority to issue commands. He chooses, however, to make an appeal, according his churches a measure of independence in arriving at a decision.

The nature of Paul's appeals, a standard feature of his letters, depends upon the situation. In Philemon he requests a slave owner to take back his runaway slave. In Romans, one of Paul's requests is for moral and spiritual support in his impending confrontation with the Jerusalem church (Rom. 15:30-33). Suiting the nature of 1 Thessalonians as a paraenetic (exhortative) letter, Paul's appeal has to do with how **to live and to please God.** When his requests require explanation or persuasion, they may be preceded by lengthy arguments, as in Romans and Galatians. In this letter little discussion is necessary, since as Paul notes once again, the church has already **learned** from Paul how properly to conduct themselves and in fact are already doing so. The term translated **learned** refers to received tradition, in this case undoubtedly catechetical instruction. Paul requests simply that **you do so more and more.**

Sexual Ethics (4:3-8)

The short paragraph is about "holiness." Three times in the space of a few verses Paul uses the Greek root *hagio-:* **sanctification** (v. 3), **holiness** (v. 7), and **Holy Spirit** (v. 8). Being holy has first to do with purity in matters of sexual conduct. The somewhat cryptically worded advice seems commonplace. It may be unnecessary to locate the reason for Paul's advice in news he received about the situation in Thessalonica from Timothy. At times, affairs within a congregation merited Paul's comment with respect to sexual practices (see, e.g., 1 Corinthians 6). The comments are so general, however, that it is difficult to view them as a response to some aberrant behavior within the church at Thessalonica.

The passage seems to reflect religious propaganda common within Hellenistic Judaism as well as in early Christianity. Like his contemporaries, Paul views promiscuity (the **passion of lust**) as a result of **not knowing God** (see esp. Rom. 1:18ff.). Conversion to belief in the one true God was to have an impact on one's sexual conduct. Such advice may represent a fixed topic in Christian instruction. It is interesting that Paul links behavior with belief in God. Abraham Malherbe argues that in antiquity ethics had little or no connection with religion. For both Christians and Jews, the life appropriate to believers is directly related to beliefs in and about God. It is, Malherbe argues, the link Paul forges between sexual purity and worship of God that is his distinctive contribution.

There may be an additional reason for advise on sexual matters even if the topic is traditional. Pauline Christianity was an experience of newness. The world for believers was a different place. Some of the differences had to do with social roles. For those who have been baptized into Christ, Paul wrote, "there is neither Jew nor Greek, there is neither slave nor free, there is neither male nor female" (Gal. 3:28). Some took the phrases to mean that those who had been initiated into the mysteries of the heavenly realm had transcended the limitations of human life, leaving behind even sexuality. Christians in Corinth apparently tended in this direction, inviting Paul's reminders about limitations that still exist even for those baptized into Christ. It is important to recognize that the life of faith is to be lived in the everyday world, and that "holiness" is about relations between men and women and about earning wages and caring for one another. The ordinariness of the advice may be precisely the point. Becoming a member of God's family through Baptism does not provide a way out of the world. The life of faith is lived in the midst of the everyday. God is concerned about wrongs against brothers and sisters. The work of the Holy Spirit leads to true community, not moral and social anarchy.

Love of the Brethren (4:9-12)

Paul begins this little section with **but concerning.** In 1 Corinthians, the phrase introduces topics from a letter the Corinthians sent to Paul ("Now concerning the matters about which you wrote," 7:1; see 8:1; 12:1; 16:1). Timothy may have brought a letter from the church to Paul, or he may have been requested to ask Paul about certain matters. That interpretation works best with Paul's comments about "those who are asleep" and "times and seasons."

Paul has nothing new to say to the congregation about *philadelphia*, brotherly and sisterly love. Earlier Paul enjoins the congregation to show love not only to one another but to everyone. This paragraph deals with relations within the family. The church, Paul believes, has been **taught by God to love one another,** as is evidenced by their behavior. Paul can only encourage them to **do so more and more.** Here, Paul is more like a cheerleader than a coach.

The injunctions that follow are particularly interesting. Paul makes three requests: (1) **to aspire to live quietly;** (2) **to mind**

your own affairs; and (3) **to work with your hands.** The behavior is important for two reasons: it will **command the respect of outsiders** and it will enable members of the church to be independent.

The injunction to work has received the most attention from commentators. Who would not work? It is possible that the problem had arisen due to intense expectation of the end-time among the Thessalonians. Like the Millerites of our century, some may have left everything to await the return of the Lord. It is clear from discussions that follow in the letter that the congregation—like Paul—believed that not much time was left. In 1 Cor. 7:26-31, Paul even recommends that the Corinthians not become too attached to their occupations in view of the impending close of the age. If this is the problem, Paul must remind the Thessalonians that they still have responsibilities they cannot shirk. Even if the end is at hand, there are jobs that must be done.

It is more likely, however, that the problem regarding work has little to do with eschatological enthusiasm. The reasons Paul gives for his advice are to **command the respect of outsiders** and **to be dependent on nobody.** The issue is what others will think of the Christian group. Abraham Malherbe has pointed out that Paul's advice is reminiscent of criticisms leveled at Epicureans in ancient society, a philosophical community that advocated withdrawal from the world as the only means of attaining true happiness.[12] Their withdrawal included abandonment of occupations. Many preferred begging to work. Thus, a major objection to their way of life was that they were leeches, living off others, a burden to society. It may be Paul detected some tendency toward such social irresponsibility among the Thessalonians and sought to head off any developments in this direction. Paul's earlier comments about working night and day in order not to be a financial burden on the congregation provide a basis for his advice. He practiced what he now preaches and can serve as a model for the congregation. A more extended discussion of the need for self-support is found in 2 Thess. 3:6-12. If the letter was written by Paul to the same congregation, the problem seems to have persisted.

The matter of social responsibility was important to Paul. On the one hand, Paul could insist that Christians recognize the new standards they had adopted at Baptism. The world was no longer the same; they had been set free (Gal. 5:1). That freedom included liberation from bondage to astrological calendars and to inappropriate social conventions. Allegiances within the family of believers had become primary. The wisdom of the world had been replaced by the wisdom of the cross that others perceived as foolishness (1 Corinthians 1). On the other hand, Baptism was not an exit visa from the world. The everyday remained the arena of discipleship. That meant living with others who had not yet heard the gospel as good news. Christians were not to adopt their standards, except to the extent Paul advises. Most philosophers would have applauded Paul's advice to mind one's affairs, live quietly, and to work. Paul is concerned about the impression the Christian church makes on the world at least so that false impediments will not be placed in the path of potential believers. Christian groups should be distinguished from those like the Epicureans who were regarded as destructive of families, socially irresponsible, and a burden to society. The gospel itself ought to be the scandal, not antisocial behavior.

Paul's advice **to work with your hands** offers a glimpse into the social realities of his congregations. Paul's churches were composed of urbanites, with a large proportion of urban poor. The way of life Paul recommended—his own—was that of an artisan, a tradesman. Learning a trade did not promise wealth, but it did offer a reliable means of support and a measure of independence. And in Paul's case, it meant he could work wherever he went.[13] Once again Paul uses himself as a model for the church.

"Those Who Are Asleep" (4:13-18)

The paragraph has to do with those who have died. In the context, the reference must be to members of the congregation who have recently died. The purpose of the section is not simply to provide information but to offer "consolation" (*paraklēsis*, v. 18) so **that you may not grieve as others do who have no hope.** The issue is not whether to grieve but how.

Paul sometimes uses the rhetorical question, "are you ignorant that . . .?" to introduce a reference to traditional material, knowledge of which can be assumed (Rom. 6:3 and 7:1). More frequently the phrase introduces new material that believers need to know (1 Cor. 10:1; 12:1; 2 Cor. 1:8; Rom. 11:25), often drawn from tradition. In these verses, Paul offers consolation by quoting a tradition about Jesus' return and the fate of believers both alive and dead.

The passage is fraught with difficulties. We might ask first what suggested to the Thessalonians that the end of the age was so near that no one would die before Christ's return or that death was no longer to be reckoned with. Evidence for such beliefs among Christians, including Paul, is not difficult to find. In his first letter to the church at Corinth, Paul speaks of the "impending distress" (7:26), by which he means the trials immediately preceding the close of the age; "for the form of this world is passing away," he says (7:31). "For salvation is nearer to us now than when we first believed," Paul wrote to the Romans (Rom. 13:11); "the night is far gone, the day is at hand." 1 Cor. 15:51-54 holds open the possibility that some who are alive will be transformed into a new mode of existence before death. The Gospels offer evidence that Jesus himself believed the end of the age was not far off (Mark 9:1; 13:30; Matt. 10:33). Albert Schweitzer argued that Christian theology was little more than an elaborate apology for the failure of Jesus to return to bring history to a close. Though exaggerated and one-sided, his views do highlight real struggles within Christian circles to understand the relationship between present and future.

Another difficulty is what to make of Paul's imagery. He opens the discussion with a standard reference to what Christians **believe: Jesus died and rose.** Even the form of the statement ("if

Jesus died and rose, thus also . . .") is common. In Rom. 6:3-11;
Eph. 2:5-7; and Col. 2:12-13, we encounter the same paralleling
of Christ's death and resurrection with that of believers. In the
Romans passage, Paul uses the same "if . . . then . . ." form of
argument. In all three instances the imagery derives from baptismal tradition. One difference, however, is the use of the verb
anistēmi ("rise") in our verse. Elsewhere Paul uses either *egeirō*
(usually passive, with the sense that Jesus "was raised" by God)
or *zōopoieō*, "make alive," also with God as the acting subject.
In the Pauline corpus, only in Eph. 5:14 and Rom. 15:2 is the
verb *anistēmi* used to refer to the resurrection, and in both cases
it is part of a quotation. Modification of traditional language must
depend here on the context in which Paul is intent upon understanding *anastasis nekrōn*, "resurrection of the dead." It may be
that the use of the verb *anistēmi* in the quotation in v. 16, **and
the dead in Christ will rise first,** is responsible for the singular
usage in v. 14.

The protasis of the clause seems awkward. We might have
expected either, "If Christ died and rose, so we too shall die and
rise," or "If God raised Jesus, so too he will bring the dead in
Christ to life." The shift to God as subject, **even so God through
Jesus will bring with him those who have fallen asleep,** seems
unwarranted; it is unclear how the "if" implies the "thus." Some
step in the argument has been omitted, perhaps the usual parallel
expressed in baptismal formulas (see Rom. 6:3-11).

There are other reasons for Paul's modification of traditional
imagery. The second half of v. 14 appears to be an interpretive
paraphrase of Zech. 14:5, "Then the Lord your God will come,
and all the holy ones with him." The verse was the subject of
creative interpretation in both Jewish and Christian circles. The
early Christian manual, the *Didache*, for example, quotes the
verse to prove that in the sequence of events at the end of the
age, believers who have died will be raised first: "and thirdly the
resurrection of the dead: but not all the dead, but as it was said,
'The Lord shall come and all his saints with him' " (Did. 16:6-7).
"Saints" is understood to mean believers who have died. The

same interpretation is implied in 1 Thess. 3:13, where Paul's use of traditional material included a paraphrase of Zech. 14:5. Matthew's strange account of the appearance of "bodies of the saints who had fallen asleep" presumes the same interpretation of Zechariah (Matt. 27:52). In the interpretive tradition, both in Jewish and Christian circles, the "come" of Zechariah was read as "bring," and the verse was taken to mean that at his appearance at the end of days God would bring the faithful dead with him. Much work needs to be done on the interpretive tradition, but there can be little doubt that Paul's comments in v. 14 reflect such scholarly work on the text of Zechariah.

Verse 14 is Paul's introduction to a **word of the Lord,** which he offers as the basis of consolation. What is a **word of the Lord?** The phrase is virtually unparalleled in the Pauline corpus. In 2 Thess. 3:1 it is a synonym for the gospel; Col. 3:16 speaks of a "word of Christ." In none of Paul's undisputed letters is the expression used, though in 1 Cor. 7:10 Paul refers to what the Lord "commands," as opposed to matters about which Paul must speak since the Lord has not (7:12; see also 7:25, "I have no command of the Lord").

Probability favors reading *kyrios* as a reference to the Lord Jesus. Then what is the **word of the Lord** Paul cites? Perhaps it is a saying of Jesus. In 1 Cor. 7:10 and Rom. 14:14, Paul appears to cite traditional sayings of Jesus. He certainly knew of such traditions even if he makes little use of them. If vv. 15-16 are from a saying of Jesus, it is one unattested elsewhere.[14]

It is also possible that **word of the Lord** should be read as a reference to Christian prophetic tradition. In ancient Israel, prophets spoke for God, using the first person singular, introducing their oracles with, "Thus says the Lord." In the NT, the author of the Apocalypse speaks for Jesus, also employing the first person singular, though the Jesus who speaks through him is clearly the one enthroned at God's right hand. Perhaps Paul's **word of the Lord** is such a prophetic utterance—a word from the Lord through the agency of the Spirit, offered for the purpose of consolation (one of the tasks of prophets, according to 1 Cor. 14:3).

Various features of the tradition favor the latter interpretation. Though the precise configuration of images is unique to 1 Thessalonians, most of the imagery is familiar to apocalyptic tradition in both Jewish and Christian circles. The trumpet is mentioned in 1 Cor. 15:52 and may derive from Zech. 9:14; the clouds are from Dan. 7:13 and are mentioned in several NT passages; the image of the Lord's coming may reflect Sinai traditions such as Deut. 33:2-3, substituting the Lord Jesus for the Lord God, and projecting the imagery into the end-times. The saying seems indicative of inspired speculation about the end-times of the sort attested in the Apocalypse of John and in Jewish apocalyptic writings, speculation often focused on biblical passages.

The words are quoted to provide the basis for consolation. The promise that **we shall always be with the Lord,** coupled with the awareness that God has made provision for those believers who have already died, offers a means by which Christians can **comfort one another.** Paul does not tell the Thessalonians that they ought not grieve the loss of loved ones; rather, he suggests an appropriate way to grieve. Paul is interested in the theological dimension of consolation; it is not mere psychological conditioning. There are reasons why Christians should not grieve like others. Their hope is built on a solid foundation. To lay that foundation Paul turns to the Scriptures and to the interpretive traditions of the community of believers. This is pastoral theology in the proper sense.

These verses have held endless fascination for Christians through the centuries, particularly when life becomes unmanageable and the prospects of the future dim. Prognostication seems almost instinctive. Every generation has had its futurists offering to reveal the secrets of tomorrow. There is something comforting about believing that history is programmed and that we possess the code. There is also something presumptuous about such views. We seem intent upon living by sight, not by faith. Paul's comments to the Romans are still appropriate: "Now hope that is seen is not hope. For who hopes for what he sees? But if we hope for what we do not see, we wait for it with patience" (Rom. 8:24-25).

We cannot, in fact, live by sight. The NT contains no code by which we can decipher the secrets of the future, even if we were to assume that such a code exists. The apocalyptic scenario Paul sketches here is one among many in the Bible. Those who seek to fashion from the numerous visions one true prophecy of the future must impose a unity on the NT that does not exist. Hal Lindsay's books are testimony to his ingenuity but say little about the future in biblical terms. We would do well to heed Jesus' warning: "But of that day or that hour no one knows, not even the angels in heaven, nor the Son, but only the Father. Take heed, watch; for you do not know when the time will come" (Mark 13:32-33).

If our hope cannot rest on one picture of the future, however, it need not be formless. Paul's response to disappointed expectations within the Thessalonian congregation was not to throw up his hands in the face of mystery or to advise blind confidence in the fates. Paul locates hope in God—a God who appears in Israel's story as one who makes promises and keeps them and whose sending of his Son is confirmation of his faithfulness. As a theological interpreter of reality, Paul finds in the Scriptures and in the experience of believers signs of God's continuing faithfulness. Christian hope is different from naive optimism. It relies not on proof nor on a complete disclosure of the secrets of the future nor on the ability of believers to think positively in the face of adversity. The Christians' hope is invested in a God with a name and a history. Real consolation can be found only through knowledge of that history and that God, in whose hands lies the future of creation.

Times and Seasons (5:1-11)

The following verses build on Paul's earlier discussion and offer some application of his visions of the future. On the one hand, the Thessalonians need no instruction about times and seasons. They themselves **know well that the day of the Lord will come like a thief in the night** (see Matt. 23:33-34). One implication is to remain alert and watchful. Paul's reference to those who speak confidently about **peace and security** perhaps echoes Jeremiah's indictment of false prophets, "They have healed the wound of my people lightly, saying, 'Peace, peace,' when there is no peace" (Jer. 6:14). Those who can discern the times know that **travail** is at hand. The image of birthpangs is an apocalyptic convention. As the birth of a new age approaches, life will become more painful, as in nature. The closer the end, the greater the tribulations. Here Paul employs the image in the negative sense. Those who foolishly suppose all is well will suddenly be rocked by distress as intense as birthpangs. For those who know the future, however, even the tribulations can be viewed as hopeful: they are the necessary prelude to the return of Christ on the clouds of heaven (Mark 13:8, 24-31). The difference between Christians and those who have no hope is not simply that they will be prepared for trials, but that they can endure them knowing what lies beyond.

Since they have been enlightened, Christians are children **of the light** and **of the day.** They know that vigilance is the proper mode of life. The image of sleep here connotes a false sense of security (see the use of the same image in Mark 13:32-37). Sobriety and wakefulness indicate a sense of expectance appropriate to those who know the times and seasons.

Being vigilant means being prepared for what life holds. Here Paul mentions the need for armor: **the breastplate of faith and love and for a helmet the hope of salvation.** The imagery is familiar from the OT and from Paul's letters (Rom. 13:12; 2 Cor. 6:7; 10:4). The most elaborate development of the theme is in Eph. 6:13-17. Armor is necessary because life involves battle against the forces of darkness. Night is not simply a passive metaphor. As in John, darkness struggles against light, seeking to snuff it out. The Thessalonians have already experienced hostility from the powers of this age. They must be properly outfitted for the struggles to come.

No matter how fierce the battles, there is reason for confidence: **God has not destined us for wrath, but to obtain salvation.** The outcome of the struggle is in God's hands. God's commitment to the elect and his ability to keep his word, revealed in the death and resurrection of Jesus, are the ground of hope. Summing up the whole of 4:13—5:9, Paul assures the church that **Christ died for us so that whether we wake** (= are alive) **or sleep** (= are dead) **we might** (begin to) **live with him.** The singular reference to Jesus' death without mention of the resurrection should not be taken to mean that somehow the two can be separated. The words may be chosen for contrast (he died that we might live). Confident in the deliverance to come, deliverance that will include even those who have died, the Thessalonians can **encourage one another and build one another up**—just as they are doing. Theological reflection has practical consequences for the life of the believing community.

Concluding Admonitions (5:12-22)

Paul makes a special appeal for leaders in the congregation (vv. 12-13). He refers to **those who labor among you, are over you in the Lord, and admonish you.** We need not think of a highly organized ministerial staff. It was some time before congregations required—or could afford—a professional clergy whose sole occupational responsibility was care of the congregation. It would be naive to imagine, however, that any group could function without some structure and leadership. Though his stay in Thessalonica was brief, Paul was apparently able to fashion some rudimentary structure. There are leaders who "care for" (the term may refer to authority—**those over you**—but its pairing with **admonish** may suggest this translation as more apt) and **admonish** members of the congregation. These are tasks of the whole congregation (mutual encouragement and admonition), but some have special responsibilities to see that they are carried out (see

Paul's list of spiritual gifts in 1 Corinthians 12 and Romans 12). Structure and leadership are not signs of disintegration; they are necessary to the life of any group.

In 5:14 Paul makes an appeal for the third time. His exhortations are of a general nature. Especially prominent is concern for **the fainthearted** and **the weak.** The strong can care for themselves. The greatness of the church, as of any society, is its ability to care for and protect the poor and the powerless.

The admonition not to repay evil for evil is familiar from Jewish tradition and may be reminiscent of Jesus' teachings. Evident here is the concern not to restrict such behavior to the family of faith. Such behavior is appropriate for **one another** and for relations with **all.** Christian faith does not encourage withdrawal from the world, for God's ultimate goal is the redemption of all creation (Rom. 8:12-23).

Three crisp phrases describe **the will of God** for believers: **rejoice always, pray constantly, give thanks in all circumstances.** They give the lie to those who view Pauline religion as sober and deadening. Awareness of the seriousness of the times and the risks of faith do not require humorless, lifeless piety. The redeemed have reason to rejoice and give thanks. Bad feelings do not have to be repressed; believers need not deny the reality of evil. God's gracious adoption makes possible a realistic piety that sees to the core of things and enables God's children to embrace life in its fullness. God's will is "abundant life" (John 10:10).

Intimately related to the life of faith are comments about the Spirit. Just as God's Spirit was at work in Paul's preaching (1:5,6), so the Holy Spirit continues to work within the life of the community to establish holiness (4:8). Christians ought not to **quench** the flames that fire imagination and zeal. Charismatic gifts were undoubtedly a feature of Thessalonian as well as Corinthian experience. Paul makes no effort to shut off the gifts, though they can lead to disorder (1 Corinthians 12–14). As in Corinthians, **prophesying**—admonishing, instructing, encouraging—is the preeminent gift of the Spirit to the church, fostering harmony and growth.

Openness to the work of the Spirit does not absolve believers from the need to **test everything.** There is nothing automatic about the operation of the Spirit. All "charismatic" manifestations are not from God. Sincerity and zeal are not sufficient. Discipleship is not an escape from having to determine in each situation what is good and what is not. Christians must "prove [i.e., test by experience] what is the will of God, what is good and acceptable and perfect" (Rom. 12:2).

■ Prayer and Benediction (5:23-28)

Paul frequently opens and closes his letters with a prayer for **peace.** Like the Hebrew *shalom*, the word should be understood to mean wholeness and well-being. Such peace is the gift of God. It is that sense of wholeness that Paul requests in his prayer for the congregation: **May . . . God . . . sanctify you wholly.** God intends nothing less than the redemption of the whole person, **spirit and soul and body.** Religion cannot be restricted to the "spiritual."

That sanctification is not understood as gradual progress toward a goal is implied in the imagery Paul uses. He prays that believers **may . . . be kept sound and blameless.** It is a matter of preserving the gift that has already been bestowed at Baptism. Those baptized into Christ Jesus have already passed from death to life (Col. 2:13); they are new creations (2 Cor. 5:17). Discipleship is life between the times, for God has not yet finished what he began. But the life of faith is not a striving for more; it is living more fully in what has already been given, knowing that even efforts to live more appropriately as "saints" (4:1-3) depend upon God who sanctifies. Christians can contemplate the future with confidence, for the God who has begun a good work will bring it to completion (Phil. 1:6). **He who calls you is faithful, and he will do it.**

Paul requests the prayers of the congregation, inviting their concern and participation in the ministry of the church beyond the confines of their community (vv. 25-26).

Paul's letter was intended to be read publicly, setting it apart from private correspondence (v. 27).

As is customary, Paul concludes with a benediction: **The grace of our Lord Jesus Christ be with you.**

NOTES

1. Ron Hock, *The Social Context of Paul's Ministry: Tentmaking and Apostleship* (Philadelphia: Fortress, 1980) 47-48.
2. E. Haenchen, *The Acts of The Apostles*, trans. B. Noble (Philadelphia: Westminster, 1971) 104-107, 509-512.
3. R. Jewett, *A Chronology of Paul's Life* (Philadelphia: Fortress, 1979), esp. the graphs at the end of the volume.
4. J. Jervell, "Paul: Teacher of Israel," in *Luke and the People of God* (Minneapolis: Augsburg, 1972) 153-184, and D. Juel, *Luke-Acts: The Promise of History* (Atlanta: John Knox, 1983).
5. See the article on "Letter" in *IDB, Supplementary Volume* (Nashville: Abingdon, 1976); also Wm. Doty, *Letters in Primitive Christianity* (Philadelphia: Fortress, 1973).
6. Malherbe's published work includes *Social Aspects of Early Christianity*, 2nd ed. (Philadelphia: Fortress, 1983) and " 'Gentle as a Nurse.' The Cynic Background to I Thess. ii," *Novum Testamentum* 12 (1970): 203-17. He kindly sent me two unpublished papers presented to the SBL Seminar on Paul, entitled "I Thessalonians as a Paraenetic Letter" (1972) and "Exhortation in First Thessalonians" (1981). Prof. Malherbe has been commissioned to write the commentary on 1 and 2 Thessalonians for the Anchor Bible.
7. Paul Schubert, *Form and Function of the Pauline Thanksgivings* (Berlin: Töpelmann, 1939).
8. Schubert, *Form and Function* 66.
9. J. Jervell, "The Problem of Traditions in Acts," in *Luke and the People of God* 19-39.
10. A. Malherbe, " 'Gentle as a Nurse.' The Cynic Background to I Thess. ii."
11. See the preface to "The Martyrdom of Isaiah" in R. H. Charles, *The Apocrypha and Pseudepigrapha of the Old Testament* (Oxford: Clarendon Press, 1913) 2:156-158.

12. Malherbe, *Social Aspects* 22-28; Hock, *Social Context* 44-47.
13. Hock, *Social Context*.
14. J. Jeremias, *Unknown Sayings of Jesus*, trans. R. Fuller (New York: Macmillan, 1957) 80-83.

ABOUT THE AUTHOR

Donald H. Juel is a graduate of St. Olaf College and Luther Theological Seminary; his Ph.D. is from Yale University. He has taught at Indiana University, Princeton Theological Seminary, and, since 1978, at Luther Northwestern Theological Seminary. Among his many publications are *Luke-Acts: The Promise of History; Living a Biblical Faith; An Introduction to New Testament Literature;* and *Messiah and Temple.*